Charles Gavan Duffy

Young Ireland - A Fragment of Irish history - 1840-45

Volume II

Charles Gavan Duffy

Young Ireland - A Fragment of Irish history - 1840-45
Volume II

ISBN/EAN: 9783744716895

Printed in Europe, USA, Canada, Australia, Japan

Cover: Foto ©ninafisch / pixelio.de

More available books at **www.hansebooks.com**

A Fragment of Irish History

1840-45

FINAL REVISION

ILLUSTRATED

BY

THE HON. SIR CHARLES GAVAN DUFFY
K.C.M.G.

VOLUME II

LONDON
T. FISHER UNWIN
PATERNOSTER SQUARE
1896

CONTENTS

Book II.

CHAPTER I.

How O'Connell and the Traversers were Tried.

PAGES

Change of Scene — Law Courts instead of Monster Meetings — Popular feeling—Foreign sympathy — Effect on O'Connell — Counsel retained for O'Connell — For the Traversers—For the Crown—Robert Holmes —"A very peaceful Party"—Would there be a fair trial?—System of Government— Crown-Solicitor Kemmis in 1811—His Jury-panel — Crown-Solicitor Kemmis in 1843-4 — Father and Son—Printed Indictment one hundred yards long — Overt Acts — Counts of the Indictment—Public Surprise—"Justice fishing with a net"—A list of Witnesses asked for—Refused—Chief-Justice's justice—Time demanded to prepare Defence—Refused—Why it had to be Granted—Devices of the Sheriff and his officials—"A mockery, a delusion, and a snare"—How a Jury was struck—All Catholics excluded—Public Meetings to protest—English Catholics 3-18

CHAPTER II.

How the Traversers were Convicted.

The Trial—Challenge to the array—Overruled by the Court—How the Jury was composed—And the Court—Attorney-General's statement—*Résumé* and analysis—The Defence—O'Connell defends himself—Comment— The Attorney-General — Startling Episode — Solicitor-General's Rejoinder—Summing-up by the Chief-Justice—Short work made of the Defence—A Partisan charge—Comments — Verdict of guilty — "The Italian Boy" . . . . 19-30 vi *CONTENTS.*

CHAPTER III.

WHAT PARLIAMENT AND ENGLISH REFORMERS THOUGHT OF THE TRIAL—THE SENTENCE.

PAGES

After the Trial—O'Connell' proposes to dissolve the Repeal Association—Editors to be excluded—Dissolution opposed—Smith O'Brien concurs—Compromise — Newspaper proprietors retire—Arbitration Courts abolished—Duties of Repeal Wardens limited—Whig promises—Federal Party active—Panaceas—Lord French's opinion—Royal Dublin Society and Smith O'Brien—Irish National Gallery projected—Meeting of Parliament—Lord John Russell's Motion on the state of Ireland—Speech—Nine Nights' debate—Sir Charles Napier—Young England—Macaulay—Irish Attorney-General's Defence — Sheil's Attack —Sir Thomas Wilde censures the Trial—Parliament refuses to consider the state of Ireland—Whig sentiment *versus* Whig action—O'Connell in London—In other English cities—Radical support—Dinner in Covent Garden Theatre—Whig Rumours—And promises—Popular feeling in Ireland—Chief-Justice Pennefather — Unexpected disclosure — Light thrown on Jury lists—Notice served for judgment—Counter-notice—Motion for new Trial—Dismissed—Arrest of judgment moved—Refused—Sentence—O'Connell's short Address to the Court — Richmond Bridewell 31-48

CHAPTER IV.

O'CONNELL IN JAIL—YOUNG IRELAND IN CONCILIATION HALL.

The new Leader—Sketch of Smith O'Brien's career—New measures—Irish M.P.s recalled—Irish representation—O'Connell's indifference—Reason—Effect—Changes by Smith O'Brien—His opinion of MacNevin—Repeal Association Meetings — Confidence — O'Brien's Challenge—Address to the Queen—O'Brien's staff—Old and new Politicians—Richard O'Gorman — Michael Doheny — Michael Joseph Barry—Discontented Unitarians defended —Presbyterian Marriages assailed—Defended by Catholics—Post-Office tampered with by Sir James Graham, the Lord-Lieutenant, and others — Sympathy with O'Connell from Belfast—From English Catholics—Decisive course taken by the *Nation*—Legal judgment subjected to criticism—Prosecuted articles republished—"Voice of the Nation"—Its teaching—The State Prisoners, Rich-

CONTENTS.

PAGES

mond Penitentiary — Prison life — Cause of indulgent treatment— Recreations—Visitors—Indignation of the Country—The privacy of prison life sacred—Proposal to release some of the Prisoners rejected by Traversers—War with France imminent — Bearing on the Irish question—Projects of the Repeal Association—Popular Education— National Literature—Influence of Davis — Le Fanu—Butt—Samuel Ferguson—Lever—Memory of Banim—Recruits—John Fisher Murray —William Carleton—Union of Ranks and Parties — London Irish Literary Association—Press recognition—*Tait's Magazine*—Lucas and the *Tablet*—*Evening Packet*—John O'Connell's hóstility . . . 49-68

CHAPTER V.

THE IRISH PRISONERS BEFORE THE HOUSE OF LORDS—THEIR DELIVERANCE.

The Writ of Error—Chief-Justice Pennefather on his Trial—Why the Trial of the Traversers was bad in law—Reasons submitted to the English Law Lords —House of Lords consults the English judges—They confirm the judgment of the Irish Court—Adjournment—Final decision of the Law Lords —Reversal of the Irish judgment—Arrival of the news at Richmond— O'Connell and the Traversers released — Triumphant procession through the streets of Dublin—Public rejoicings all over Ireland— Opinions of the English Press—Effect upon Peel 69-77

Book III.

CHAPTER I.

IRISH PARTIES AFTER O'CONNELL'S DELIVERANCE.

"Leader incapable of leading" — Mental condition of O'Connell—"The doctrine of instalments"—Retrograde decision—First Meeting of the Association after O'Connell's release—Futility of his proposals—Their abandonment—Subsequent Meetings—Idle talk—Opportunity lost— Banquet—Darrynane—Rumours of a Whig Alliance—Federal developments—The Dublin Corporation—Grey Porter's scheme of Local Legislatures—Tory and Liberal adhesions—Sequel of Lord Hawarden's story—*Note* 81-93

CONTENTS.

CHAPTER II.

RECREATIONS OF THE YOUNG IRELANDERS.

Weekly *Symposia*—Answers to Correspondents—Disguised contributors—A note from MacNevin — *Bons - mots* — Davis's and Smith O'Brien's enthusiasm for the study of Irish—Indifferently responded to—Banter—Anti-Gaelic proclivities—Excursions—A trip to Darrynane—Kilkenny—"The divine valley of the Blackwater"—Cork—Father Matthew—Lakes of Killarney—Gougaun Barra— Incidents of the journey—O'Connell's mountain home—Letters from Davis—And to him—John O'Hagan and M'Carthy 94-106

CHAPTER III.

THE FEDERAL CONTROVERSY.

O'Connell at Darrynane—Result of a month's retirement—Declares himself in favour of Federation—Dismay of the *Nation*—O'Connell abandoning Repeal—Public remonstrance addressed to O'Connell by the Editor—Widely discussed—Whig and Tory Comments—Barrett of the *Pilot*—The *Evening Post* — A Castle Stipendiary— Sincere Federalists—Sharman Crawford—English Whigs—French Press—Silence of the Repeal Association—The *Nation*—Important result of Duffy's remonstrance—O'Connell breaks with Federalism—" The red-hot poker"—O'Connell's action in the Federal Episode—Failing intellect—Extravagant abuse—A great opportunity lost—Collapse of the Federal movement—*Note* 107-124

CHAPTER IV.

RELIGIOUS INTRIGUES AT HOME AND ABROAD.

Young Irelanders to be punished — Concocted slanders— "The Young Liberator"—O'Connell's disreputable adherents—The *Pilot*—Davis attacked—*Dublin Review*—Honest controversy—The young priests on the side of the *Nation*—Davis to O'Brien and Duffy—His indignation and strong Protestant feeling—Another letter to O'Brien—The Author's judgment on the Religious Question—O'Connell's Letter to Davis (see *Appendix*)—Rally of Young Ireland round Davis—He takes the chair at the Association—Rumour of a new Concordat —O'Connell's letter to the bishops—Mr Petre—"The Propaganda"—Warning to the Irish bishops—Disregarded—The Duke of Wellington's admission of failure—*Note* 125-135

CHAPTER V.

PEEL'S CONCESSIONS TO IRELAND.

A little blarney—O'Connell's proposals a blank—Meeting of Parliament—Peel's Irish proposals—Endowment of Maynooth and Middle-Class Colleges—Welcomed by the *Nation*—Meeting for the encouragement of Irish manufactures—Tresham Gregg's oration—O'Connell's eulogium—Important recruits to the Association—Grey Porter's speech—A standing difficulty—Report of the Devon Commission—Miserable condition of Ireland—Patience of the People—Why Down was peaceful and Tipperary disturbed—Maynooth Bill—English outcry—Petitions—Opposition of Irish Protestants—Ulster Synod favourable—Peel defends his policy—War with America threatened—Peel's "Message of Peace" to Ireland—Parliamentary gladiators—Macaulay—His declaration—Smith O'Brien's reply—Gladstone resigns office—Bill becomes law—Note 136-150

CHAPTER VI.

THE WORKSHOP OF YOUNG IRELAND.

New Projects—The '82 Club—Davis's oratorical success—Eminent artist on Nationalising Art—New national literature—Projected History of Ireland—Existing histories reviewed—Project takes another form—"Library of Ireland"—Immense success—"A new mine, closed for two hundred years"—Designs unaccomplished—Carleton—Dr Madden—Lever—Influence exerted by Davis on Irish art, literature, and social progress—John Dillon's Report on the Law of Landlord and Tenant—Dillon to Duffy—Davis to Lane—Attempt to publish Mangan in England—Criticism on the men of the ancient Confederate period—Literature supplanting oratory 151-164

CHAPTER VII.

THE PROVINCIAL COLLEGES.

Bill introduced—Its main principles—Perfect Religious Equality—No Sectarian Teaching—A College for each province—Well received in Parliament—First discordant notes—A Catholic objection—Sheil—Sir Robert Inglis and the "Godless Colleges"—In the Repeal Association—Davis and majority in favour of the Scheme—Minority against, including

O'Connell—Proposal to make the Association neutral—Negatived by O'Connell—His trenchant criticism—His proposals—John O'Connell's speech—Davis's reply—Discussion closed by O'Connell—The measure advocated in the *Nation*—Different standpoints—Accepted by the Bishops with Safeguards—Smith O'Brien—A Scene in Conciliation Hall —Explanations—A pathetic moment—Apparent reconciliation—Davis's last public words—Mistaken policy of O'Connell—A truce—Father John Kenyon—*Note* 165-181

CHAPTER VIII.

THE OPPOSITION TO THE BILL.

O'Connell and O'Brien—Attend Parliament to demand amendments—Peel's difficulties — Davis's letters to O'Brien — Secession mooted—John O'Connell's invidious design—Davis sees through it—Letters to O'Brien and Lane—Wide controversy—Influential Catholic opinion in favour of the Bill—O'Connell and his son return from Parliament—Condemn the Bill—It becomes Law—Certain Bishops agree to give it a fair trial—But afterwards withdraw their support—Disastrous result—Personal testimony to the disadvantages Irishmen labour under competing with State-Educated Colonists — Peel's third measure for Ireland — An abortive Land Bill—Davis thinks of going circuit—National Levee at the Rotunda—Literary projects—An ominous figure—*Notes* . 182-190

CHAPTER IX.

THE VICE-TRIBUNATE OF JOHN O'CONNELL.

Scattering for the holidays—Darrynane—Cahermoyle—Davis in charge of the *Nation*—Duffy's trip to the north—His companions—Mitchel—Martin— John O'Hagan—Incidents of travel—Character of the "Plantation" country—Lord Roden's Bibles—Mountains and Mists—Grave of Thomas Russell—"Tea and Thomas"—Banbridge — Armagh — News from Dublin — Vice-Tribune playing the Dictator — Breaking faith with Protestant Members—Enniskillen Meeting—Orangemen of Fermanagh and Tyrone—Duffy suddenly called home—First acquaintance with Thomas D'Arcy M'Gee—Davis's opinion of him—Letter from Mitchel— *Note* 191-198

CONTENTS.

CHAPTER X.

THE DEATH OF DAVIS.

PAGES

Author's return to the *Nation* office—Davis in town at his "Curran"—State of the National cause—O'Connell insults France and America—Repeal Associations broken up in the United States—Hopes of Irish Union dispelled—Indignation of Dillon and MacNevin—A conspiracy to ruin the *Nation*—Announcement of Davis's illness—His notes—*Facsimiles*—Getting better—No importance attached to Davis's illness by his friends—Sudden Relapse and Death—Funeral—The Author's estimate of Davis's character—Influence of his writings—His friends dispersed—Dillon — MacNevin — O'Hagan — Pigot — Daniel Owen Maddyn — Faction busy — Calumny — Editor of the *Nation* — Young blood—Memorials of Davis—Memoir—Publication of his Poems and Essays —Portrait—Statue — Progress of Nationality — Tribute by Samuel Ferguson 199-223

APPENDIX.

Readers of the *Nation*—The Federal Controversy—O'Connell's Letter to O'Brien on the Federal Plan—Extract from the Federal Project, enclosed in the foregoing Letter—O'Connell's Letter to Davis—Peel's Concessions and the Young Irelanders—The Library of Ireland—Maurice O'Connell on Davis 227-236

INDEX 237-240

LIST OF ILLUSTRATIONS.

VOLUME II.

1. READING THE *NATION*. (*From an Oil Painting by Henry MacManus, R.H.A.*) . . . . . *Frontispiece*

2. WILLIAM SMITH O'BRIEN . . *Facing page* 49

3. RICHARD O'GORMAN. *Two Portraits* . ,, 52

4. MICHAEL DOHENY . . . . ,, 54

5. THE TRAVERSERS, 1844 . . . . ,, 63

6. LEAVING KILMAINHAM . . . ,, 75

7. WILLIAM CARLETON . . . ,, 97

8. THOMAS FRANCIS MEAGHER. *Two portraits* ,, 102

9. "THE POKER TRICK" . ,, 121

10. REV. C. P. MEEHAN . . . . ,, 157

11. SKETCHES OF T. F. CONWAY AND RICHARD BARRETT . ,, 174

12. JOHN MITCHEL . . . ,, 191

13. JOHN MARTIN . . . . . . ,, 193

14. THOMAS D'ARCY M'GEE . . . ,, 197

BOOK II.

YOUNG IRELAND.

BOOK II.

CHAPTER I.

HOW O'CONNELL AND THE TRAVERSERS WERE TRIED.

THE scene changes from exulting musters and processions of the people to the grave procedure and dilatory processes of a court of law; but there was no falling off in interest, and the incidents are certainly not less instructive to the political student than those already passed in review. The bulk of the nation were disappointed and puzzled, but not alienated, by the change of policy; and they turned with unabated solicitude to the new contest between their veteran tribune and his opponents. Throughout Europe and America the prosecution was watched with mingled interest and wonder. It was regarded, at first, as an attempt to punish a renowned Irishman, by the agency of an Irish court and an Irish jury, for having striven to raise his country in the scale of nations; an attempt which foreigners might well deem maladroit and hopeless. But after a little, when the nature of the agencies relied on for success became better understood, there was a new issue raised—the system of government and jurisprudence established in Ireland was placed on its trial before mankind. It will repay those who desire to understand a system by which Irishmen of moderate temper were made rebels, and thoughtful men in foreign countries made sympathisers with rebels, to study the incidents of this memorable trial.

The suppression of the Clontarf meeting was a humiliation to O'Connell, but it is probable that his arrest was a relief. It transferred the contest to a field where he was at home and a master. He was confessedly the greatest advocate of his day; the practice of criminal courts, the method and machinery of State prosecutions, and the devices by which verdicts are obtained or evaded, were all familiar to him. But he did not rely solely on his own resources. He retained the foremost men at the Bar, and engaged the attorneys most skilful and experienced in *Nisi Prius* courts. Two counsel and an attorney were assigned to each of the traversers (as the gentlemen charged with conspiracy came to be called after they had traversed the indictment), and these counsel included Mr Pigot, afterwards Chief Baron; Mr Monahan, afterwards Chief Justice of the Common Pleas; Mr Moore, between whom and the Great Seal of Ireland only an accident intervened; Mr Whiteside, afterwards Lord Chief Justice; Mr Jonathan Henn, reputed to be a lawyer of wider and riper knowledge than any of these eminent men, but who loved the sport of Isaac Walton better than angling for preferment; Richard Sheil, the most accomplished rhetorician in the House of Commons, and a number of juniors, among whom were Mr O'Hagan, afterwards Lord Chancellor of Ireland, and Sir Colman O'Loghlen, afterwards Judge Advocate General in England. The agents were men of as much note in their own profession. Pierce Mahony, sometimes called the Prince of Attorneys, who twelve years before had organised the Leinster Declaration against Repeal, and given a heavy blow to the movement in 1833; William Ford, noted for having advocated the desperate device of "exclusive dealing" in the Catholic Association; Peter M'Evoy Gartlan, and John M'Namara Cantwell, were names of significance in Ireland; and Thomas Reilly, who was less widely known, was destined a little later to give a remarkable recruit to the national cause in the person of his son, Thomas Devin Reilly. The skill and pertinacity of these well-trained litigants of the shorter robe made them invaluable in such a contest. Barry suggested that they should be called the "Traversers' Brass Band," and the title not merely stuck, but has since been borrowed and employed with less success by Mr Punch.

The Crown was also represented by men on the highroad to the bench. The Attorney-General, Mr T. B. C. Smith, afterwards Master of the Rolls, was son of a remarkable Irish judge who left a reputation for eccentric ability, indolence worthy of a lotus-eater, and a partisanship abnormal even in his class and day. Mr Smith was a well-informed lawyer, with an active intellect sometimes disturbed by sudden fits of irritability, less attributable to a bad disposition than to a bad digestion. But passions ran too high to make such an allowance, and on his first outbreak of temper O'Connell took occasion to remark that his disposition towards the Traversers was probably not sweetened by the recollection that his father was censured by Parliament on the motion of the Traverser Daniel O'Connell, and he himself defeated at Athlone by the Traverser John O'Connell. Surrounded by the trappings and formalities of a court of law where he was much at home, Mr Smith had a certain prim dignity; but he was so meagre, unwholesome, and ghastly that elsewhere he looked like an owl in the sunshine. The Solicitor-General, Richard Wilson Greene, afterwards a Baron of the Exchequer, was a lawyer of greater ability and resources, but subject also to fits of morbid and eccentric humour. The other counsel for the Crown included Mr Brewster and Mr Napier, each of whom reached the office of Lord Chancellor, half a dozen men selected from the Tory Bar for professional or political reasons, and Robert Holmes, whom men wondered to find in such society.[1] Mr Holmes was brother-in-law of Robert Emmet, who has left an historic name as a martyr for Irish liberty; and he had been imprisoned in early manhood as a sympathiser with that generous enthusiast. This imprisonment was said to be so strict that it was only on his release he learned the tragic fate of his friend. Mr Holmes's writings against the Union were still quoted for their fierceness and pungency; and he had retained so much of his early opinions as induced him to refuse promotion from the Irish Government whatever men were in power. He still wore a stuff gown after nearly half a century of practice, and when he had become in effect leader of his circuit and Father of the Irish Bar. With two of the Traversers his personal relations were such as gave an unpleasant aspect to his appearance among the prosecuting counsel. O'Connell, who was habitually unjust to the men of '98, flung at them the absurd epithet of "miscreants." They were miscreant of English authority in Ireland, but there is no group of men in history to whom the reproach, in its vulgar sense, was less applicable. After they had become political exiles they rose to eminence in the Old and New worlds in arms, arts, science, and the liberal professions. Mr Holmes resented this

---

[1] The counsel for the Crown, in addition to those named above, were Mr Sergeant Warren, Mr Bennett, Q.C.; Mr Freeman, Q.C.; Mr Martley, Q.C.; Mr Tomb, Q.C.; Mr Smily, and Mr Baker. The agent was Mr Kemmis, Crown Solicitor. It was noted as a strange fact that the young barrister who had encountered O'Connell in the Corporation debate was not entrusted with a brief by the Government. When in later times Attorney-General Smith became Master of the Rolls the junior bar had a bad time with the dyspeptic Judge. One of them quoted a couplet from Goldsmith's description of the pedagogue in the "Deserted Village" to paint their daily experience in the Rolls:—
"Full well each boding trembling learned to trace
The day's disasters in his morning face."

injustice, and there had been frequent and fierce encounters between him and O'Connell at the Bar. Mr Barrett, who considered it his *rôle* to embrace and exaggerate his patron's quarrels, had assailed Mr Holmes in the *Pilot* with scurrility so offensive that the old man, half a dozen years before the date now reached, had sent him a challenge. Knowing nothing of Mr Barrett, he said he had enquired whether he was a gentleman, and finding him gentleman enough for his purpose, he called upon him to become responsible for his foul language. Mr Barrett replied that he was under recognisance to keep the peace, arising out of a conviction for seditious libel. Mr Holmes, who was not to be baulked by such an impediment, offered to lodge the amount of the penalty with trustees for the "benefit of the gentleman's heirs or creditors." Mr Barrett, however, did not choose to fight, even on those liberal terms, and the incident had long made sport for the Dublin newspapers. Even Repealers could not refrain from so tempting a theme. "We're a very peaceful party," Morgan John, the most jovial of the second generation of O'Connells, used to say; "Uncle Dan has registered a vow in Heaven not to shed blood, and Dick Barrett another vow in the Head Police Office." It is proper to note that Mr Holmes was in a measure bound by the rules of his profession to accept the retainer sent to him by the Crown, and that he did not exhibit the least animus against the defendants in the course of the proceedings.

The question first mooted among all classes was, Would there be a fair trial? A fair trial in a political case was a phenomenon which in Ireland had not been seen in the memory of living man. In State prosecutions the law was wrested to the interest of the Crown as systematically in the reign of Queen Victoria in Ireland as it had been wrested in the reign of Charles I. in England. The jury panels and the jury itself, it was feared, would be as carefully packed for a conviction as panels and jurors had been packed in Middlesex under the Stuarts. And this fear was not confined to ignorant or prejudiced persons. Lord Cloncurry, a Privy Councillor, publicly declared that up to the time of O'Loghlen and Perrin an impartial and unpacked jury in Crown cases where Catholics were concerned was a thing quite unknown. And "the time of O'Loghlen and Perrin" was distant just half a dozen years. Mr Henry Grattan revived in the public memory the fact that when Lord Fingal was arrested, and the Catholic delegates tried in 1811, the jury panel produced by Mr Kemmis, the Crown Solicitor, was proved to have found its way out of the pocket of Sir Charles Saxton, the Under Secretary, in Dublin Castle. Mr Kemmis's son was now Crown Solicitor, and the Sheriff's office was still in the hands of persons bred in the practice of empaneling accommodating juries. In Dublin the Sheriff himself was appointed by the Crown; in London he was appointed by the Corporation, and so he had been appointed in Dublin while the Corporation was an Orange lodge; but when it was opened to the whole community the power was taken away. It was much feared that these well-disciplined officials would decide the State prosecution before a witness was examined or an indictment found. There was no doubt a probability that a Minister so cautious and circumspect as Sir Robert Peel would permit nothing very gross to be done; but on this slender foundation rested the whole chance of a fair trial.

On the second of November the indictment was sent to the Grand Jury; but it was only found a true bill after five days' deliberation. One cause of delay was its inordinate length, for which there was no precedent in that museum of obsolete instruments of torture—the State Trials.

The printed indictment handed to the Court was nearly a hundred yards long. When it was made up into a book it covered fifty-seven folio pages, like the pages of the *Times*. In this huge document there were forty-three overt acts set out; sixteen of which consisted merely of attendance at monster meetings. It was charged against the three journalists, as part of the conspiracy, that they reported the speeches made at these meetings. Fifteen other overt acts consisted in attending the ordinary meetings of the Repeal Association, where speeches of O'Connell's, alleged to be seditious, were delivered, and the plan of the Arbitration Courts adopted; and, as respects the three journalists, in "unlawfully, maliciously, and seditiously" reporting these transactions in their newspapers. Another overt act was the "endeavour to collect a meeting" at Clontarf. Ten of the eleven remaining overt acts were charged against the newspapers. Mr Barrett had published in the *Pilot* a letter from a Catholic clergyman on the "Duty of a Soldier," and an article on the "Irish in the English Army," which with certain speeches of O'Connell's on the absence of promotion from the ranks, and an article in the *Nation* on the "Morality of War," were the evidence relied upon to establish the charge of endeavouring to cause dissatisfaction among her Majesty's troops.

Six other overt acts were publications in the *Nation;* four of them consisting of leading articles, one a poem,[1] and another a letter proposing that the modern names of places in Ireland should be abandoned, and the old Celtic names revived. And, finally, there was a general charge that all the conspirators did on divers days, and in divers places, seek to carry out their conspiracy by the not altogether unprecedented method of holding meetings, collecting money, making speeches, and adopting resolutions.[2]

The best skill of the Crown lawyers had been devoted to frame an impregnable indictment, and the contest over this important instrument was the most stubborn and decisive in the trial.

It was distributed into eleven counts, in each of which all the defendants were charged with having unlawfully, maliciously, and seditiously combined, conspired, and confederated with each other, and with divers other persons unknown, for the purpose of committing the offences imputed to them. The first count charged a conspiracy to raise discontent among Her Majesty's subjects, and to incite seditious opposition to the Government ; to stir up ill-will between Her Majesty's subjects, especially between Irishmen and Englishmen ; to excite disaffection in the army ; to assemble large meetings for the purpose of intimidation ; and to bring into hatred and contempt the Courts of Law. The ten other counts varied these charges for the purpose of bringing them with more certainty within the rules of criminal pleading. The aim of the preliminary documents called pleadings in an action or trial is to determine a simple intelligible issue to be sent to the jury ; but this stupendous document raised so many separate issues that to answer it, or even to understand it, was difficult. The Lord Chief-Justice of England afterwards described in memorable language the confusion it was calculated to create.

"The pleaders who drew this indictment," he said, "may mean one thing. the judge another, the jury a third, and the jury if asked whether the party was guilty in the only sense in which the law would condemn him might in that sense have acquitted him, whilst a fourth sense might perhaps be discovered by the Court of Error for these ambiguous phrases."

When the indictment was published the first feeling was one of profound surprise. The Attorney-General, before the bill was found, had

---

[1] "The Memory of the Dead."—See "Spirit of the Nation." The prosecution drew attention to a poem whose rare merits when they became known won it a reputation which, after more than half a century, is still fresh and universal. The author was John K. Ingram, a student of Trinity College, Dublin, then a youth under age, who has since risen through the offices and dignities of his university to become Senior Fellow and an accomplished man of letters.

[2] The attendance at the monster meetings was set out in the indictment, meeting by meeting, and the whole number exceeded three millions and a half. A movement of the people so profound and universal, had it occurred in England, would be sufficient not merely to re-adjust the legislative machinery of the State but to change the dynasty. If in Ireland it was to be answered only by a State prosecution, what, then, was Ireland? Edmund Burke, speaking of the American Colonies, had answered the question. "The Government against which a claim of liberty is tantamount to high treason, is a Government to which submission is equivalent to slavery."

declared that he was prepared to disclose "as wicked and foul a conspiracy as ever disturbed an Empire," and here was nothing to be disclosed; nothing which had not been done in public places without any design or desire of concealment. If the Traversers had been guilty of an overt act of conspiracy in attending monster meetings or meetings of the Repeal Association, it was an offence which the whole community shared. The meetings were open to everyone, and almost everyone had attended some of them. If the journalists were guilty of overt acts of conspiracy in reporting the meetings, it was a common offence, for they were reported by every journal in the island, Tory, Whig, or National. It was felt to be very probable that some of the defendants in speeches or writing had violated the strict law of seditious libel. Whether they had not usurped the prerogative of the Crown in establishing Arbitration Courts was a question of law which it would be rash to prejudge. But there was a belief nearly universal that no conspiracy existed or could be proved. And in truth no conspiracy did exist, in law or in fact, between the persons charged with this offence in the indictment. Some of them literally did not know each other; some of them existed in a still completer state of alienation, for they had ceased to know each other; some would probably not have conspired under any circumstances, conspiracy being a dangerous recreation; and others would certainly never have conspired, combined, or confederated for any serious purpose, with certain of the persons whom the law officers associated with them in the bill of indictment.

The public were puzzled to understand why so improbable an offence was charged, till they learned that it enabled the Crown to make the defendants responsible for each other's acts—to make O'Connell responsible for newspaper articles and correspondence which he may never have read; to make others responsible for his speeches which they certainly had never heard delivered; to make Mr Tierney responsible for transactions which had happened eight months before he took part in the movement, and Mr Barrett for the proceedings of an Association of which it was ultimately discovered he had never become a member. An indictment for conspiracy is a peculiarly ingenious instrument of destruction: it is not necessary for the Crown to prove that an agreement was entered into at any time or place; the jury are at liberty to infer its existence from subsequent transactions; and for the accused to prove that such an agreement never took place is, of course, impossible. The method had another important consequence. Had the Crown prosecuted any of the monster meetings as an unlawful assembly, the question of its legality must be tried in the county where the meeting took place, by men necessarily familiar with its character; but by charging a number of the meetings as overt acts in a conspiracy, the question might be remitted to a jury of Castle tradesmen who had never seen a monster meeting. "Criminal Justice," a Tory writer exultingly declared, "had formerly fished with a hook, but she now fished with a net."[1]

She had no longer, however, the advantage of fishing in muddy waters; whatever was done in this case must be done under a flood of penetrating light. It is difficult to doubt that Sir Robert Peel was possessed by the desire attributed to him, that a decent fairness and moderation might be observed, but he had to act through agents trained in a widely different policy. The importance of the case and the constitutional prudence of the head of the Government exercised some restraining influence, but men do not easily put off the habits of a lifetime, and enough of the original spirit remained to enable a philosophical observer to estimate the character of State prosecutions in Ireland in cases which were protected by their obscurity.

At the outset the traversers' counsel applied for a list of witnesses examined before the Grand Jury, some or all of whom must also be examined on the trial. The veracity and character of witnesses are circumstances upon which the weight of their testimony depend. Witnesses called to prove important facts might be persons unworthy of credit, or who had forfeited all character in their own districts by evil lives, or who were notoriously absent from the transactions they pretended to describe. But how was this to be proved if the traversers heard their names for the first time when they were produced in the witness-box? In England the practice, in all indictments for conspiracy, is to furnish the list as a matter of course. In the then recent Chartist trials it had been furnished; the Traversers' counsel demanded whether the same thing could be refused in Ireland. The Crown lawyers were of opinion that it could and ought to be refused. Admitting the English practice, they contended that a contrary practice prevailed in Ireland. The humane and liberal policy of later legislation, which extended the privileges of the accused and narrowed the harsh prerogative of the Crown, was still, they declared, unknown in the Four Courts, and it was now to be judicially determined whether an Irishman charged with conspiracy in Dublin should enjoy the same safeguards as

---

[1] *Quarterly Review*, Dec. 1844.

an Englishman tried for the same offence in Westminster. When the Court delivered judgment Mr Justice Perrin was of opinion that there ought to be an uniform practice throughout the United Kingdom; but the majority of the Court ruled otherwise. The judgment of the Chief-Justice reads like one of the amenities of Jeffreys to the State prisoners of James II. "Their defence," he said, "if any defence they have, does not depend on the names of the witnesses, but the nature of the charge. . . . The defendants would not be a whit benefited by knowing whether the names of the witnesses are A B or C D." And so it was determined, literally in the face of Europe, that there should be one law for political offences in England and another in Ireland.[1]

On the 21st of November the Traversers pleaded, and it became necessary to fix a day for the trial. Their counsel read a joint affidavit from the solicitors, asking for a delay on account of the unprecedented body of evidence which they had to collect or digest. The indictment charged a long roll of overt acts occurring in widely separated districts, and extending over a period of nine months; and it appeared by the "bill of particulars" that all the speeches, resolutions, and documents, and all the acts done at the several meetings, as well as the entire contents of thirty-four numbers of the *Pilot*, thirty-nine numbers of the *Nation*, and forty-one numbers of the *Freeman's Journal*, would be made evidence. With such a vast variety of facts to be inquired into, if they were limited to the time ordinarily allowed to prepare a defence, it would amount to a manifest denial of justice. In order that they might have two months to perform their arduous duty, they asked that the trial should not take place earlier than the 1st of February.

The Attorney-General did not consider that these facts justified delay; the Traversers, who were themselves present at the meetings or reported them in their newspapers, must necessarily be familiar with all the circumstances, and could not suffer by a speedy trial. The rejoinder was complete. There were some of the Traversers who were not present at a single monster meeting, others who were present at only one or two, some of them owned no newspaper; and it was certain that not one of the eight Traversers had read the whole of the hundred and twenty-four newspapers for which it was proposed to hold them responsible. To become acquainted with so vast a body of facts in a

---

[1] The names never were disclosed till after the verdict, and then it was discovered that twenty-three witnesses had been produced before the Grand Jury, of whom only nine were subsequently examined at the trial and subjected to the test of cross-examination.

few days was manifestly impossible. This argument, however, did not prevail with the Court or the Crown. But there was another ground taken up by counsel from which it proved to be impossible to dislodge them. The Crown was about to move for a special jury (that is, for a jury of a class over which the Crown has most influence), and the special jury list was at that moment undergoing the ordinary annual revision before the Recorder, and would not be in legal operation before January. An affidavit was read from Mr Mahony, which let in a flood of light on the art of panel-making as practised under sheriffs appointed by the old Corporation or the Crown. He had applied at the sheriff's office for a copy of the general jurors' book, and a list of the special jurors for the current year; but both applications were refused. As a last resource he went to the office of the Clerk of the Peace and inspected the returns made by the collectors of Grand Jury Cess from which the General Jury List is made up. Upwards of eleven thousand houses in Dublin were rated at the amount which qualified the owner to be on the jury list, but the list of persons liable to serve, furnished by the collectors, amounted to less than five thousand; and among the five thousand there were more than four hundred whose Christian names, by which alone they could be identified and summoned, were omitted. The latest Special Jury List open to inspection disclosed more alarming discrepancies. It was supposed to contain the names of all persons in the city of Dublin qualified to serve as special jurors. Peers, baronets, and their eldest sons, persons entitled to the style of esquire, all wholesale traders, and retail traders worth five thousand pounds, were entitled to be placed on the list. But it contained only three hundred and eighty-eight names in all, and of this small number upwards of seventy were disqualified or incapable of serving; some being dead, some disabled by bodily infirmity or non-residence, and the remainder excluded by statute as city magistrates or members of the Corporation. The omissions were not accidental, but systematic; of the three hundred and eighty-eight, only fifty-three, or less than one in seven, were Catholics. And these fifty-three were further diminished by the circumstance that thirty of them were among the seventy who were disqualified. Out of the three hundred and thirty-three Protestants forty were disqualified or only one in eight; out of fifty-three Catholics thirty were disqualified, or more than one in two, leaving only twenty-three persons professing the Catholic religion on the special jury list for the Catholic city of Dublin. Mr Mahony was able to affirm, from an experience of more than a quarter of a century in the practice of his profession, that instead of twenty-three there were at least three hundred Catholics in Dublin entitled to act as special jurors. It is highly probable from the current of their decisions that the Court would have held these facts to be quite irrelevant, and gravely pronounced the list to be unexceptionable; but there were other facts which could not be conveniently ignored. A few days before, the Recorder, in the process of revising the list for the coming year, took occasion to state that he had complained to successive sheriffs of its imperfect condition, and that he now hoped, with the aid of counsel and agents (who attended for the purpose on behalf of the Traversers), to be able to form for the first time a full and fair jurors' book. The Recorder in question was Mr Frederick Shaw, member for Dublin University, and one of the Privy Councillors who had signed the proclamation against the Clontarf meeting. Mr Shaw was a Parliamentary personage of considerable importance, and at this time was becoming somewhat discontented with Peel, of whom he had been an efficient supporter. In the face of his admission, which he might feel it his duty to repeat in the House of Commons, it would have been perilous to proceed; and the law officers said that after what had fallen from so eminent a judge they would consent to a delay. They proposed to fix the trial not for the 1st of February, but for the first Monday of the ensuing term, the 15th of January, the date at which the new jurors' book would come into operation.

The jurors' book, such as it was discovered to be in 1843, probably contained a larger proportion of Catholics than had been placed upon it at any time since the Revolution of 1688, and for five generations the property, liberty, and lives of Irish Catholics had been made the sport of a permanent conspiracy of Crown officials, acting with the audacity which long impunity creates. In recent times it was known that a small knot of broken-down citizens of safe politics were enabled to live by the trade of being special jurors. They were always in court their confederates in the Sheriff's Office and the Crown offices knew they were to be relied upon, and they went into the jurors' room to earn the fee paid in such cases with as much regularity as the sheriff's bailiffs took their place outside the door. This was the highest court of criminal jurisdiction in the kingdom, and the most scrupulous in its procedure; in the utter darkness of a petty sessions, where the naked peasant had often to face an angry master sitting as his judge, only a morbid imagination can picture the horrors sometimes transacted. Yet English statesmen and publicists have found it difficult to understand why the law was not trusted or venerated in Ireland.

The revision of the jury list now became the point of public interest, and the Recorder gave it assiduous attention. The rate-collectors' books supplied the names of all rate-paying citizens, and with care and patience the full and fair jurors' book which he proposed to frame seemed at length likely to be attained. But the officials of the Sheriff's Office, who had stuffed panels and packed juries for a lifetime, were not easily baffled. The special jury list was indeed increased from 388 to 717 names,[1] but they had executed a manœuvre equivalent to picking the best trump out of a pack of cards. It was this transaction, to be presently detailed, which Lord Denman afterwards described as one which rendered trial by jury in Ireland "a mockery, a delusion, and a snare."

On the 3rd of January the agents in the case, accompanied by counsel, attended before the Clerk of the Crown to strike the special jury which was to be sworn a fortnight later. Sharp practice was still the order of the day. The Attorney-General had issued summonses for this meeting before the special jury list was in legal existence, and since it had come into existence the Sheriff had refused a copy of it to the Traversers. The statute under which they were proceeding gave each party the right to make certain objections to jurors; the Crown had the list and would be prepared with objections, but how could the Traversers be prepared, if they did not know the names? Hitherto the uniform practice had been to furnish the list; the practice was so unbroken that it assumed the strength and character of law. They therefore demanded a copy and a postponement for a few days in order to scrutinise it. The Clerk of the Crown, who is the presiding officer on these occasions, remarked that there was no affidavit, and in the absence of legal proof that the Sheriff had refused the list he could not entertain the application for postponement. The agent for the Traversers replied that the Sheriff was then present in the room, and might, without inordinate inconvenience be asked whether he had not refused. But this was an expedient so informal that the official gentleman would not condescend to have recourse to it. Counsel, however, succeeded in extracting from the Sheriff an admission that the list had been refused, and a postponement till twelve o'clock next day was at length recorded, that the Traversers might be enabled to

---

[1] A more careful revision in later times raised the number to 1100.

exercise the right conferred on them by law of objecting to persons to whom a legal objection existed.

But the gentlemen of the Sheriff's office were not at the end of their resources. No copy of the list was ready; but they were willing to read it aloud and allow the agents—the attendance of their clerks being forbidden—to copy the names with their own hands. Could anything be fairer or more obliging? Copying the names, addresses, and additions of seven hundred and seventeen persons, to be written by gentlemen long unaccustomed to that class of manual labour, occupied till half-past eight o'clock at night; and as the jury was to be struck at twelve o'clock next morning, the Traversers were welcome to such scrutiny as they could accomplish in the interval.

When the parties met at noon next day, Mr Whiteside, with a grave and decorous reserve very trying to the temper of those who knew the facts which had been discovered in the interval, complained that, by some quite unaccountable mistake, the names of sixty persons who had been adjudicated on by the Recorder and duly entered on the Common Jury-book as special jurors were altogether omitted from the list from which it was now proposed to strike the jury. Among those omitted were some of the most eminent, wealthy, and respectable men in the community. Nearly one-tenth of the special jurors of the city were dropped out, and he submitted that the officer could not proceed to strike a jury from so defective a panel. These facts he proposed to establish by calling on the Clerk of the Crown to produce the Common Jurors' book, where the names omitted from the special jury list would be found recorded. Mr Brewster, who was afterwards acclimatised in the mild region of Conservatism as a Peelite, was at this time a fierce and even truculent Tory, who had only recently emerged from the boisterous contests of a criminal court. On behalf of the Crown he flatly objected to the book being produced or referred to; their business was to strike a jury, and to striking a jury they must confine themselves. Mr Ford, who was in attendance as solicitor for O'Connell, grew impatient at this fencing with foils. He exclaimed vehemently that there had been "an infamous tampering with the list;" the names of many of the best known Catholic gentlemen in the city had been illegally suppressed; and he protested against using the panel under such shameful circumstances. The Clerk of the Crown, who had lived all his life in the atmosphere of Protestant ascendancy, in the jury-box as well as in the State, and who was accustomed to the vulgar discontent of the majority, overruled this objection and gravely proceeded to strike the jury from the mutilated list. And so the first stage of this great trial commenced under an angry sense of foul play, which speedily spread from the Crown Office to the city, and from the city to the whole country. If English government in Ireland was on its trial before the great international court of public opinion the evidence was becoming critical.

Striking a special jury, according to the system which then prevailed, was a mixed game of chance and skill. As many cards as there were names on the jurors' list were put into a ballot box, where they were, or ought to be, well shaken; then forty-eight cards were drawn out and the names on the jury list corresponding with the numbers on the cards so drawn constituted the panel. The forty-eight names on the panel were reduced one-half by each party striking off any twelve they thought proper; and of the two dozen who remained the twelve who first answer to their names in court on the day of trial must be sworn on the jury. Experienced players are said to have great advantages over novices in the method of placing the cards in the box, and in the method of drawing them out of the box, but these are mysteries on which the uninitiated speculate in vain.

Upon the present occasion there were eleven Catholics among the forty-eight jurors drawn. The practice is for the attorney on each side to strike off a name in his turn. Mr Kemmis on behalf of the Crown struck off one after another, as the opportunity arose, every Catholic on the list. He had often done so before in administering what was called justice in Ireland, but the business was no longer transacted in silence and darkness. Each exercise of his power was followed by a bitter commentary from Mr Cantwell. "There goes the first Papist," he cried; "another Catholic," and "another" till the work was completed. Next morning it was known throughout the United Kingdom, and speedily known over Europe and America, that the most eminent Catholic in the Empire, a man whose name was familiar to every educated Catholic in the world, was about to be placed upon his trial in the Catholic metropolis of a Catholic country, before four judges and twelve jurors among whom there was not a single Catholic. The effect which this transaction produced on the public mind in Ireland may be compared to the effect produced in England by some of the most offensive aggressions of James II. Yet James never tried a Protestant gentleman in Middlesex before a bench and a jury composed exclusively of Catholics. The seven bishops were tried before a Protestant jury, which in England was putting them on their country, but the English Government, a century and a half later, dared not put O'Connell on the country in Ireland.

Jury-packing was not new, but so gross an application of the practice to a victim so distinguished wounded the national pride as keenly as if it were new. An aggregate meeting of Catholics was immediately summoned to address the Crown on the subject of this "insult and wrong" inflicted on the "emancipated Catholics" by direction of the Queen's Ministers. The requisition was signed by a number of gentlemen who never were Repealers, but steady partisans of the Whigs before and since this transaction. Names like William Murphy of Smithfield, D. R. Pigot, Dominic Corrigan, Matthew Corbally, Francis Codd, John Ball, Thomas Galway, and Walter Sweetman, were not smirched by contact with popular agitations;[1] and still less other names destined, four years later, when the Whig Government were prosecuting another batch of Irish Nationalists, to have their sincerity submitted to a sharp test. One may still read appended to the requisition against jury-packing the names of James Henry Monahan, Attorney-General during the State prosecutions of 1848; James O'Brien, one of the Crown Counsel, aiding him on that occasion; and Thomas Redington, Under Secretary for Ireland, as well as the names of Richard Sheil and Thomas Wyse, who held office out of Ireland during the same memorable period.

At the aggregate meeting some of the most eminent of the requisitionists declared that the exclusion of Catholics from the jury was an intolerable wrong, and that the previous omissions of Catholics from the special jury list afforded grounds for suspicion that foul dealing had been practised. By this time it was ascertained that the number of Catholics omitted amounted to thirty, being more than the entire number on the list before it was revised. On the new list as it now stood, the names of Catholics were about one-fourth; of the names improperly omitted there were more than one-half. All the great towns followed the example of Dublin, and a little later the English Catholics addressed the Queen on the subject. The English Catholics were not Repealers, and were reputed to be but lukewarm in their sympathy with Irish interests; but their pride as a class and their sense

---

[1] English readers will need to be told that Mr Pigot afterwards became Chief Baron, Dr Corrigan became a baronet, a member of Parliament, and President of the College of Physicians in Ireland; and Mr Ball became Under Secretary for the Colonies, and was better known in later times as President of the Alpine Club, and an accomplished man of letters.

of justice were wounded by this transaction. Many of them were influential by wealth and station, and they had relations with the great Catholic States of Europe, where their complaints would be sure to find an echo. Nine English and Scottish peers and a large number of country gentlemen, among whom the historic names of Talbot, Howard, Vavasour, Weld, Townley, Langdale, and Maxwell were conspicuous, took part in this protest.

While the trial was still in its preliminary stages one of the Traversers, Father Tyrrell, died. His death was attributed to fatigue, endured on the night before the Sunday fixed for the Clontarf meeting. When the news of the proclamation reached him he was in bed; he immediately got on horseback and spent the greater part of a bleak October night in the open air, making arrangements to prevent his parishioners from going to Clontarf. A week later he was arrested for conspiracy, and in a few weeks he was carried to his grave.

CHAPTER II.

HOW THE TRAVERSERS WERE CONVICTED.

WHEN the day appointed for the opening of the State trial arrived,[1] the interest was intense and nearly universal. In the city business seemed to have stopped suddenly like a clock that had run down. From an early hour two living currents set in opposite directions, one towards O'Connell's house in Merrion Square, from which a civic procession accompanied the Traversers, the other to the Four Courts where the trial was to take place. Every warehouse, every office, every workshop, contributed to swell these agitated streams. In the great hall of the Courts it had become necessary to fence the entrance to the Queen's Bench with barriers of solid oak, and here only the Traversers were permitted to pass. The eager crowd of their friends strained against the barrier for the chance of a glance within, or flowed out along the quays on both sides of the river, waiting impatiently for news of a contest, which, instead of yielding any decisive result that day, was about to occupy weeks, and even months, in its languid course. The court was crammed in every part, the precincts of the bench itself were invaded by fashionable toilettes, and the public interest was represented by more reporters than the Press of England and Ireland had ever before sent to a single court.

When the jury list was called over, and the first juror was directed to take the book in his hand, the Traversers' counsel interposed with a challenge to the array. A challenge to the array is a proceeding which calls in question the legal competence of the panel, and prays that it may be quashed. Public opinion had been appealed to with respect to the exclusion of Catholic jurors, but the legal question was now to be tried whether the jurors' book, with so many names abstracted from it, complied with the requirements of the statute regulating juries.

The case of the Traversers was logically complete; there had confessedly been fraud, and fraud would vitiate the judgment of the

---

[1] 15th January 1844.

highest court in the realm; *a fortiori* it vitiated the proceedings of the subordinate court of a Recorder. On any theory the panel could not stand; either the Recorder himself caused a fraudulent list to be made out, which beyond controversy would be a fatal objection under the statute; or, as the Traversers believed, some person without his knowledge had made up the list in its defective condition, in which case it was not a list "made up by the Recorder" as the law required. The statute directed him to frame a list containing the names of "all" qualified persons; it was admitted that the existing list did not comply with this direction; and, if the Crown persisted in using the panel framed from it, the Traversers would be denied their right to be tried by a jury constituted according to law.

The Court made up its mind promptly on the demurrer. Judge Perrin was of opinion that the challenge ought to be allowed, as the list had been falsified to the extent of omitting the materials for five entire juries. As respects inconvenience, judges should not regard the consequences of their decision; the inconvenience must be remedied by those whose province it was to make laws. Chief-Justice Pennefather and the majority of the Court, however, overruled the challenge and allowed the demurrer. Names had been omitted by some mistake, but the list still contained seven hundred and seventeen names from which a jury might be fairly selected; a better panel could perhaps have been made, but the omission did not render the proceedings null and void.

During this legal argument it would have been considered highly indecorous to allude to the fact that half of the jurors omitted from the panel were Catholics. The Court would have regarded such a statement as wholly irrelevant, and not a little offensive, and counsel were too discreet to risk it. But in angrier times, which were not far distant, these official proprieties, as we shall see, proved too fragile and artificial a barrier to restrain men contending for their lives and fortunes from uttering the naked truth.

A jury was at length sworn to make a true deliverance between the Crown and the Traversers. It was skilfully selected if the aim was to constitute a tribunal sensitive to the opinion of the propertied classes. It was composed of a half-pay officer, a fashionable gunsmith, four wine merchants, a pianoforte maker, a surveyor, a tanner, a wholesale grocer, a dealer in porcelain, and a retired attorney, who in the end proved useful to the Crown in framing the verdict over which the laym stumbled.

Though there was not one Catholic among the twelve, it was noted that there was one Englishman; as among the four judges, though there was not one Catholic, there was also one Englishman. Mr Justice Burton had come to Ireland as a clerk to John Philpot Curran before the Union; his national prejudices, however, were considerably modified by long residence in the country, and he was not a man in any case to be consciously swayed from the right. But he was old, and found it nearly impossible to keep his faculties in a state of activity, and he had no clear idea of constitutional rights. Chief-Justice Pennefather, descended from a family of Puritan "Undertakers," gorged with lands and offices during the penal times, but still on the watch for Ministerial favours for his kith and kin, had been a fierce politician, and could scarcely regard one who questioned English Supremacy or Protestant Ascendancy in Ireland except as a personal enemy. He was a skilful lawyer, but his law and his skill were as much at the service of the Crown as those of the supplest judge who found favour with the Stuarts. Mr Justice Crampton also had been a vehement Tory at the Bar, and his appointment to the office of Solicitor-General by the Whigs in 1832 had first alienated O'Connell from that party; but on the bench he aimed to be a discreet judge and contrasted favourably with some of his colleagues. Mr Justice Perrin had been Attorney-General under the Whigs, and with the Solicitor-General Mr O'Loghlen had first instituted the practice of selecting juries in Crown cases with an approximation to fairness. These personages so bred and disciplined could no more escape from the influence of their nature and training than ordinary mortals.

The Attorney-General's statement of the case occupied two days, during which he spoke for nearly twelve hours. Public interest has seldom been more painfully strained than it was when he began; but before he concluded it had become languid and intermittent. He had promised to disclose a foul and wicked conspiracy; and if he had been able to prove secret consultations, correspondence with soldiers and foreigners, a military organisation or private drilling, it would have barely justified language so emphatic. But there was not a single fact relied on which was not long familiar to his audience. Speeches of O'Connell, articles from the popular journals, and endless extracts from English jurists to illustrate the law of conspiracy, sandwiched between little staid sentences of prim commonplace, constituted the interminable speech. An eye-witness, one of the Traversers indeed, has enabled us to recall this curious scene.

"Men who had expected a lofty and solemn impeachment soon sickened under the weary monotony with which Mr Smith read his litany of extracts. Drip, drip, like water from a rusty pump, the familiar facts fell from his lips. Piece by piece he threw up the bill of indictment, as he swallowed it, without mastication or digestion. Sustained attention became impossible, and he soon travelled his weary way alone. No eye was turned towards him, no ear listened to him but those of a few old imperturbable lawyers. At one of the most important points of the indictment might be seen two of the Traversers reading newspapers, one copying documents for his defence, two writing autographs in ladies' albums, one noting a brief, and the rest absent from the Court, while the majority of the junior Bar were joking *sotto voce*, the audience eating sandwiches or chatting—a painter making sketches of the ladies in the gallery—fully half the jury fiddling listlessly with their pens, the other half making painful exertions to do their duty—two or three of the counsel for the defence reading their briefs, and one of the judges fast asleep."[1]

This speech, so hard to listen to, was not wanting, when it came to be read, in method, or even in a certain persuasiveness. What was new, however, may be compressed into a paragraph or two. Mr O'Connell was not bearding English law in Ireland for the first time or by new methods. In 1831 he agitated for Repeal, and Lord Althorp warned Parliament that the direct tendency of his language and conduct was to incite insurrection. Lord John Russell on the same occasion declared if he succeeded the result would be the destruction of the British Monarchy in Ireland and the establishment of a ferocious republic. Then and now he had recommended submission to the law, but it was submission to the law till he was ready to break it successfully. The monster meetings assembled and dispersed peaceably, because the time for action had not come. He asked the people attending them, "Will you be ready when I want you again?"—a part of the scheme being to complete the organisation before the signal was given. He inquired whether they could not walk in order after a band as well as if they wore red coats, and if they could not obey Repeal Wardens as well as if these persons were called sergeants or captain. He assured them that there was a natural military strength in Ireland such as few countries possessed; her enclosures made every field a redoubt where cavalry could not charge infantry, and her roads were defiles. Was this language employed for the purpose of petitioning Parliament or promoting

---

[1] *Nation*, Jan. 20th.—As I was the writer of this sketch I can vouch for the strict accuracy of all the details. The somnolent judge was Burton. The wits made constant sport of this habit, *ex. gr.*
"Nota Bene, who says—Is it Shakespeare or Sancho?
See the moonlight that's sleeping (like Burton) in banco."
M'Carthy's "Scrapes of a Sawbone."

a constitutional movement by legal agencies? So lately as September he had assured his adherents that if his present plans were frustrated they had sufficient resources remaining for success; they might increase the potato culture, and leave the entire cereal harvest uncut; and they might abandon the use of excisable articles. To leave the corn to rot on the ground, to cripple the public revenue—these were the legal and constitutional methods by which the Irish Parliament was to be restored.

In describing the formidable instrument which the jury wielded in an indictment for conspiracy the language of the Attorney-General became clear and precise.

The mere confederacy to do an illegal act constituted the crime, though the purpose was never accomplished. It was not necessary to prove the conspiracy; the jury might assume its existence if the conduct of the accused justified the assumption. Neither was it necessary that they should be of opinion that the defendants were guilty of every portion of the conspiracy; if they were guilty of any portion of it, that was sufficient to justify a verdict against them.

Witnesses were then produced. For seven days the tedious process of proving facts which were of common notoriety, and of reading public documents and public journals, went on. Ten days were consumed in the *mêlée* of the Bar. Each Traverser was heard by counsel except O'Connell, who defended himself; and Greene, the Solicitor-General, made a reply of remarkable clearness and vigour which occupied nearly three days. Some of the speeches for the defence were reputed at the time to be marvellous efforts of forensic oratory, but read a generation later, there is a mocking and artificial tone in this hired advocacy of a national cause which is painfully disappointing. The duty of counsel was to obtain a verdict, and to this end all higher aims were subordinated; their tones were pitched to the compass, not of a nation, but of a *nisi prius* court; and the Traversers were often mortified by ignorant banter of historical names and events which they honoured.[1]

---

[1] Mr Sheil spoke on behalf of John O'Connell, Mr Moore on behalf of Father Tierney, Mr Hatchell of T. M. Ray, Mr Fitzgibbon of John Gray, Mr Whiteside of Charles Gavan Duffy, Mr M'Donough of Richard Barrett, Mr Henn of Tom Steele; O'Connell's defence of himself concluded the series of speeches to the jury. Mr Whiteside, a man of large presence and sonorous voice, was supposed to have won the crown in this rhetorical contest. His speech was pronounced to be a masterpiece of advocacy, but my personal impression did not correspond with this opinion. It wanted the subtle charm of sincerity, and some pulses keenly sensitive to that wonderful instrument, the human voice, were unmoved by it. In the *Irish Monthly* for February 1877, a private letter from one of the Traversers to a *Dublin Reviewer*

The case upon which the counsel for the defence relied, stripped of whatever was merely temporary or technical, may be briefly stated :—

The jury were not empannelled to try whether the Repeal of the Union was desirable or undesirable, but to try whether the Traversers were guilty of the specific offence of conspiracy.

The offence of conspiracy consisted of an agreement to do something illegal. Unless there was an especial agreement for this object among the persons indicted there was no conspiracy. Agreement was essential; each of the defendants might entertain in his own mind an illegal intention, and yet this would not constitute the offence unless they had combined and confederated for a common object. There had been no attempt to prove any agreement for an illegal purpose. They were agreed to bring about the Repeal of the 40th George III., called the Act of Union, but that was a perfectly legal object. The effect of this distinction was signal; if men combined for a legal purpose, and if in the prosecution of the common design one of them transgressed the law, he was answerable for his own offence, but he did not implicate the innocent. Thus every one of the overt acts in the indictment might be proved, and yet it would not follow that the jury would be justified in convicting the Traversers of conspiracy. Why so? Because these overt acts might not have been done in pursuance of an illegal agreement. If meetings were illegal, why were they not separately prosecuted? To know them to be illegal, and yet encourage them to proceed, would amount to unpardonable baseness in the Government.

There was another notable departure from English practice. The Traversers were charged with a new offence—the offence of procuring the attendance of large numbers, for the seditious purpose of obtaining changes in the constitution of the country by intimidation and the exhibition of physical force. But the assembly of the people in large numbers did not constitute illegality. On the contrary, whatever England holds most dear in her institutions was obtained by the method now indicted as unlawful. The exhibition of physical force, though not the employment of it, was an ordinary and constitutional agent in movements to procure reforms from Parliament.

When the privileges of the English Parliament were invaded, the English people did not stand on scruples; they took the field, struck down the monarchy, and dragged their sovereign to the block. But there was no need

---

(C. G. Duffy to Peter M'Evoy Gartlan) is published, and a paragraph is worth quoting : " To say there is not a sentence in Whiteside's speech that is not effective is to claim for him what is true of no living man, and is eminently untrue of him. There were many weak, some ill-judged, and several highly objectionable passages ; and his manner throughout was a mixture of the declamatory and the familiar, begotten upon a bad debating society style by the habit of squabbling with ;Mr M'Donough. There is perhaps no reason why you should say this in so many words ; but really there ought to be some shade in your picture, as the glare is too much for moderate eyes. I conceive you have committed the same error with respect to O'Connell. Posterity are entitled to know that he never delivered a speech so carelessly and ineffectively as this one. Let them interpret the fact as they please— and it is capable of a highly favourable construction—they have a claim, at all events, to have it stated in a journal that looks to be a magazine of historical materials." As a rhetorical effort Sheil's speech was superior to Whiteside's.

to go back for examples to distant times. When the Whigs wanted to carry the Reform Bill of 1832, a hundred and fifty thousand men assembled in Birmingham and threatened to march on London. A resolution not to pay taxes was passed, and was applauded by Lord Fitzwilliam. Cabinet ministers became correspondents of the Birmingham Union. Cumber was reduced to ashes, Bristol was in flames, and the Whig Ministers, instead of dissociating themselves from popular opinion, which had plainly violated the law, proposed to swamp the House of Peers, and declared that the whisper of a faction must not drown the voice of the people.

But none of these English confederacies was indicted for conspiracy to procure changes by means of intimidation. Even in Ireland no precedent could be discovered for this charge. For the last three generations the history of Ireland was occupied chiefly with popular organisations for the attainment of one public object or another. Almost every object sought was now the law of the land, and had been conceded because it was demanded by organised opinion.

But they were not indicted for a conspiracy to intimidate the legislature. The ordinary agents for obtaining or resisting constitutional changes were popular power, popular enthusiasm, and popular determination. Let the twelve gentlemen in the box hold a meeting to accomplish some legitimate public purpose, and as they were but twelve the Press would ignore their meeting and the Government disregard it. But let twelve hundred of the same class meet for the same object and the reporters would flock to hear them and the Ministers might hearken. But suppose twelve hundred thousand men met for the same object, they must be listened to; and they would no more be conspirators, or an illegal assembly, in the last case than in the first.

There was another startling novelty in this indictment. It charged the Traversers with a conspiracy to promote ill-will among the Queen's subjects in Ireland against her subjects in England. This was an offence never before heard of in criminal law. If it were an offence, on what evidence did it rest? The Traversers seeking to convince their audience that a Repeal of the Union would be beneficial had recourse to the most powerful arguments that could be employed—illustrations from past history. It was not alleged that they falsified facts or misquoted history; and if past history was calculated to produce ill-will between the two peoples that was a fact to be deplored, but it was no fault of the Traversers.

The indictment charged the Traversers with a conspiracy to excite discontent and disaffection. If this charge was supported in a court of law there was an end of all chance of getting rid of bad laws and obtaining good ones! How was it possible to convince men that a new law was necessary, or that an existing law ought to be amended or repealed, without a risk of exciting discontent among those who profited by the law as it stood?

It charged them also with a conspiracy to create discontent in the army. What was the evidence for this charge? Certain speeches of Mr O'Connell, in which he expressed an opinion that non-commissioned officers ought to be promoted, instead of a system of purchase prevailing; a letter from Father Power, and an article from the *Nation* on the conditions which render a war just and necessary. The Attorney-General did not prosecute the priest who wrote the letter, or the paper which published it, but made it part of a conspiracy by persons who never saw the writer and never read the letter. This was not fair dealing. Why were those Traversers who had no control over the newspapers to be made responsible for them? Mr O'Connell was treated as if he were editor of the *Freeman*, the *Pilot*, and the *Nation*. If a prosecution for conspiracy were instituted in England against the Anti-Corn Law League, would it be reasonable to hold Mr Cobden and Mr Bright responsible for every article in the *Chronicle*, the *Globe*, and the *Sun?* The most notable conditions of a conspiracy were wanting. Mr Barrett was not a member of the Repeal Association, Mr Ray spoke but once, Mr Tierney had attended but one of the monster meetings, a meeting in his own parish, at which none of the other Traversers were present; Mr Duffy had not attended even one; and Mr O'Connell had no connection with the newspapers. If several persons were each ignorant of the acts of the others, it was settled law that under such circumstances they could not be considered guilty of them; yet Mr Tierney was indicted for speeches, writings, and transactions which had occurred eight months before he joined the Association or had any communication with the other Traversers.

O'Connell defended himself. His speech, which was not addressed to the jury but to the world, was a justification of his principles as a Repealer. But it was not eminently successful—the materials were necessarily borrowed from familiar sources, and were not relieved on this occasion by freshness of treatment or vigour of delivery.

This was the case for the defence, and on this case the Traversers were entitled to a verdict of acquittal. For whatever were their aims or their acts, they were not guilty of the offence charged in the indictment: they had not conspired together for an illegal purpose. Of O'Connell it may be confidently asserted that he was no more guilty of conspiracy than of bigamy. But when the Solicitor-General had replied, and the Chief-Justice had charged the jury, the case was brought back to the narrow issue whether or not the municipal law had been violated; that issue by which English judges in all centuries have sought to trammel popular power, and under which nearly every function which Englishmen venerate in their constitution would, in its first exercise, have been pronounced illegal and criminal.[1]

The Solicitor-General's reply was vigorous but narrow. He admitted that a Repeal of the Union was the object the Traversers had in view, but they sought to accomplish an object not in itself illegal by illegal means: first by the exhibition of physical force, whereas an Act of

---

[1] A startling incident interrupted the course of the defence. Mr Fitzgibbon vexed the Attorney-General by a personal reflection, and the law officer who was "prosecuting seven gentlemen for an imputed misdemeanour immediately sought to commit a felony on his own account"; he sent a hostile message to his learned friend. It was an incident which might have brought the prosecution to an ignominious close; for counsel menaced in the performance of their duty by threats of personal violence from the representative of the Crown might have thrown up their briefs and retired. But the Court, with a benevolence none of which it reserved for the benefit of the Traversers, interfered, and the quarrel was composed.

Parliament could only be properly repealed by the uncontrolled action of the Legislature.

Their meetings were orderly; the charge was not that they were disorderly, but that they were held for the unlawful purpose of alarming and intimidating the people of England and the Legislature of the empire. Mr O'Connell suggested that the time might come when the manufactories of England and the City of London would be burned by Irishmen. Was it not plain that the object was intimidation? and intimidation was the offence charged in the indictment. At Mullaghmast Mr O'Connell told the people that in '98 there were brave men at their head, but there were also many traitors who left them exposed to the sword of the enemy. The enemy!—that was the king's army. He told them that it was an ill-organised, a premature, and a foolish insurrection; but they had a leader now who would never allow them to be led astray. What was the meaning of "led astray"? It meant that their present leader would not let them break out too soon, but teach them to wait for a regular course of organisation and preparation. Mr O'Connell in addressing the jury had an opportunity of explaining or qualifying his language, but he had not done so in a single instance. It was a fact of great significance that Mr O'Connell had not attended Parliament or adopted any measure to raise the question in a constitutional manner. On the contrary, all authority was concentrated in the Association. There was scarcely a public department in the State whose functions it had not usurped, and scarcely a public officer whose duties were not assumed by some one or more of the Traversers. One of them had taken on himself the office of Lord Chancellor and regulated the administration of justice; another that of Prime Minister; and above all, there was a Chancellor of the Exchequer and a Treasury.

The temper of the Chief-Justice had been sorely tried by the delay, by the unexampled plain-speaking of counsel, and by the comments of the Press. His turn had now come, and he was determined to make short work of the defence. Grown grey in the exercise of arbitrary authority, confident from long impunity of protection in Parliament and completely hardened against opinion at home, he forgot that on this occasion he had the civilised world for an audience, and proceeded to deliver himself as if the Queen's Bench was a court of final judgment, and that his charge would find no echo beyond the circular road. A Whig peer, who had been Lord Lieutenant of Ireland, afterwards declared in the House of Lords that when he came to read the charge in a newspaper he could not persuade himself in the first instance that he was not still reading the Solicitor-General's speech for the prosecution.[1] A "lapsus" of the Chief-Justice during the trial lent this criticism a keen edge. In criminal cases the presiding judge ordinarily regards himself as the prisoner's counsel, but in laying down a

---

[1] Lord Fortescue.

principle of law the Chief-Justice observed that he was speaking "under the correction of the gentlemen of the other side"; the other side from this prerogative judge being the side of the defence. His main purpose seemed to be to supply oversights or deficiencies in the case for the Crown, and he applied himself to carry it out without shame or reserve. He told the jury that he saw no great difficulty in the law or the facts. He bade them put out of their minds the idea that the offence of conspiracy necessarily implied secrecy, as had been suggested; if the parties conspired to overawe Parliament and cause alarm and terror in Her Majesty's subjects, publicity and not secrecy might be the fittest agent. Suppose the object of collecting together these hundreds of thousands was not to commit a present breach of the peace, but to deter the Legislature from exercising a deliberate and unbiassed judgment on public questions, that was an illegal object. The speeches at these meetings were generally made by Mr Daniel O'Connell, but others of the Traversers seized the opportunity of displaying themselves.

The cards of the Association, of which the Crown Counsel had not made much use, seemed a very serious offence in the eyes of the judge. One of them, he remarked, had on the face of it inscribed in green colours an enumeration of the powers, population, and resources of Ireland relatively to other countries, and it concluded with a sort of chorus "And yet she has no Parliament." To disseminate upon these cards that from their strength and consequence the people of Ireland ought to have a Parliament, and yet had not one, was to disseminate a statement of matters upon which the members of the Association had no right to make a decision. Others of them contained portraits of persons implicated in rebellious or treasonable practices.

The case of Mr Tierney was full of difficulties to many friends of the Government, but it presented none to the Chief-Justice. The jury were invited to mark that though he only joined the Association the day after the Mullaghmast meeting, "he had a little pet meeting of his own in his own parish the day of the Tara meeting." Nothing that was said or done there had been pressed by the Crown as of any consequence, but he attended the Repeal Association on the third of October—only a fortnight before the prosecution commenced— and it was for the jury to consider whether his speech on that occasion did not fall in with the common design of the defendants. Why did he introduce such topics as English perfidy and cruelty, Irish victories and English defeats? It was for the jury to say whether they were brought forward, after the lapse of two or three hundred years, to promote Christian charity and peace? Was his speech not in unison with the speech of Mr O'Connell detailing the massacres at Mullaghmast and Wexford? Did the jury see here anything of community of purpose and design? It was for them to say.

Before the judge had finished some of the critical audience who listened to him pronounced that he had misdirected the jury, a blunder which would render the trial void; and others were of opinion that he had disgraced the Irish Courts before the world by the temper of his charge. "Mr Daniel O'Connell" was not a decorous form to employ in speaking of a man who in his own profession was his undoubted superior, and who had refused a judicial office of the same rank as the Chief-Justiceship; and if the object of the Traversers, as he alleged, was to indulge in the vanity of "displaying themselves," that was not an illegal object, and was scarcely compatible with the belief that they were engaged in the formidable conspiracy charged in the indictment. When he spoke of the class of persons whose heads were engraved on the Repeal cards, it was difficult to restrain an impatient junior from reminding him that one of them was copied from the frieze of the hall where the Traversers were on trial,[1] and others from the walls of the University, carved or painted at a time when Ireland had a Parliament and was not ashamed to commemorate her historical men. Several of them were anterior to William Wallace and Robert Bruce, whom their countrymen were not forbidden to honour, though one was a proclaimed traitor and the other died on an English gallows. The picture of Parliament brooding over the public interest in a solemn stupor on which the disturbing voice of the people who created it must never obtrude was in the highest style of judicial rhetoric; but in truth it is a species of nonsense which is only talked by men in full-bottomed wigs. Parliament has never made any serious political change except under the goad of public impatience, sharply applied; and the special charge of intimidation, which the learned judge considered so formidable in this case, proved on investigation before a superior court to disclose no legal offence whatever. The Constitution confers rank and authority on judges, and fences them round with

---

[1] This was Odlam Fodlah, who gave to ancient Ireland a constitution and a code; a hero as worthy of national veneration as Alfred or Charlemagne. But this modern Puritan had the same ignorant contempt of him as may be supposed to have marked the first Pennefather who carried a knapsack and a ramrod.

immunity that they may be able to do justice without fear or favour; when they employ these advantages to promote party or personal objects they are justly regarded as amongst the basest of mankind.

The jury accepted the opinions so energetically pressed upon them. After a little decent delay they convicted all the Traversers—Mr Tierney, who had joined the Association only five days before the Clontarf meeting, as well as Mr O'Connell or Mr Ray, who had been members from its foundation. Mr Tierney was convicted on one count only, while some of the Traversers were convicted on several, and others on all the counts; but they were alike declared guilty of the crime charged in the indictment—unlawful and seditious conspiracy. The trial had lasted twenty-five days, but the result was confidently predicted from the moment the jury were sworn. O'Connell himself at that time whispered to one of the Traversers that the Attorney-General was moderate in only charging them with conspiracy, as these twelve gentlemen would have made no difficulty in convicting them of the murder of the Italian boy.[1]

The sentence, according to the practice in misdemeanour cases, was postponed till the opening of the ensuing term.

---

[1] The murder of the Italian boy was a mysterious crime which had recently caused an intense sensation in Dublin and baffled the skill of the police.

CHAPTER III.

WHAT PARLIAMENT AND ENGLISH REFORMERS THOUGHT OF THE
TRIAL.—THE SENTENCE.

THE Government had obtained a verdict, but it remained to be seen whether they had not bought it too dearly. Counsel in the case and eminent English lawyers who were consulted, agreed that good grounds existed for an appeal to the House of Lords by writ of error; a process which if successful would quash the entire proceedings. Under these circumstances the obvious policy of the Association was not to accept the law laid down in the Queen's Bench as final, till the appeal was heard. But the lawyers, who were in general anti-Repealers, and his old allies among the Irish Whigs, who had party ends in view, "both-eared" O'Connell on the necessity of rendering the Association prosecution-proof for the future, and he determined to act as if the law of Pennefather could not be disputed.

Immediately after the conviction a meeting of the General Committee was summoned to deliberate on the situation. The Committee was an overgrown cabinet, but a cabinet wanting whose concurrence the leader could no longer act, without serious danger of a catastrophe. O'Connell opened the conference by a proposal which amazed and dismayed the best of his associates. He was of opinion that the Association ought to be immediately dissolved and the Arbitration Courts abandoned. He was prepared to found a new Association, of which no newspaper proprietor would be a member, and whose wardens would receive instructions and perform duties different from those which had been made the subject of such serious rebuke in the Queen's Bench.

To abandon the Association which had organised the country, which was the heir and representative of the monster meetings, and which great political parties in France and America had treated on the footing of a national government, was to lay down our arms. A divorce from the national Press might prove nearly as disastrous a mistake. Since the struggle for Irish liberty had been transferred from the field to the forum, it had been commonly organised in newspaper offices. It was through a popular journal that Swift, that Charles Lucas, that Flood and Grattan, had successfully renewed the contest with English ascendancy. And in the Catholic struggle Sheil had accomplished as much with the pen of the journalist as with the voice of the orator. As regards O'Connell himself, his control of the people sprung in a large degree from his authority as a counsellor who had advised them successfully in contests with the law, and to abandon the Arbitration Courts, for whose legality he stood pledged, almost amounted to an abdication of his functions. At best the remedy was futile; for in truth it was not the Repeal Wardens, the newspapers, or the popular courts, but his own menacing speeches which had proved the dangerous feature in the indictment. Nevertheless, had the proposal been made in a public meeting of the Association, it would probably have been carried, so lively was the fear of dissension and so habitual the deference towards the leader. But in the Committee a vigorous free opinion had always prevailed, and here was an occasion, more stringent than any that had hitherto arisen, to exercise it.

The young men opposed this policy in language as moderate as men could employ, suddenly brought face to face with such an emergency. They would regard the dissolution of the Association, they declared, as a fatal wound inflicted on the cause. O'Connell might take any course he thought advisable on his own motion, and his great authority would no doubt induce the people to consider it favourably; but the course now proposed he could not take with the advice and consent of the General Committee, for the bulk of the Committee would not advise it or consent to it. Nor would they pledge themselves to follow him into a new Association, if the Association which had accomplished so much, and whose legality the Crown had not seriously questioned, was sacrificed to the prerogative law of Chief-Justice Pennefather.[1]

Smith O'Brien, who held somewhat the position of an umpire, concurred generally in the proposal of O'Connell, but Dr Gray leaned to the opposite opinion. The contest became critical. On one side was the leader, and on the other many of the men of most mark and capacity in the movement, including two of the convicted conspirators. O'Connell, who was too sagacious to attempt forcing his way while

---

[1] "It was not contended by the Attorney-General that the Association was an illegal body, nor do I pronounce any opinion one way or other upon that subject."— Mr Justice CRAMPTON.

there was any chance of winning it, asked was he, or were men who might be induced to join hereafter, to be responsible for everything written in the newspapers? He was reminded that the law of conspiracy in this respect was still to be tested by appeal; that Mr Barrett had thought proper to plead that he was not a member of the Association, but that this fact had not prevented his being convicted as a conspirator, or saved the others from being held responsible for his writings. At this critical moment I proposed that all the proprietors of newspapers should resign, rather than the Association should be dissolved. Someone else suggested that the Arbitration Courts might be maintained by the people locally, without direct control by the Association. To avoid an open rupture, and to keep the Association intact, this compromise was finally adopted. At the next meeting, Dr Gray, Mr Barrett, Alderman Staunton, and Mr Gavan Duffy sent in their resignations, and the proprietors of provincial journals followed their example. The Arbitration Courts were informed that all connection between them and the Association was at an end, and in a little time they died out. New Repeal cards, shorn of all historical association, were prepared. And the Repeal Wardens, on the motion of Mr John O'Connell, were directed to confine themselves strictly to the duties of collecting Repeal rent, obtaining signatures to petitions, and watching over the preservation of peace till new regulations were issued.[1]

It was understood that these concessions to opinion outside the Association were to be rewarded by considerable Whig achievements on behalf of Ireland and in defence of the convicted conspirators. The Federal party were growing in importance. Mr Patterson, one of the members for London, and Joseph Sturge were named as among its English recruits; and Irish Whigs of great position and possessions showed an increasing desire that something might be conceded which would strengthen the connection between the two countries, and furnish an excuse, if not a justification, for the abandonment of the extreme popular demand. At a meeting at Charlemont House it was agreed to

---

[1] Mr Doheny has made an allusion, the only one which has hitherto been published, to this transaction. "Immediately after the close of the State Trial, as well as I can remember, Mr O'Connell proposed the dissolution of the Association, with a view of establishing a new body, from which should be excluded all the 'illegal' attributes and accidents of the old. The suggestion was resisted by Mr O'Brien and all those understood to belong to the Young Ireland party. They protested against such a course as false, craven, and fatal, and Mr O'Connell at once yielded to their vehement remonstrance."—Doheny's "Felon's Track."

urge upon Parliament a number of reforms, among which the most notable was a proposal that the Imperial Parliament should hold a session in Ireland once every three years. Lord Charlemont affirmed that Pitt had this project in view at the time of the Union, and it was known, within a narrow circle, that the English Archbishop of Dublin, Dr Whately, still put faith in it. The idea was also thrown out of creating a Secretary of State for Ireland responsible to a majority of the Irish members. The Duke of Leinster, the Earl of Meath, the Earl of Charlemont, and other Whig peers, approved of the scheme, and it was hinted that two of them, Lord Stuart de Decies and Lord Milltown, if these demands were not conceded, would join the movement for Repeal. A little earlier the *Edinburgh Review* had advised the holding of an occasional session of Parliament in Dublin, and the project promised to become a Whig panacea.[1] But Lord Ffrench, who was invited to join the movement and refused, brought its practical value into question. What the country required, he said, was not an itinerant, but a domestic Legislature; not merely a resident, but a native Parliament; a Parliament of men not educated in habitual ignorance of Ireland and contempt of Irishmen.

O'Connell's Whig friends were eager that he should go to England to cultivate this friendly sentiment, and after the contest in the General Committee it was a question of anxious consideration whether it was a greater danger that he should go or stay. Davis thought that the balance of risk, in the temper of mind that led him to propose the dissolution of the Association, was in remaining in Ireland.

"If O'C. were firmer," he wrote to Smith O'Brien, "I would say he ought not to go to England; but fancy his speeches at ten meetings here with the State Trial terror on him. I fear we must keep him out of that danger by an English trip till Parliament meets, and then all will be well."[2]

The Irish Tories, like the Whigs, had been talking occasionally a speculative and conditional nationality; but the sentiment had scarcely gone beyond the point where it was employed as a menace to a Minister

---

[1] The article in the *Review*, which covered a wide field of speculation, was written by Mr Senior and revised by Lord John Russell, and probably prompted by Mr Senior's friend, Dr Whately. See "Macvey Napier's Correspondence." The project of an occasional Session of the Imperial Parliament in Dublin, however, was first mooted by William Cobbett, and will be found in a list of proposed reforms which he circulated, generally known as "Cobbett's Propositions."

[2] Cahermoyle Correspondence, Nov. 18th. The Cahermoyle Correspondence are papers in possession of Mr O'Brien's eldest son, kept at the family seat, Cahermoyle, County Limerick.

not sufficiently amenable to their advice. Two incidents, however, proved decisively that the asperities of the past were dying out. The Royal Dublin Society was a Conservative camp; four years earlier Archbishop Murray had been blackballed in it for no intelligible reason except that he was a prelate of the Catholic Church. Smith O'Brien desired to become a member, in order to turn it to account for literary and antiquarian purposes. He refused, however, to be proposed by any of his friends, or to be made the subject of a canvass; he simply sent his name to the Secretary as a candidate, and on a ballot he was elected by a majority of a hundred and five to five. At the same time, mainly by the influence of Davis and John Pigot, a Society was formed for the establishment of a National Gallery in Dublin. It contained amongst its council and officers Tory or Whig, and Nationalist, noblemen and gentlemen, in about equal numbers, and it laid the basis of what has now become a flourishing public institution.

Parliament met on the 1st of February,[1] before sentence was pronounced, and the speech from the Throne was framed to ward off criticism from the State Trial. "I forbear," the Queen was made to say, "from observation on events in Ireland, in respect to which proceedings are pending before the proper legal tribunals." But the Opposition could not be driven off from so tempting a theme. The Government were immediately assailed by skirmishers with a shower of questions respecting the Jury, the Chief-Justice's charge, and the Attorney-General's duel. As soon as the dilatory forms of Parliament permitted, Lord John Russell moved a party motion on the state of Ireland. A party motion is a motion designed to displace the Government or to damage them with a view to their future displacement, and it will be instructive to note the opinions which men who hoped soon to govern the empire held of the recent transactions in the Court of Queen's Bench in Dublin. The temper of the times seemed to have transformed the frigid Whig statesman into an Irish tribune. He spoke with a vigour and directness which startled his audience, and uttered truths which may still be pondered on with advantage.

Ireland was filled with troops, the barracks were fortified, a regiment was recently drawn up in the Castle yard, and preparations made as if the outbreak of civil war was hourly expected; did not these facts justify him in believing that the country was occupied but not governed by those who held the reins of power? In England the Government was a government of opinion, in Ireland it was notoriously a government of force.

[1] 1844.

Let the house consider the administration of justice as it was illustrated by the State Trial. Nominally the laws in Ireland were the same as in England, but were they administered in the same manner? In Ireland the sect to which a man belonged, the form in which he worshipped his Creator, were grounds on which the law separated him from his fellows and bound him to the endurance of a system of the most cruel injustice. Sir Michael O'Loghlen, who had travelled the Munster Circuit for nineteen years, declared that in criminal cases it was the habitual practice of the Crown to set aside all Catholic and all Liberal Protestant jurors, and it was his conviction that the same practice prevailed on all the other circuits in Ireland ; and so it had been in the late State Trial. Could the same thing have happened in Yorkshire, Sussex, or Kent? Was this the fulfilment of the promises made at the time of the Union? Was it wonderful that the poorer classes, instead of having recourse to the public tribunals, should fly to violence? Their insubordinate habits sprang from that fatal system which denied a man on account of his creed the advantages of a free administration of justice.

The nature of the charges levelled at the Traversers amazed the leader of the Opposition as much as the unfair character of the tribunal. They had been indicted for exciting ill-will among the people of Ireland against the people of England. Did the Government know of no man in England who had done the same thing, just transposing the words "Ireland and England"?

Was there no eminent person who had endeavoured to excite that feeling among the English people by calling the people of Ireland aliens? Had that person been prosecuted by the Attorney-General in a speech of eleven hours? or if the offender was protected by having uttered his words in Parliament, was he at least debarred from the confidence of the Crown? On the contrary, he was at that moment at the head of the magistracy and the law of England, prosecuting to conviction some of the ablest men in Ireland, on the charge of having excited ill-will against England.[1]

The debate lasted for nine nights, and was in the main a contest between Whigs and Tories for the possession of the Treasury. But some statements and admissions were made, the significance of which outlives the party conflict.

Sir Charles Napier, in a speech which smacked of the freedom and bluntness of his profession, invited Englishmen to make the case their own.

Napoleon had once an army at Boulogne to invade England, and forty-three ships of war down Channel. If he had effected a landing in England (and speaking recently to Marshal Soult, that accomplished soldier

---

[1] Lord Lyndhurst, at that time Chancellor, had on a former occasion spoken of the Irish as "aliens in blood, language, and religion." He was himself the son of an Irish emigrant, and was born in one of the North American colonies, which had since become the United States.

thought if the fleet were well manned it might have been done) the great General with 200,000 or 300,000 veterans might have conquered England. If he had conquered England and brought over French bishops and French priests, and forced on the English a religion they did not like, would not the English be anxious to drive every man Jack of them out of the country, religion and all? And if the Irish were treated as a conquered people, it was no wonder if they would do the same sort of thing.

Young England, a group of cultivated young men who professed to disregard party aims and traditions, reiterated the protest against misgovernment which they had made on Smith O'Brien's motion in the previous Session. Mr Smythe,[1] who was often their spokesman, uttered a truth on this occasion which arrested attention by a courageous boldness reaching almost to genius. He detested all extremes, he said, but considering who the Irish people were, if Ireland must be ruled by faction, he would rather see it governed in the spirit of Tyrconnell than in the spirit of Cromwell. The founder and guide of the new party, who were still imperfectly understood by Parliament, disturbed Tory prejudices more rudely by proposing to reverse their entire Irish system in Church and State. The duty of a wise English Minister, in Mr Disraeli's opinion, was to effect by policy all the changes which a revolution would effect by force. He foreshadowed the changes such a Minister should undertake by describing the evils under which the country suffered. "A starving population, an absentee aristocracy, an alien Church, and the weakest Executive in the world: this was the Irish question."

In a party contest in those days Mr Macaulay was always on duty. On this ocasion he opened his historical *camera obscura*, and invited men to note that it was only Whigs or Tories with Whig opinions who had known how to govern Ireland.

Three great statesmen had conceived plans for the pacification of that country, each on a system of his own. That of Cromwell was simple and strong, if it was not also hateful and cruel; it might be comprised in one word constantly uttered in the English army at that time, "extirpation." But he died before his plan was completed, and it died with him. The policy adopted by William III. and his advisers was in seeming less cruel, but whether in reality less cruel might be doubted. The Irish Catholics were to live, multiply, and replenish the earth, but they were to be what the Helots were in Sparta or the Greeks under the Ottoman, or men of colour in Pennsylvania. They were to be excluded from every office of honour and profit, every step in the road of life was to be fettered by some galling restriction. If he desired military glory, the Catholic might gain it in the

---

[1] Afterwards Lord Strangford, and the hero of Lord Beaconsfield's novel of "Coningsby."

armies of Austria or France; if political success, in the diplomacy of Italy or Spain; but at home he was a mere Gibeonite. The third was Pitt's. He had projected the Union, but the Union was only a part of his plan; he wished to blend not only the parliaments but the nations. The disabilities of the Catholics were to be removed, and their clergy and the education of their youth to be adequately provided for. Had his plan been carried out, the Union with Ireland would perhaps be as far out of the reach of agitation as the Union with Scotland. But he was not permitted to carry it out. And Canning, who followed him and adopted his policy, as a reward for his foresight, was hounded to death—the House knew by whom.[1]

When Canning was carried to his grave in Westminster Abbey the Catholics began to rely on themselves for success, to array that formidable display of force, just keeping within the limits of the law, which afterwards produced such memorable consequences. Before he was two years in his grave it led to a result which their noblest advocates had been unable to achieve—they were emancipated. Was it not inevitable that from that moment there should have been an opinion, deeply rooted in the minds of the whole Catholic population, that from England, or at all events from the powerful party which then governed England, nothing was to be got by reason or by justice, but everything by fear? Hence, when the concession of Catholic Emancipation was made, it deserved no gratitude and obtained none.

The skilful rhetorician then took up the recent transactions for review.

As respects the exclusively Protestant jury, the technicalities of law might be on the side of the Crown, but why had they regarded such a case merely from a technical point of view? In the trial of an alien, where prejudice was likely to arise, the law mercifully provided a remedy. Was he tried by twelve Englishmen? No; their ancestors knew that this was not the way in which justice could be obtained. Half of the jury must be of the country where the offence was committed, the other half of the country to which the prisoner belonged. The Tories were ready enough to call the Catholics of Ireland aliens when it suited their purpose, but the first privilege of alienship they practically denied them, and he invited the House to mark what sort of a prisoner they had got hold of by these unfair methods. Go where you might on the Continent, dine at any *table d'hôte*, travel upon any steamboat, enter any conveyance, from the moment your speech betrays you an Englishman, the very first question asked is, "What has become of Mr O'Connell?" It was a most unhappy fact (but it was impossible to dispute it) that throughout the Continent there was a feeling respecting the connection between England and Ireland not very unlike that which existed with respect to the connection between Russia and Poland.

All the details of the trial, with which we are familiar, the motions made, the opposition of the Crown, and the decisions of the Court, the Irish practice in criminal cases, and the English practice, were fought over again by the Attorney-General for Ireland and Mr Sheil. The

---

[1] To wit, by Peel.

Catholics were not set aside as Catholics, Mr T. B. C. Smith insisted, but as Repealers. Could he try the accused by partisans of their own? Several of the excluded jurors, Mr Sheil replied, were Repealers, but assuredly not all. He had in his hands affidavits from two gentlemen who were set aside, declaring they were not in any manner connected with the Repeal movement. And when the Government were so solicitous not to put Repeal partisans on the jury, how came they to put anti-Repeal partisans on it?

One of the jurors, Mr Faulkner, had been sheriff in the old Corporation, from which all Catholics were excluded. He had taken part in a furious meeting against municipal reform four years ago, in which O'Connell was denounced as the disgrace and scourge of this generation, who by the aid of a crafty and ambitious priesthood was organising the Irish Romanists to rebellion. Had this juror not already prejudged the question to be tried? Mr Thompson, another juror, was in the new Corporation as a Tory member, and in the previous year, when O'Connell had made his memorable motion for Repeal, had seconded an amendment promising to support and maintain by every means in his power the legislative Union between Great Britain and Ireland. Was he unprejudiced in the premises? Six other jurors were men who had habitually voted against O'Connell at the Dublin election. Were these persons indifferent between the Crown and the Traversers? O'Connell might have said, like Louis XVI., "I look for judges, and I find none but accusers here."

But the speech which produced the most profound and lasting impression was that of Sir Thomas Wilde. It was a party speech, doubtless, but he spoke with the authority of a man in the front rank of his profession, who had been the official head of the English Bar, and whom, it might be reasonably assumed, a still greater distinction awaited. He spoke not only with the authority, but necessarily with the reserve and caution which such a position imposes. The manner in which the offence had been charged by the Crown was a method, he declared, most unfavourable to public liberty; and its adoption was lamented in Westminster Hall as a disgrace to the law. The trial was on a par with the indictment; when it was discovered that so many Catholic names had been abstracted from the jury list, it was the cleai duty of the Crown to consent that the panel should be quashed. But on the contrary they upheld it. Was not that act, he demanded, one of dishonour? Could any weight be attached to a verdict so obtained? It was no verdict. Of the Chief-Justice's charge he expressed a grave disapproval.

Mr O'Connell's defence consisted in this contention: You charge me with uttering certain expressions with a certain intent; you select certain passages from my speeches; I call on you to read the whole of these speeches by which those sentences are qualified. And during the defence the time was chiefly occupied with reading passages other than those which the Crown had cited. But not one word of the matter thus read was referred to in the summing-up of the Judge. The Solicitor-General had got particular passages printed on pieces of paper for his reply, and as he read them the learned Judge said, "Hand them up to me." These passages were read in the summing-up to the jury, and the points which were most violent were left to the jury without a sentence of the qualifying passages. On these premises he was prepared to affirm and maintain the cardinal proposition that Mr O'Connell had not had a fair trial.

The debate was damaging to the Government, but they were strong in supporters who were beyond the influence of debate, and a majority of ninety-nine refused to consider the state of Ireland. In the Lords, the Marquis of Normanby raised the same question, but was met by a similar majority.[1] And the noble friends of the Administration were even more secure from being converted by debate than the majority in the Commons, for by virtue of the system of proxies they included in their number Lord Ellenborough, who was in Calcutta; Lord Saltoun, who was in China, Lord Tweeddale, who was in Bombay; and Lord Sidmouth, who might reasonably be considered to be in his grave.[2]

These were noble sentiments, it must be confessed, which were delivered in defence of public liberty by eminent statesmen. And there are enlightened Englishmen who cannot forgive Ireland that she has not felt bound by ties of eternal gratitude to defenders so magnanimous. But alas! nations cannot live upon noble sentiments any more than they can live upon wind. Five years later Lord John Russell and Mr Macaulay were in office, having Sir Thomas Wilde and Mr Sheil for colleagues, and juries were packed in political cases in Ireland, as we shall see, without scruple or shame, precisely as they had been packed under the Tories. And Mr Disraeli was since called three times to a commanding political position, but he never found leisure to effect by policy the changes which a revolution would effect by force.

During this debate O'Connell went to London and became im-

---

[1] The majority in the Lords was 97.
[2] Speech of Thomas Duncombe. Lord Lansdowne renewed the subject a little later on a motion for the instructions issued to Crown Law Officers relative to the challenging of juries. The practice of exclusion, he said, was so inveterate that there were cities in Ireland where for generations a Catholic had not sat on a jury. After the practice of admitting them had been tried the happiest results followed. He could quote the opinion of the most eminent Law Officers, Crown Solicitors, and magistrates, that from that moment it became known that Catholics were to act upon juries, the administration of justice was improved, and Catholic jurors did their duty in an exemplary manner.

mediately the object of party intrigues. When he entered the House of Commons, accompanied by a number of Irish members, the Opposition received him with clamorous applause, and the member in possession at the moment invited Peel to consider what he would gain by sending such a man to jail? He attended a meeting of the Anti-Corn Law League at Covent Garden, and the theatre rang with applause. A little later he was invited to Birmingham by the Radicals, headed by Joseph Sturge, who assured him that if the franchise were extended to the industrious classes a perfect union between the countries would be established. He was invited to Manchester and received in Free Trade Hall, where Sir Thomas Potter proposed a resolution, insisting that "full, complete, and equal justice should be accorded to Ireland." He subsequently visited Liverpool and Coventry, and in each town his reception was enthusiastic; but in each town, as if they were moved by a common impulse, or schooled by a common prompter, the aim of the meetings was such concessions to Ireland as would render repeal of the Union unnecessary. These ovations concluded with a dinner to the convict in Covent Garden Theatre. The notable persons present were chiefly English Catholic peers and English Radical commoners. The Earl of Shrewsbury and Sharman Crawford, with both of whom O'Connell had maintained fierce controversy, forgot their feuds and attended; and Dr Bowring and Sir John Easthope headed a muster of Radical members. The official Whigs, however, kept away; not one man who had then attained, or who has ever attained, to office was present. The relation of that class to O'Connell at all times was one which a proud man would scarcely have brooked. They had vehemently denied in Parliament having any alliance with him, when such a denial was not only uncourteous but substantially untrue. They apologised for having invited the foremost man of his race to the official hospitalities of Dublin Castle; and pleaded that the judicial office which they proffered him was not an office connected with the administration of criminal law, at a time when the Irish Bench was thronged with bitter partisans, and seven million of Catholics did not see one man of their blood or creed in the ermine: and the social relations which existed between him and the leaders of the Administration subsisting by his support were such as may well amaze a later generation. When Guizot was ambassador in London in 1840 he desired to meet the great Tribune, who filled a larger space in the thoughts of France than Althorp or Melbourne. But O'Connell was never at Holland House, or Lansdowne House, or any other of the official houses where the ambassador was invited; and it was only by the good offices of an Irish lady, whose husband was whipper-in for the Whigs, that they at length met.[1]

In 1833 he had been willing to accept office, and the position of Attorney-General was suggested to him. Dazzled it may be by the prospect of carrying over to the side of the people the formidable authority which Saurin wielded in the interest of the Protestant Ascendancy, he consented; but the haughty prejudice of Lord Grey rendered the negotiations abortive.[2] Finally they offered him the employment in which the eloquence and vivacity of Curran had been stifled; to become Master of the Rolls would be a preferment carrying no political consequences, and he refused. But his refusal was a half measure; he accepted favours from the Whigs for his family and friends, and even exacted them on occasions; and in return he enabled them still to count upon him as a steady ally in their party contests.

O'Connell's reception in England, following the modifications to which the Association had submitted, led to sinister rumours. Certain Irish Whigs began to whisper that Repeal would be dropped, and remedial measures, of which they had a plentiful supply on hand, substituted. The Whig journals in London exhorted the Irish leaders to remember the sympathy exhibited during the State Trials, to note the reception accorded to O'Connell in England, and to enable Lord John Russell to give practical effect to the goodwill of his party by frankly abandoning a measure altogether unattainable. The verdict of the packed jury would never be enforced, and justice for the future would be fairly administered. In the recent debate, however, Lord John Russell had specified his Irish policy, and it was ill calculated to second these intrigues of his partisans. The reforms proposed by the Irish Whig peers were not alluded to. The promises of the great towns to O'Connell were passed over in silence. The project which

---

[1] Guizot's "History of My Times," 8th April 1840. "I felt surprised at never meeting in this Whig circle a man with whom the party had long been connected, and whose support was indispensable to them, the celebrated Irishman, Daniel O'Connell. I expressed this one day to Mrs Stanley, now Lady Stanley of Alderley, daughter of Lord Dillon, an estimable lady, whose husband was at that time whipper-in for the Whigs. . . . 'Do you wish to know Mr O'Connell?' said she to me, 'Yes, certainly.' 'Well, I will arrange that.'" In Liberal circles which were not official the same coldness prevailed. "The leading Liberals," says Mrs Grote in the life of her husband, "avoided contact with the Liberator, as he was called, and we ourselves never but once met him in private society, and then it was at Mr Charles Buller's, in Westminster, at dinner."

[2] Mr M'Cullagh Torrens's "Life of Lord Melbourne," vol. i. p. 120.

he had himself privately sanctioned in Mr Senior's party manifesto in the *Edinburgh Review* was forgotten. He was prepared to propose some modification of the Irish Establishment, chiefly for its proper benefit as an establishment, some security for future improvements made by tenant farmers, if made with the consent of their landlords, and some promotion of Catholic barristers and politicians. Had he done all he proposed it would have merely thwarted the more effectual reforms which came later. And had he offered even these effectual reforms at once, the people of Ireland would have been disgraced in the eyes of Europe if they consented to abandon their claim to a national existence. In truth, the hopes of the Whigs were insensate. If O'Connell proposed the retrograde movement they desired he would have retired, like Dumouriez and Lafayette—leaving his army behind. He could have broken up the National party or rendered it no longer formidable to its enemies; but it was beyond his power to make it take service with the Whigs. The danger, however, was one which might pass away; it would only be precipitated by controversy, and the *Nation* touched it lightly, simply declaring in relation to the sinister rumours that capitulation would be treason. MacNevin, however, to whom political badinage was perpetual sport, wrote that "Whig sympathy at this time was not surprising; there always was an English party who pitied Ireland—the party who were not at the moment profiting by her plunder. Henry II. pitied her under the sword of Strongbow, and there was probably an Irish party in the bodyguard of Jack Cade. Ireland had not been kindled into flames, however, merely to boil the *pot-au-feu* of a few Whig barristers.' If some who have lived in later times, when professions of goodwill to Ireland have been followed by decisive action, should consider these sentiments flippant and ungracious, they shall see by-and-by how the perfervid Whig orators conducted themselves when they returned to office.

The popular feeling in Ireland was divided between indignation at the Chief-Justice and wrath at the jury-packing. Reasonable men were ready to admit that the English Government was entitled to defend itself resolutely against a movement which threatened its existence; but they denied that it was entitled to defend itself by agencies which polluted justice. The feeling against Pennefather was gratified by an unexpected disclosure. Since Municipal Reform, the Corporation of Kilkenny, with all its records, had passed from the control of the Tories to that of the Nationalists, and some angry Nationalist published an opinion which the Chief-Justice, when a practising barrister twenty years before, had given to the old close corporation. It was necessary to advise a search with a view to infer the non-existence of a certain patent granted by King James before the Revolution of '88, and Mr Pennefather suggested a device for making the search secure which was supposed to throw unexpected light upon other things besides his integrity.

I advise that a person should be produced to prove that he has made search among the Corporation papers, the records at the Rolls or Auditor General's Office, and in the Birmingham Tower, for any anterior patent, and that none such had been found. Good care should be taken to employ some one in the search who has never heard of the Charter of James II., and wherever he goes to search that charter should be kept out of his way.

As this convenient person was required to search the public records of the State, upon whose integrity private rights and national interests depend, the method by which the charter was to be kept out of his way was a secret which would have supplied a valuable clue to the management of public offices in the good old times. It was suggested that it enabled one to surmise by what contrivance the jurors' list had been manipulated. The disinterred opinion moved some moral indignation and a good deal of rhetorical wrath; but no one who knew Ireland felt greatly surprised. It was in this manner the interest of the Undertakers had been conducted since the Revolution. Irish history was elaborately written, and Irish journals were established and maintained to present the affairs of Ireland to the English people with the same ingenious provisions for withholding the truth. In the present day the books from which Englishmen commonly obtain their sole knowledge of Irish transactions are books constructed on the same principle; some one is employed who is ignorant of notorious facts, and keeps his eyes fast closed against patent evidence. An irreverent junior in the Four Courts, suspected of Young Irelandism, capped the Chief-Justice's device by declaring that when he had next occasion to advise a negative search, he would suggest that care should be taken to employ a blind man for the purpose.

Notice was served on the Traversers that they would be called up for judgment on the 19th of April: but the case was not yet ripe for judgment. The Traversers replied by a notice to the Crown that they intended to move for a new trial. The grounds specified in the notice were various, but the most important was misdirection of the jury. For this part of the case they relied on the facts that the Chief-Justice admitted improper evidence; that he misled the jury as to the effect of the evidence properly admissible; that he stated with strong comments against the Traversers the evidence offered for the Crown, and omitted to make any observation on the evidence favourable to the Traversers, or the inferences which the jury were at liberty to deduce from it; that he read to the jury extracts from the speeches and publications relied on by the Crown, and omitted to read the portions of the same speeches and publications relied on by the Traversers, and that he expressed his opinion on the facts of the case and demeaned himself generally in a manner calculated to control the judgment of the jury and lead them irresistibly to the conclusion that the Traversers were guilty.

These were weighty charges to sustain against a judge in his own court, and all the more so that the Chief-Justice, contrary to general expectation, determined to preside when the motion was heard.

The case for a new trial had been carefully considered in the recess, and was argued with remarkable ability.

The points chiefly insisted upon by counsel will be presently stated in the judgment of the Lords.

The argument lasted nine days, and when it had concluded the Court intimated that it would take time to consider its judgment. The judge who hesitates is supposed to be in the position of a besieged castle which parleys, and rumour immediately declared that the verdict was about to be set aside. The Government Press was fearful that the Traversers would escape, and for a time the Chief-Justice found little mercy at their hands. He was paying the penalty so often exacted from the partisan who lets his zeal outrun his discretion.

When judgment was at length delivered, rumour for a moment seemed to be justified in predicting the collapse of the entire proceedings; for the judges of his own court were not in accord in sustaining the Chief-Justice's law. Mr Justice Perrin on two material points concurred with the Traversers. As respected Mr Tierney's case, the Chief-Justice commented on it in a manner that had misled the jury. He had asked them, were such and such sentiments uttered for the purpose of promoting Christian charity and peace? But that was not the question which the jury had to determine, but whether the Traverser had been guilty of the crime of conspiracy, and guilty to the extent imputed to him in the indictment. The verdict against him ought therefore to be set aside.

Mr Justice Crampton, without adopting every sentence and sentiment of the charge, approved of the manner in which the Chief-Justice had put the evidence against all the Traversers, except Mr Tierney, but as respects that Traverser he wished that a verdict of acquittal had been returned. He was sorry the attention of the jury was not more pointedly called to his case. The Crown might release him by entering a *nolle prosequi*—if there was no mode of releasing him adopted he could not satisfy his conscience as a judge without declaring that there ought to be a new trial.

Mr Justice Burton thought that a new trial ought to be refused as regarded all the Traversers, including Mr Tierney; and the Chief-Justice was also coerced by a sense of duty to sustain his own charge in all particulars. This was the result of a trial which had lasted from January to May. One of the judges thought the verdict was substantially wrong as respects all the Traversers; another thought it was fatally wrong as respects one of them. Only one judge, and that judge an Englishman, sustained it, apart from the official who was regarded as simply fighting his own battle. The verdict had been obtained by means of a mutilated panel, a packed jury, and, as it now appeared, by means of a charge which half of the Court pronounced to have been illegal. What would the Government do under the circumstances? What the Government did was not very discreet or very magnanimous. They entered a *nolle prosequi* in the case of Mr Tierney, and gave notice to the other Traversers that they would be forthwith called up for judgment on the disputed verdict.

On Thursday morning, the 30th May 1844, the Traversers were called up accordingly. When O'Connell entered the Court a crowded audience welcomed him with peals of applause which could not be repressed, and a large section of the Bar stood up to receive him—a deference ordinarily only paid to judges.

Before sentence was pronounced there was yet another question to be considered, which faction promptly declared to be frivolous and impertinent, but which to-day, under an amended criminal practice, has become a motion of course. The Traversers were about to sue out a writ of error, and counsel moved that whatever judgment the Court might think fit to pass should not commence till a future day, to be fixed at its discretion, so as to enable this appeal to be made before their imprisonment commenced. It was contrary to the principle of law and justice that men should be first punished, and then an inquiry instituted whether the punishment was a legal one. The Court were of opinion that they had no power in criminal cases to make a judgment commence *de futuro*, and the application was refused. But if the Court had no remedy the Crown lawyers had a very simple one; they could have refrained from calling up the Traversers till the appeal was determined, but they insisted on immediate judgment.

Judge Burton, who had often been O'Connell's competitor, often his associate at the Bar, pronounced sentence.

The object of the Traversers was to obtain a Repeal of the Union by means which he could not say were not violent, for excitement, intimidation, and terror were violent means, but without bloodshed. He believed the principal Traverser had that design rooted in his mind, and that it was by his great influence the country had been preserved from civil war. But he had told the people that if he had found it impossible to succeed he should leave them to themselves ; and in case of aggression they would know how to act. The Court, however they might lament it, were bound to consider that exhortations to keep the peace did not take away the character of conspiracy from the proceedings. With respect to the principal Traverser, the sentence of the Court was that he should be imprisoned for twelve months, pay to the Crown a fine of £2000, and give security in £5000, and his personal security in a like amount for his good behaviour for the period of seven years. The sentence of the other Traversers was nine months' imprisonment, a fine of £50, with security for £1000, and their personal security for the same amount for a similar period of good behaviour ; all the Traversers to be imprisoned till the recognisance was completed.

Mr Ford could not be restrained from asking in an audible whisper if it was for preserving the country from civil war O'Connell was required to give securities to keep the peace. And O'Connell himself suggested that the judge's opinion seemed to be that his only conspiracy was a conspiracy to prevent an insurrection.

The judge, while he spoke, appeared to be deeply moved; but he was feeble and nervous, and as he had recently sustained the Chief-Justice in his illegal charge, no one regarded his maudlin sympathy; it was a fair trial the Traversers required at his hands, and this they had not found. O'Connell rose and spoke a few words with dignity and self-possession.

"I will not do anything so irregular," he said, "as to reply to the Court, but I am entitled to remind Mr Justice Burton that we each of us have sworn, and that I, in particular, have sworn positively that I was not engaged in any conspiracy whatsoever. I am sorry to say that I feel it my imperative duty to add that justice has not been done to me."

The Junior Bar, with a generous forgetfulness of their interest, received this declaration by raising a thrilling cheer for Repeal of the Union. It was taken up by the audience in the Queen's Bench, echoed in the great Central Hall of the Four Courts, and prolonged by the crowd who lined the quays into the heart of the city. Had Ireland been a country governed by the opinion of its own people, that cheer would have been as significant and decisive as the cheer of the camp at Hounslow Heath when the seven bishops were acquitted. But Ireland was not in that fortunate position.

Richmond Bridewell, the healthiest of the city prisons, was assigned as the place of duress, and the Traversers were locked up in the sheriff's room till arrangements were completed for their removal. The Hall of the Courts was occupied by a strong body of police, and the State prisoners, as they had now become, passed through a private passage to the rear of the Courts, where carriages were ready to convey them under escort, and by an unexpected and circuitous route, to prison. But these precautions were unnecessary. O'Connell's last act had been to issue an address exhorting the people to keep away from the exciting scene of these transactions. "Let every man," he said, "stay at home. Let the women and children stay at home. Do not crowd the streets, and, in particular, let no one approach the precincts of the 'Four Courts.'" It was impossible that such a command should be literally obeyed, but it was obeyed in spirit. There were considerable crowds round the Courts and the prison, but they were orderly and self-restrained.

CHAPTER IV.

O'CONNELL IN JAIL—YOUNG IRELAND IN CONCILIATION HALL.

O'CONNELL was in jail; and if the Government had locked up the spirit and soul of the national movement in Richmond Penitentiary, they had accomplished one main purpose of the prosecution. But if the spirit and soul were not imprisoned, but remained outside, more determined and dogged than before the trial, able to live apart from the national leader, and destined to outlive him, the purpose was scarcely accomplished. And this is exactly what had happened.

It was necessary to make provision for the management of public business, and by the express desire of O'Connell the leadership was entrusted to Smith O'Brien. It is scarcely possible to conceive a man less like O'Connell than his successor. Grave in demeanour, measured in language, cold in manner, precise and even prim in dress, and possessing neither humour nor popular eloquence, O'Brien had none of the dazzling gifts by which the multitude is accustomed to be wooed. But he was endowed with moral qualities very serviceable to such a cause at such a time—firmness of purpose that neither danger nor ruin could subdue; veracity that made his casual statement as reliable as the sworn testimony of ordinary men; quick and generous sympathy with whatever was noble or true; and under reserved manners the frankness and cordiality of a generous gentleman. He had a remarkable faculty of getting work done, for he was entirely free from jealousy, and took that strenuous interest in the labours of his associates which is the surest bounty to enlist the young. And these qualities were not liable to be disturbed by accidents of temper or fortune. It was admirable to note how speedily a lofty and confident tone was restored to the Association by his unaffected determination never to recede, and a practical aim, by the seasonable proposals which he introduced and carried out. He had been a hardworking member of Parliament for twenty years, and long an active member of the Society for the Diffusion of Useful Knowledge, and this training qualified him to carry to another stage the political education of the people. He entered on his task with a systematic industry which men commonly bring only to some personal pursuit. He conferred daily with the most active minds in the Association, pondered over their consultations, reduced them to agenda, carried them to Richmond Prison for further consultation with O'Connell and his fellow prisoners before any final step was taken, and then worked them out with the minute care a great merchant or banker bestows on the details of his business. During the State Trial he had formed a Parliamentary Committee of the best available men, and this Committee now became the motive power of the organisation. It had proved its capacity by valuable reports on the fiscal relations between Ireland and England, on the parliamentary and municipal franchise, on foreign tariffs, English aggression in India, and other questions of public polity, and it was about to further prove its capacity by fertility of resources and fitness for action as a popular executive. In all this work O'Brien received the same aid from Thomas Davis that Washington got from Alexander Hamilton.

One of the first measures taken was to summon the Repeal members to attend Conciliation Hall instead of the House of Commons, and during the imprisonment the chair was every day taken by a member of Parliament, unless when preference was given to some more conspicuous adherent. Mr Tierney, for example, who had been prosecuted for attending a single meeting, took the chair and renewed his adhesion to the policy and purposes of the movement. Mr Arabin, who was Lord Mayor elect of Dublin, immediately took the chair and identified himself with the national party. The weekly attendance was in excess of the ample accommodation of the new Hall, and the weekly rent exceeded the amount received during the flush of the monster meetings.

It was determined to contest every representative office from that of Town Commissioner upwards; and that it might be done effectually the registry was ordered to be revised, and a staff of barristers and attorneys volunteered to superintend this work. The state of the Parliamentary representation at that time was a public scandal. No general election had taken place since the country was organised, and while more than seven-eighths of the people had declared for Repeal, less than a fifth of the Irish members were Repealers. And some of them were men who brought no moral weight to the cause.[1] O'Brien aimed to increase

---

[1] Of the 105 Irish members 43 were Tories, 36 Whigs, 7 Federalists, and 19 Repealers. The Repeal members were Daniel O'Connell, Maurice O'Connell, John O'Connell, Sir Valentine Blake, Henry Grattan, James Kelly, Caleb Powell, Edmund Burke Roche, Nicholas Maher, Pierce Somerset Butler, John O'Brien, Mark Blake, Cornelius O'Brien, J. P. Somers, John J. Bodkin, James Power, Hewitt Bridgeman, Robert Dillon Browne, Martin J. Blake, and William Smith O'Brien. The Federalists were D. R. Ross, Thomas Wyse, and Morgan John O'Connell.

the number, but still more to improve the character, of the representation. It may seem a proposition too certain for controversy that a system which rests on opinion and moral suasion must be impaired while its agents are persons in whom it is difficult to place confidence. But the extraordinary belief that a man may be a scamp and even a knave in his private relations, but of steady honour as a representative, found adherents in Ireland. The belief has invariably proved as ill founded as the reliance of a skipper who works his ship with Lascars; they are content with small pay, and yield implicit obedience in quiet times, but at a moment when courage or devotion is required, they fly to the long-boats and hen-coops. That a man of the practical capacity of O'Connell should be indifferent to the character of his adherents is only to be accounted for in one way. What he wanted was implicit obedience, and implicit obedience is a virtue which ordinarily lives alone. The system, no doubt, answered his immediate purpose. Followed into the House of Commons by a retinue of foolish and often disreputable persons, he was a conspicuous figure in public life and a powerful factor in affairs; but it was at the complete sacrifice of a more important purpose. The character of Irish representatives was fatally lowered. The assembly which they were sent to persuade or defy came to regard them as the equivalent in politics to Grub Street in letters. And though there were men of honour and men of capacity among them, it was inevitable in a hostile assembly that they should be judged not by their best but by their worst members. The first remedy O'Brien proposed was to reduce election expenses to a minimum; for men who are expected to use their position in Parliament for public ends ought not to be required to purchase the right of using it. He proposed that by way of example Hely Hutchinson should be elected for Tipperary free of expense. But Mr Hutchinson would not consent to enter Parliament. He then suggested MacNevin.

"I look upon him," he wrote to Davis, "as a man of real genius, with great capacity for public affairs; but as one who wants a great deal of discipline. A couple of years' training in the House of Commons, where he would probably at first encounter many disappointments, would lop off some of his exuberances and chasten his action, which is too theatrical. In the meantime, if he gives himself up to hard solid work, such as his analysis of Kane, ... we will make of him a statesman of whom Ireland will hereafter be proud."[1]

The tone of the public meetings was marked by good sense and

---

[1] Davis's Papers, Dec. 16, 1844.

self-respect, and by a confidence in ultimate success which was entirely genuine. The Unionist Press resented this tone in a defeated party, and intimated that the Government would shut up Conciliation Hall and prohibit the collection of the Repeal rent. This was a danger which O'Brien was peculiarly fit to encounter. He immediately announced that if such a step were taken he would ask the Association to place him in the chair, and he would try in his own person the legality of this aggression on the right of public meetings. He was not prepared to shed one drop of Irish blood, but he was ready for any extremity of personal endurance in defence of the legal rights of the country, and he knew that there was an honourable emulation among the members of the Committee who should be the next victim in such a struggle. As a daily reminder of his new studies, he resolved not to taste wine or any intoxicating liquor till the Union was repealed, and he invited other Repealers to follow his example. The manner in which he discharged this obligation is very characteristic of the man. Neither the perils of insurrection, the sufferings of a fugitive, the lingering tortures of imprisonment, the tedium of exile, nor the defeat of his cause, could induce him to consider himself released from its obligation.[1]

The tone which animated these proceedings was very welcome to the bulk of the national party. The Repeal Association was in their eyes the true legislature and executive of Ireland, possessing the consent and confidence of the nation from whom all legitimate authority springs; and they longed to have its position reasserted and the highest ground it had reached re-occupied after every attack upon its authority.

Among the men associated with O'Brien in this work Maurice O'Connell and O'Neill Daunt represented the original school of Repealers; Davis, Dillon, MacNevin, Barry, and Richard O'Gorman the new school. O'Gorman was a young barrister, and the representative of a family with whom O'Connell had been at feud since the time of the Catholic Association; but he and his father, a merchant of the class of whom John Keogh was the highest type, thought the imprisonment was an occasion when past differences ought to be forgotten, and they joined the Association. The young men spoke constantly in the public meetings and worked daily with

---

[1] After his return from Van Diemen's Land to Europe he was induced, under professional advice, to take a little claret for medicinal purposes.

Dublin, 1848.

Richard O'Gorman Jr

JUDGE O'GORMAN.
New York, 1890.

O'Brien in committee. It was plain that the cause no longer depended on the life of O'Connell, but had a distinct life of its own. Had his death found the national party still united, we may surmise, from the experience of this interregnum, the character it would have maintained. A recruit was admitted into the staff of the *Nation* during these proceedings who deserves to be mentioned. Michael Doheny had been a country schoolmaster, and by native vigour emerged from his humble condition and made himself a barrister in a country, and at a period when the feat was no slight test of power. He had followed O'Connell into all his defunct Associations and through his doubtful alliance with the Whigs. But unlike most of the old agitators, he had preserved his individuality and a certain independence of opinion. In the Committee he was generally found supporting the reforms and developments projected by the young men, and he exhibited a lively desire to be associated with them. At first this desire was by no means reciprocal. He was considerably their senior, his tastes and recreations were different, his appearance was not prepossessing, and more than one of them entertained a vague distrust of him. He has himself stated the case with a modesty and candour which disarm criticism. "I do not know to what circumstances I owe the happiness of their trust and friendship. My habits, my education, my former political associations, disqualified me for such association." But vague objections disappeared before his sincerity and zeal, and he became at length an occasional writer in the *Nation*, and a confederate of Davis and his friends. A curious result followed. In discussion in committee on subjects suddenly arising, he sometimes spoke with admirable vigour and distinctness; in the public meetings, when there was any leisure for preparation, he was always in danger of becoming florid and declamatory; but in his writings, when he could choose his time and subject, he totally abandoned his natural manner and ran into a fantastic imitation of the style of Davis. In Davis, his peculiar style was the result of a powerful imagination lighting up a wide range of knowledge, and the imitation resembled the original (as Mr Carlyle said on a similar occurrence) "as the reflection of a man's face in a dish-cover does." Remonstrance and ridicule, or what he feared more than either, the frequent rejection of his articles, failed to cure him. "My friend," exclaimed MacNevin, "why don't you circulate your sterling native Cronebawns,[1] instead of giving us change for a

---

[1] Copper coins, named from the mine where the copper was found.

guinea of Davis's in one-and-twenty bad shillings?" But to the end of his life he continued to speak, as a rule, well and naturally, and generally to write ill and artificially.[1] The most practical and persuasive of the young orators was M. J. Barry, and though in the end he lost heart and faith in the cause, it is impossible for anyone who was a daily witness of his life to doubt that he served it at that time *toto corde*, and with an alacrity and industry which he never bestowed on his personal interests.

The discontent excited by the unfair trial was increased by other transactions at this time, in which the Government came into conflict with powerful and sensitive interests. A legal decision in England had taken one of their meeting-houses from the Unitarians, on the ground that it was originally granted to a different sect. If the intention of the founder could be pleaded against long possession, it was a plea which would entitle Catholics to multitudes of churches and glebes throughout the Three Kingdoms; but the Catholics thought it dishonest to disturb the possession of the Unitarians, and they gave them effectual assistance in Parliament and in public meetings in defending their property. The stricter Tories in both Houses, and many orthodox dissenters, passionately resisted any relief; and when an Act was at last obtained securing the property of dissenting congregations who had been twenty years in possession, the Unitarian Synod of Ulster passed a vote of thanks to the Catholics for their assistance in obtaining the settlement. Another legal decision brought into question the validity of Presbyterian marriages, and the wealthy and intelligent dissenters of Ulster took immediate steps to protect themselves. The Government seemed indisposed to help them, and for a time Peel was assailed from Presbyterian pulpits and platforms with a wrath commensurate with the tender interests at stake. The Catholics recognised the injustice and helped the Old Lights as they had helped the New Lights to fight their battle successfully. While the discontent was at its height a few northern Protestants joined the Association. John Mitchell wrote to me at Richmond, announcing Mr John Martin, one of his old school-fellows, as a recruit.

"The Presbyterians here are nearly frantic about the Chapels Bill. Could

---

[1] "The Felon's Track" (New York, 1850), from which the extract quoted above is made, is a pamphlet in which Mr Doheny gives some account of his connection with Irish affairs. It contains curious specimens of his original and acquired style, and is a strangely chaotic and incoherent performance.

they not be goaded into throwing up that dirty *Donum* of the devil?[1] At the very least some of them will become Repealers. *Ça ira.* All things tend that way. Some from patriotic motives and some from party ones, some from high, some from shabby ones, will join the conspiracy for Old Ireland. But if there be a single member of the Association that has joined it for the pure love of justice and of his native land, that one is John Martin."[2]

Catholics had also at this time a special complaint against the Government. An Act had lately been passed to regulate charitable bequests, which some ecclesiastics regarded as a new penal law. It forbade lands to be bequeathed by the dying for any charitable or religious object, and it created a board with powers which were regarded by some as deliberately undermining the authority of bishops. And while large sections had these special causes of complaint, the whole community was moved to anger by the discovery that the privacy of the Post-Office was violated. It was ascertained in England that the Home Secretary, Sir James Graham, had caused the letters of Signor Mazzini to be opened and communicated to a foreign Government; and in the Parliamentary inquiry which ensued, it became known that the same system was in full operation in Ireland. Whigs and Tories had alike exercised the odious power—Lord Anglesey, Lord Mulgrave, and Lord Morpeth, when they were idols of the people, as well as Lord de Grey and Sir Edward Sugden in the current year. The letters of sixty persons had been tampered with in Ireland since the Reform Act transferred power from the aristocracy to the middle classes. Thus important interests had recent and special grounds for discontent with the Government.

Among the meetings held universally throughout the country to address the State prisoners, one attracted peculiar attention. For more than a generation Belfast had held aloof from every national organisation; on this occasion men fairly entitled to represent the enterprise and intelligence, as well as the hereditary liberality and hereditary Protestantism of the capital of Ulster, adopted an address of sympathy to O'Connell, which was national in the sense of embracing nearly every opinion in the nation.[3]

---

[1] The Regium Donum was a grant by the State to the Presbyterian congregations. It was abolished at the same time as the Irish Establishment, in 1867.
[2] Banbridge, June 14, 1844.
[3] Robert James Tennent, Robert Grimshaw, and Robert M'Dowell took a lead in procuring the adoption of this address. Mr Tennent, a man of remarkable ability, afterwards M.P. for Belfast, was the head of the family whose name Sir Emerson Tennent adopted on his marriage.

"Some of us," said this remarkable document, "are hostile to Repeal of the Union; some of us look upon it as an extreme measure for which the time is not yet come; some of us are in favour of a system of legislation for domestic purposes; and some of us may be numbered among the warmest and most zealous supporters of the principles for which you yourself contend."

Belfast had once been the nurse of Irish liberty. It began to be hoped—for it was then easy to excite hope in Ireland—that she might perhaps return to her early faith.

An address, not intrinsically more important, but which made a profounder impression, emanated from the Catholic aristocracy and gentry of England. It was the more remarkable because they were supposed to have been deficient in gratitude to the Emancipator; and there was a story, which few Irishmen could hear without wrath and scorn, that he had been blackballed in their London Club. On this occasion they employed language of grave and measured censure, which was very impressive. After condemning the policy which had subjected him to prosecution for the hitherto unknown crime of constructive conspiracy, they complained that he should have been tried by a jury of which every member held political and religious opinions opposed to his. A few years earlier such a jury would have convicted him of conspiracy for organising his countrymen to shake off the trammels of religious ascendancy. And they expressed surprise and indignation that a sentence so procured should have been carried out before the legality of the verdict had been fully established. To these statements names were subscribed which in every capital of Europe were recognised as affording a substantial guarantee of their accuracy.

The *Nation* steadily seconded O'Brien, and there was no lowering of tone in the press any more than in the Association. Refraining systematically from personalities of all sorts, it was felt necessary to show no symptoms of shrinking before the truculence of the Queen's Bench. Its doubtful law was not only subjected to unreserved scrutiny, but the partisan judges were treated as history treats Jeffreys and Norbury. A new and costly edition of the "Spirit of the Nation" was published, containing the poem which the Attorney-General had prosecuted, and scores of others of the same character, set to appropriate Irish airs. A collection of leading articles entitled, "The Voice of the Nation," was issued, containing the prosecuted "Morality of War" and essays on the main branches of national polity. The day on which the imprisonment commenced some of the national journals appeared in mourning, but the *Nation*, on the contrary, was printed in green ink to typify hope and constancy. One contributor, an Englishman, taught the people, in verses which soon became household, that what was pronounced a State crime was in truth a clear and necessary duty :—

> " Conspire ! conspire !
> Singly, ye shall be weak as water,
> Singly, like sheep to slaughter,
> By tyrants evermore you shall be led ;
> Singly ye are as saplings which a breath
> Bends to the earth, a wand broken as soon as bent ;
> Sorrow and shame and death,
> These are the portions sent
> To nations by division rent,
> Therefore conspire."[1]

The doctrine of O'Connell had been scornfully formulated in the Tory Press—"Gather a million of shillings, keep quiet, and then the sky will fall, and you'll catch Repeal." The hope which the *Nation* taught was not an insensate confidence that liberty would come after a certain interval, but the creed that it might be won by commensurate labours and sacrifices, and not at all otherwise. Two weeks after the imprisonment commenced this was the language held :

We are not men who bid the people to expect Repeal in the change from leaf to fruit in any year. We have never said it was certain. It is not certain ; for if the people do not persevere with a dogged and daily labour for knowledge and independence they will be slaves for generations. It is not at hand, for the Protestants must be in our array, or foreign war must humble our foe. Ireland must be united, or our oppressor in danger, ere we can succeed by moral force ; but we ask those who require knowledge, discipline, and civic wisdom as guarantees for our fitness for nationality —Has not Ireland done something to solve their doubts and satisfy their demands?

In Parliament, Ministers were invited to contemplate the result of their labours, and twitted with ignominious failure. "You have imprisoned three newspaper proprietors," exclaimed Mr Sheil, "and the Irish Press is as bold and as exciting as it was before. Eleven thousand copies of the *Nation* circulate every week through the country, and administer the strongest provocation to the most enthusiastic spirit of nationality which the highest eloquence in writing can supply."

It is time to turn for a moment to the State prisoners.[2] O'Connell

---

[1] S. Dixon in the *Nation* of March 23, 1844.
[2] Of the State prisoners three were Protestants—Gray, Steele, and Barrett ; the others Catholics. These were their ages at that time—O'Connell, 69 ; Steele, 55 ; Barrett, 51 ; Ray, 44 ; John O'Connell, 34 ; Gray, 30 ; and Duffy, 28. By birth they were connected with all the provinces—three of them with Leinster, two with Munster, and one each with Ulster and Connaught.

and his associates were in jail, but the imprisonment, as far as personal inconvenience was anticipated, turned out an agreeable surprise. Richmond Penitentiary is under the control of the Corporation of Dublin, and the Board of Superintendence were not disposed to use their power in an offensive or arbitrary manner against their distinguished countryman. The Governor and Deputy-Governor were authorised to sublet their houses and gardens to the State prisoners; members of Mr O'Connell's family, and of the families of the other prisoners, came to reside with them; they employed their own servants; from the first day presents of venison, game, fish, fruit, and the like began to arrive; and after a little they found themselves established in a pleasant country house, situated in the midst of extensive grounds, bright with fair women and the gambols of children, and furnished with abundant means either for study or amusement. They breakfasted and dined in common, but generally spent the evening apart with their personal friends, each prisoner having a separate sitting-room at his disposal. A gymnasium was set up for exercise, a spacious canvas pavilion erected in one of the gardens for dining in the open air, and each man settled down to some specific work which would occupy the forenoon. O'Connell proposed to write the "History of his Life and Times," and had a collection of the necessary books of reference set on shelves round his study. The journalists did their ordinary work with scarcely any interruption, and some of the other prisoners did a little amateur journalism. During the first month of the imprisonment, John O'Connell and T. M. Ray contributed to the *Nation*, the former his "Repeal Dictionary," afterwards issued in a volume, and the latter a couple of lively political squibs which none of us had expected from the laborious and saturnine secretary.[1] It was whispered that the two youngest prisoners were taking lessons from Moore Stack, a noted teacher of elocution, had foils and masks for fencing, and even horses in one of the great yards for daily exercise. After a little time, a

---

[1] "Letters from London," one in prose and one in verse. I surmise from the correspondence of the period, rather than remember, that the editor shut up in prison was disposed to take his ease and shirk work. In the middle of the second month Davis writes:—"What will you do with Maddyn's long story? Keep, publish it, or send it back. Have you reviewed the magazines? Mind, I'll not give the Black Cabinet unless you have the magazines done in time. I am just going to write it, and shall not see you, as I dine out to-day; but shall to-morrow. I extirpated the historical error of the 'Stone of Fate from Dathi' (a ballad by Davis) and now defy your criticism thereanent. Can you let me have the 'Invasion'? (a novel by Griffin.)"—Davis to Duffy, July '44.

weekly journal called the *Richmond Gazette*,[1] the circulation of which was strictly limited to one copy in MS., was read aloud after dinner every Friday, and John O'Connell, who was indefatigable as a Master of Revels, projected private theatricals, and got "Julius Cæsar" into rehearsal. No Cassius being forthcoming among the convicted conspirators, he brought from the outer world beyond the walls, his cousin, Maurice Leyne, to undertake the part; and Leyne, then little more than twenty years of age, and as Irish in sympathies and purpose as Robert Emmet, took so heartily to some visitors from the *Nation* office, that he gradually became attracted to the Young Irelanders, and finally cast his fortunes with them for the remainder of his too brief career.

But plans of study and seclusion were interrupted by the stream of visitors. For a time the whole day was occupied in receiving public and private friends, strangers of distinction, and deputations from public bodies. The names of visitors were ordinarily published, and they included all the men of mark in the National party, and many who did not belong to it. At the end of a week it was necessary to subject the stream to some control; a card from O'Connell and the other State prisoners was published in the newspapers announcing that no person

---

[1] *The Richmond Gazette* came to an untimely end. It consisted chiefly of squibs and burlesques, the best of which, or at any rate the only one that lingers in my memory, was a gentle pleasantry of John O'Connell's, entitled "The Industrial Resources of Richmond Prison," describing the occupations and amusements of the State prisoners in terms parodied from Dr Kane's famous book then just published. It was edited by the four junior prisoners in turn, and at length one of them, to whom it was no amusement to play at newspapers, when his turn came round inconveniently soon, made the leading article a "Farewell Address," pleading the limited circulation as a legitimate ground for abandoning the undertaking. As the writers had never hesitated to season the articles with a *soupçon* of satire at each other's expense, the farewell address, in thanking the contributors, ventured also to thank Mr Barrett for not having contributed, as this fortunate circumstance enabled the editors to declare that they had not published a line which, dying, they would wish to blot. Perhaps some of the other follies of the time ought not to be altogether omitted. Tom Steele, in a sportive mood, named a hillock in one of the gardens "Tara," and a bench in the other "Mullaghmast," and exhibited his playthings to visitors with the grave enjoyment of Uncle Toby. It was his high jinks to defend Tara, with half a dozen picked men, against Edmund Burke Roche and an equal following; and the man approaching sixty, who was endowed with enormous strength, held his own against the young squire in the flower of manhood. In the evening, when O'Connell and the students had retired, there was a "sederunt," it was understood, over pipes, where Steele and Barrett presided, and about which it was the sport of the prisoners to indulge in pleasant exaggerations. Describing the imprisonment at some social meeting afterwards, Mr Barrett said, "It was a happy time, that rustication in Richmond, for we had leisure to drink (hear, hear, and ironical cheers from his late fellow-prisoners), we had leisure to drink wisdom and experience from the lips of the Liberator."

would be admitted any day before twelve or after four o'clock, or admitted at all on Monday or Wednesday. Our immediate political associates came every day, and the dinner-table was never set for less than thirty persons. O'Connell was a genial and attentive host, full of anecdote and *badinage* while the ladies remained, and ready, when they withdrew, for serious political conference or the pleasant carte and tierce of friendly controversy. An artist's studio and a daguerrotypist's camera were set up within the precincts to multiply likenesses of the prisoners, and the caricaturists made more amusing ones without the trouble of a sitting.[1]

This sort of imprisonment scandalised pedants and bigots; and the Lord Lieutenant in the third week ordered that admission should be subject to rules, and that deputations should not be received in any case. Deputations had already arrived in town whose names filled columns of the daily papers, and one morning a procession of civic functionaries in their robes of office presented themselves at the gates. They were informed by the governor that their reception as a deputation was forbidden, and they proceeded to O'Connell's residence in Merrion Square, where they were received by Maurice O'Connell on the part of his father, and afterwards came individually and unofficially to pay their respects to the prisoners. The distinction was not worth much, but it seemed to have satisfied the scruples of the Government. Next day a meeting was held at the Mansion House, when a municipal declaration was adopted, condemning the conduct of the State trials, and claiming for Ireland a fair share in her own government. It was sent for signature to every municipal body in Ireland, and Londonderry united with Limerick, and Armagh and Newry with Clonmel and Kilkenny, in furnishing adherents to it. In the end it received five hundred and sixty signatures of elected representatives of the people.

---

[1] There was a portrait of O'Connell engraved from a miniature of Carrick published at this time, which represents with great fidelity what he was at the era of the imprisonment. It exhibits a man of vigorous frame and commanding countenance, both, however, depressed by age and beginning to be marked by decrepitude He sat in Richmond to a young artist named N. J. Crowley, then rising into notice, who produced an ideal O'Connell, a tribune in the height of his vigour and inspiration, bearing only a distant and fanciful resemblance to the original. This portrait became the property of Dr Gray. The same artist painted the editor of the *Nation*, and felt bound to bestow upon him a dreamy, poetic head which might have passed for Shelley's—a grace nature had denied him; and the achievement gave rise to a *mot* by O'Connell which is worth recording. "Is not that very like Duffy?" Crowley demanded, producing the head in question for the inspection of O'Connell. "Hum," said O'Connell, looking from the portrait to the original, "I wish Duffy was very like that."

Though the convicted conspirators took their imprisonment gaily, it moved the gravest indignation of the country and of other countries. The Catholic bishops framed a form of prayer beseeching God that grace might be granted to O'Connell to bear his trials with resignation, and that he might be soon restored to liberty for the guidance and protection of the people. A special prayer-book containing this prayer was printed and obtained a large circulation. Catholic colleges in France and Germany sent addresses to the man who was familiar to them as the Catholic champion, reminding him how blessed were they who suffered persecution for righteousness' sake; and the Belgian and Rhenish journals brought news that prayers for his deliverance were offered in the churches from Ostend to Dusseldorf.

The relation of the prisoners to the Association and the newspapers was not in any manner disturbed, and an open communication with the political world was maintained by means of a weekly bulletin read in the Association by O'Connell's youngest son and namesake, then barely arrived at manhood. At first it merely announced that his father and the other prisoners were in good health, and by degrees it grew into something like a brief review of the public affairs of the week, and there was no attempt or desire to conceal further than was necessary by the regulations of the Penitentiary that the voice from the prison was the voice of O'Connell.

I have always regarded the Richmond imprisonment as subject to the rules which protect the privacy of domestic life. The State prisoners were in effect a household, of which O'Connell was the head; and though the most searching criticism could find little with which to reproach him or them, a narrative of their familiar talk and every-day life, especially of the familiar talk of the historic prisoner on his own hearthstone, is not, I think, permissible. The incidents which may properly be described are incidents which were designed to have some public result. After the imprisonment had lasted a few weeks, the Government Press[1] suggested that the prisoners might, as an act of grace, be discharged from custody, with the exception of O'Connell. But his associates, who were not disposed to avail themselves of this somewhat contemptuous lenity, adopted a resolution declaring that they would reject any proposal of this nature; that, on the contrary, as they were fully identified with O'Connell in the proceedings for which he was assailed, they would not pay the fines imposed by their sentence,

---

[1] The *Morning Herald* and *Standard*.

or enter into the recognisances required until his imprisonment had expired.

But there was another influence to which they would gladly have owed their deliverance. The foreign policy of Ireland, which seemed a dream for twelve months before, was now an important factor in controlling the policy of the Empire. A quarrel was ripening between France and England. The Democratic Press of Paris and the Parliamentary Opposition were eager for war, and war seemed imminent. But in the temper of Ireland that country at lowest would be closed as a recruiting field, and it might well be that France would find active allies there. O'Connell felt persuaded that Peel would not declare war without unconditionally releasing the State prisoners, and a man so skilled in foreign politics as Lord Palmerston arrived at a similar conclusion.[1] The foreign quarrel had two branches. Prince de Joinville, who was an admiral in his father's service, had recently published a pamphlet to demonstrate that the Navy of France was at length in a condition to cope with the Navy of England. And this exasperating *brochure* was followed by aggressions in the Mediterranean which, while they were only in contemplation, the English Press described as too offensive to the honour and too injurious to the interests of the Empire to be permitted. The case was this: The French Government had a dispute with Morocco, and it seemed probable that they would seize that country and colonise it, as they had seized and colonised Algiers; but Gibraltar draws its supplies in part from Morocco, and would be nearly worthless as a fortress if two coasts of the Mediterranean were occupied by France. Another dispute was long smouldering in the Southern Ocean, originating in the pretensions of an English Consul, named Pritchard, to direct the policy of Queen Pomare of Tahiti, after she had placed herself under the protection of France. News at length came that Prince de Joinville was bombarding Tangiers, and it was said he would blow down the walls of Richmond by the same operation.[2] After Tangiers, Mogador

---

[1] "There is a talk of the Queen going to Ireland in September, and it is said that O'Connell is to be let out to smoothe the way for her visit. I suppose that now that the Government have been compelled to look at a war with France as a possible contingency, they think they may as well turn over a new leaf in regard to Ireland, and try what conciliation will do for them in that country."—Lord Palmerston to his brother, 1844. Lord Dalling's "Life of Palmerston."

[2] There hung in the dining-room a map of the Mediterranean, on which the State prisoners followed the story of the expedition. O'Connell wrote on it: "On this map I watched the progress of the French armies and navy during our unjust captivity, and I present it on the 5th September 1844, the closing day of that

THE TRAVERSERS OF 1844.
(*From a large Italian Lithograph*)

was bombarded; but England did not interfere except to counsel the Emperor of Morocco to concede all that the French Government demanded. In Tahiti, where Pritchard had, in the language of Sir Robert Peel, been subjected to a "gross outrage accompanied by gross indignity," a thousand pounds were accepted as an adequate *solatium* for his wounded honour and the wounded honour of his country, and the contest was declared to be at an end. Sir Robert Peel and his colleagues were angrily assailed for having truckled to France, and they had no good answer to make. In truth, England was beginning to practise the foreign policy in which she has since made such notable progress; for to shrink from foreign war was the necessary complement of her defiance of the Irish people.

Books upon the history and condition of Ireland were now published in France, Prussia, and Belgium, and portraits of the conspirators were to be found in every town and village between the Atlantic and the Pacific, and in every city on the Continent of Europe. More than a quarter of a century later, when these transactions were nearly forgotten by a new generation in Ireland, I was startled to find for sale under one of the piazzas of Turin a large lithograph designated "Capi e Promotori della Questione Irelandese"—being no other than the convicted conspirators of 1844.[1]

The Association, in pursuance of its new policy, offered a prize for the best essay on a constitution for Ireland, and exhorted competitors to remember that "the difficulties of the case must not be evaded, but frankly stated, and the means specified by which they might be best met." There were three hundred Repeal reading-rooms in existence, and it was resolved to increase them to three thousand, and to make them centres of organisation and union. Education had long been a luxury forbidden under heavy penalties. In later times it was an instrument of proselytism; it was determined to turn it into an effectual weapon of defence. The Celtic race, though obstinate in its habits, is very susceptible of discipline; no peasant is so easily transformed into a soldier; no peasant girl so speedily acquires ease and intelligence by living among the cultivated classes. The enthusiasm of the time which had enabled an entire nation to become water-

---

captivity, to my valued and cherished friend, Charles Gavan Duffy, one of the successful Traversers."—Daniel O'Connell, M.P. for the County of Cork, Richmond Bridewell. (This map is now in the Melbourne Museum, of which I am one of the Trustees.)

[1] Reproduced on the opposite page.

drinkers would, it was hoped, enable them to submit to other discipline and other sacrifices. It was admirable to see how young men of all ranks entered into this idea. Townsmen took up the defence of farmers, who were unable to assert themselves before a landlord armed with a merciless code; the ancient seats of piety and learning had been wantonly desecrated as granaries, cattle-sheds, and ball-courts, or as quarries for the neighbouring squire or parson; and young peasants volunteered to become their guardians till the time arrived when a National Government would take them in charge. This progress was obvious; but there was progress more important which could not be measured. Davis possessed the rare faculty of exciting impatience of wrong without awakening the deadly hatred of those who profit by it; and it was only in after years men came to know how deeply the new ideas penetrated among cultivated Protestants. Joseph Le Fanu was the literary leader of the young Conservatives, and Isaac Butt their political leader; both were at this time engaged, privately and unknown to each other, in writing historical romances which would present the hereditary feuds of Catholics and Protestants in a juster light to their posterity. Their books were published anonymously, and not for some years after they were begun; but I can state, on their authority respectively, that they had constantly in view in pursuing their task to gratify the new sentiment which the *Nation* had awakened.[1] Samuel Ferguson, more essentially a man of letters and more indisputably a man of genius than either, broke through the hostile silence of the *Dublin University Magazine* by predicting with generous exaggeration that, if no untoward event interrupted their career, the time would come when the national writers in Dublin would be read with something of the same enthusiasm in Paris as men in Dublin were reading Béranger and Lamartine. Mr Lever, who winced under contemptuous criticism in the *Nation* (for the young men rejected his drunken squires and riotous dragoons as types of the Irish character), could not altogether resist the same sentiment; his historical stories took a tone so national that his cautious Scotch publisher demanded if he was "Repealising like the rest."[2] Even in Ulster, the home of prejudice in later times, they had reason to know that their songs found favour, and, like Moore's, were heard in unwonted places.[3] And in the stronghold of

---

[1] The romances in question were "Torlogh O'Brien," a story of the wars of King James, by Le Fanu; and "The Gap of Barnesmore," by Butt.
[2] Fitzpatrick's "Life of Charles Lever."
[3] "I am passionately fond of the old Irish melodies, and have long been picking them

bigotry, in the office of the *Evening Mail*, at the feet of the astute parson who directed its politics, there was growing up a lad who in a few years broke away from hereditary prejudice to become the laureate of Irish treason.[1]

History and historical poetry, which elsewhere are the food of patriotism, were wholly excluded from public teaching in Ireland, and it was well entitled to be regarded as a notable event when professors of Trinity College and professors of Maynooth, Protestant and Catholic clergymen, Conservative and National barristers and journalists, were seen side by side in the Rotundo while Moore Stack recited ballads and speeches alternately from the classics of Irish literature and the recent writings in the *Nation*.[2] A little later a similar combination took place on behalf of the widow of John Banim, a writer intensely national in his scope and spirit, and whose name at an earlier period would certainly have frightened away Conservatives. A committee, selected alternately of Repealers and Conservatives or Whigs, was organised to purchase her an annuity, but was relieved from the duty by the frank concession of a pension by Sir Robert Peel, impressed perhaps by the unprecedented phenomenon of such a combination.[3] Society, which in Dublin was like a British camp, began to open its doors to the young orators and

---

up wherever I could find them. Indeed, I was familiar with most of the airs in Moore before his Melodies were heard of. My father had an enormous store of old scraps of this kind, and when a child he used to sing them to me in Irish. You would hardly expect this from an old black-mouthed Presbyterian." — James M'Knight, LL.D., Editor of the *Belfast News-Letter*, to C. G. Duffy. "These ballads make their way even into the barracks, and generally into the public-houses frequented by our Irish soldiers. They are full of fire, and the writers cannot be ordinary men. We therefore call attention to them, and trust all officers will exert a salutary vigilance over any attempts to introduce them into the army." — *Naval and Military Gazette*.

[1] "Myles O'Reilly" was the *nom de plume* in the Irish American Press of Charles G. Halpine, whose father was editor of the *Mail* during the State trial.

[2] Moore Stack was the gifted actor who, under the stage name of Moore, interpreted the latest creations of Sheridan Knowles and Leigh Hunt in Covent Garden, till religious scruples induced him to retire from the stage.

[3] The names of the committee deserve to be recorded :—Daniel O'Connell, M.P., John Anster, LL.D. (the translator of "Faust"), Smith O'Brien, M.P., Isaac Butt, LL.D. (then leader of the extreme Conservatives), Dr Kane (afterwards Sir Robert Kane), John O'Connell, M.P., Charles Lever (the author of "Harry Lorrequer") Torrens M'Cullagh, LL.B. (later M'Cullagh Torrens, M.P.), Thomas Davis, Samuel Ferguson (afterwards Sir Samuel Ferguson, Deputy-Keeper of the Records in Ireland), Thomas O'Hagan (who became Lord O'Hagan), William Carleton (author of "Traits and Stories of the Irish Peasantry"), E. B. Roche, M.P. (since Lord Fermoy), Joseph Le Fanu (author of "The House by the Churchyard," etc.), Charles Gavan Duffy, Hubert Smith, M.R.I.A., Thomas MacNevin, Dr Maunsell (editor of the *Evening Mail*), Gray Porter, James M'Glashan (proprietor of the *Dublin University Magazine*), and M. J. Barry.

poets, and the "Songs of the Nation" were heard in drawing-rooms where nationality had never penetrated since the Union, except in the disguise of Moore's Melodies. Good old Tories shook their heads and predicted perilous consequences. There was a story of a dowager who, after one of the national songs, gathered her flock and carried them off in a pretended panic, crying, "Come away, my dears, before we are piked out."

The writing of the *Nation* was chiefly done by those who founded the journal, but the occasional contributors at this time show how widely sympathy had spread. Among them were William Carleton and John Fisher Murray, habitual writers in the Conservative periodicals. Carleton, long lost to the race from which he sprang, had caught fire from the society of the young men, and renounced his bigotry for ever. Among them also were others doubly welcome as the heirs of historic names in Ireland. It stirs the heart to hear how the descendants of William Wallace fostered the genius and fortunes of Robert Burns; and there are some who will not read unmoved that the son of Dr Drennan, the patriot poet of '98, the grandson of John Keogh, the Catholic leader of that era, O'Reilly of Breffni, the representative of James II.'s Irish Chancellor, and the son of MacDermott, still known in Ireland as Prince of Coolavin, came to the aid of the founders of the *Nation*. It was justly regarded as a fact of significance that an Irish Society for the purpose of social and intellectual intercourse between Irishmen, irrespective of political or religious differences, was established in London at this time, in which might be found, side by side (in its prospectus at any rate), men hitherto so hostile in party conflict as the Marquis of Londonderry and the Marquis of Clanricarde, Lord Castlereagh and Lord Rossmore, Frederick Shaw and Anthony Blake, Emerson Tennent and D. R. Pigot, W. H. Gregory and Morgan John O'Connell; representatives of literature and art like Dr Croly and Fr. Prout, Maclise and M'Dowell; such recruiting sergeants of hostile forces as Captain Taylor and Dr Cooke Taylor; John Doyle, who was delighting London by bantering all parties indiscriminately in his H. B. sketches, and young lawyers who were writing in the *Nation* and lecturing in Repeal reading-rooms.[1] The Irish cause had not changed

---

[1] It consisted mainly however of two political parties, according to one of the principal Conservatives engaged in organising it. Mr Emerson Tennent wrote to me—"It goes on charmingly, and is a real national reunion. But who are its members? They are as nearly as possible one-half high Tories and Conservatives—and one-half Repealers. But a single Whig never crossed its threshold. Though urged, entreated, and implored, they won't do it."

its purpose but only its agencies; the clamour of monster meetings was replaced by a power as silent as electricity.

The modified character of the national movement did not long escape comment. *Tait's Magazine*, which spoke with authority in those days, regarded it as "far more formidable and menacing than during the era of the monster meetings. The Repealers were doing a more dangerous thing now than reviling the Saxons: they are imitating them, educating themselves and one another into a most Saxon sturdiness of purpose and persistency of action."

In the *Tablet*, Frederick Lucas, who afterwards proved himself to possess rare powers of political organisation, judged it in the same manner.

"Never," he said, "were both the leaders and the led more deeply in earnest or more assiduous in their labours. The contest had become less noisy, and this deceives the vulgar, but it has in exactly the same proportion become more real, more true (shall we say it?), more honest, and more respectable. It has now become a recognised fact that the struggle for Repeal may be a long one; and all parties are girding themselves up for that march through the wilderness which is to prepare them for the possession of the promised land. . . . And in the meantime the years of pilgrimage will not be wasted. They will be spent in earnest, anxious, painful efforts to acquire knowledge and discipline, and every spiritual, moral, and intellectual quality which can accomplish and adorn freedom."

The *Evening Packet*, the most violent of the Government journals in Ireland, shrieked out that no device of treason hitherto invented had proved so mischievous as the Reading-rooms were destined to become, and that the moderation of the leaders was a mask for the worst purposes.

But the men who had designed this policy knew better than their opponents to how many dangers it was liable. A Celtic people will make great immediate sacrifices and endure the extremity of ruin for a cause they love. They will return again and again to a purpose with clinging but fitful devotion; but they do not willingly settle down into the patient pursuit of an end which is confessedly distant and even doubtful. And they are easily turned aside by novelty.

Mr John O'Connell, who regarded the succession to the popular tribunate as his entailed estate, and did not look with equanimity on possible competitors, was the first to demur. An incident which might have led to disastrous consequences was attributed—rightly, I am persuaded—to his occult influence. Mr Dillon Browne, a type of the Irish member who disgraced the Irish cause, made a speech in Conciliation Hall in the absence of O'Brien, hostile to the policy which the Association was working out with so much care. Mr Browne's speech was a matter of no importance, but, when he had concluded, Mr Daniel O'Connell, junior, moved a vote of thanks to him for his well-timed counsel, and the *Pilot* in its next issue applauded this judicious recognition of public merit. No one believed that a timid young man, who had hitherto not got beyond reading his father's weekly bulletin, would have ventured on this step on his own responsibility, or that Mr Barret would have applauded an irregular proceeding without authority. Davis was deeply moved, less by the incident than by the disposition and design which seemed to lie under it. He wrote to O'Brien, then in the country, like a man who was stunned by a sudden blow.

"When you write to Richmond notice the fact that Mr O'Connell's son moved a vote of thanks to Mr Dillon Browne without the consent of the Committee, and did so because of Mr Browne's opposition to the Charities Bill, which in its present form a majority of the Committee approved. What is worse, he did so after Mr Browne had made a speech adverse to our whole policy, attacking the Federalists, calling on the people to turn them out, and this because they did not aid his opposition to a useful measure. I have made up my mind if such conduct be repeated to withdraw silently from the Association. . . . There are higher things than politics, and I never will sacrifice my self-respect to them."[1]

Davis, who never shrank from enemies in the front, threatened secession in his disgust at being hamstrung from behind; but to such a man secession in any other sense than changing the nature of his labours was impossible. O'Brien was disposed to treat the matter lightly. In his reply he recommends patience and forbearance, and indeed sermonised generally on the necessity of self-restraint in a manner very trying to a man who was not in the least thinking of himself, but solely of the public cause.[2] The offence was repeated in the *Pilot* in terms which argued a set purpose, and some explanation why conflicting counsel was offered to the people was becoming urgent.[3] Events, however, were at hand which swept the transaction into obscurity.

---

[1] Cahermoyle Correspondence.—Davis to O'Brien, August 20, 1844.
[2] Davis Papers.—O'Brien to Davis.
[3] "There was a disgusting article in the *Pilot* last night; one which, I think, Barrett would never have dared to write without the knowledge of his masters. It must be dealt with one way or the other; and I wish you would come out as early as you can in the morning to talk it over. I think it desirable to have O'Connell discountenance, or countenance it, whichever he chooses, that we may deal with it accordingly. The gist of it is an attempt to stop the Repeal Reading-rooms."—Duffy to Davis. Richmond Prison. Davis Papers.

CHAPTER V.

THE IRISH PRISONERS BEFORE THE HOUSE OF LORDS: THEIR DELIVERANCE.

WE must now turn to the story of the appeal against the judgment of the Queen's Bench. In October the writ of error was opened before the House of Lords by counsel for the Traversers. An appeal to the Lords seemed an expedient so desperate that for a time no one believed it was seriously contemplated. A man so skilled in gauging public opinion as Lord Palmerston thought that the prepossession of the Court could scarcely be overcome. "The case in favour of O'Connell," he wrote to his brother, "must be strong indeed if the decision is given in his favour. The Court will certainly be against him."[1] But eminent English counsel insisted that there was a case which was irresistible, and it was resolved to make the experiment.[2] It was Chief-Justice Pennefather and his learned brethren, and the Irish Law Officers who were now upon trial. The Chief-Justice's abnormal charge did not fall within the review of a court of error, which can only deal with matters on the record; but of the matters on the record everything essential to a fair trial was called in question, as tainted with error or malice. The offence for which the Traversers were tried was not, it was contended, legally charged in the indictment. The jury which tried them was not a lawful jury of the country. The verdict which the jury found was not a legal verdict. And the judgment of the Court, as entered on the record, was bad in law and ought not to stand.

The counsel in the case succeeded in the hard task of disentangling these grave objections from legal technicalities, and making them intelligible and of vivid interest to the whole community.[2]

---

[1] Lord Palmerston to his brother, June 5, '44.—Lord Dalling's "Life of Palmerston."
[2] The counsel for the Traversers before the Lords were Sir Thomas Wilde and Messrs Peacock Hill and Fitzroy Kelly, the late Chief Baron. The Crown was represented by Sir William Follett, the English Attorney-General, and Mr Smith, the Irish Attorney-General. Sir Frederick Pollock, who had advised the Crown in the early part of the case, was now a Judge. To Mr Peacock is attributed the credit of having hit the chief blot in the indictment.

The offence was not legally charged: some of the counts in the indictment were so framed as to disclose no offence. For example, the counts charging the defendants with conspiring to exercise intimidation did not specify the persons whom they intended to intimidate. These, in the pleader's language, were "bad for generality." Some counts set forth several distinct conspiracies, when only one conspiracy could be properly charged. These, in the same language, were "bad for duplicity." All the counts were perhaps bad, but if one was bad it was contended that the judgment could not be sustained.

The jury was not a legal jury of the country: it was taken from a spurious list, and the opportunity of correcting this spurious list had been denied.

The verdict was not a legal verdict: there were findings upon more offences than were charged in the indictment or pleaded to by the defendants. Three of the defendants were found guilty of all the five charges set out in the counts, seven of them were found guilty of three of these charges, and eight were found guilty of one of them. But the very essence of criminal conspiracy was one common object, and one object common to all. If there was a conspiracy, say of three out of the eight, for an object different from the object of the eight, it could not in law or in justice be dealt with as one conspiracy. The charge was conspiracy, and a man must be acquitted or convicted of it; it could not be divided into two or three parts. The jury were sworn to try one issue, and they had found on no less than three distinct issues.

The judgment of the Court was bad: in one respect the sentence was clearly unlawful, as the defendants were to be detained in prison not only until each of them paid his own fine and entered into his own recognisances, but till all the others had paid their fines and entered into their recognisances also. The indictment contained six distinct charges, each of which, if proved, aggravated the guilt; and the sentence was "for the aforesaid offences." But if the verdict on any count was bad, the Traverser must necessarily have been sentenced for an offence of which he was not legally convicted. On these grounds it was submitted that the judgment of the Queen's Bench in Ireland ought to be reversed.

It is customary for the House of Lords in important appeals to ask the assistance of the English Judges, and a number of questions were framed to elicit the opinions of these learned persons upon the main points of the case. On a day appointed answers were read by the Chief-Justice of the Common Pleas [1] on behalf of the majority of his brethren.

In reply to a question, whether all or any of the counts were bad in law, they stated that the sixth and seventh counts were clearly bad, as they failed to specify with sufficient certainty the illegal purpose of the agreement entered into between the defendants. It was left in complete doubt whether the "intimidation" charged was to be directed against the peaceable inhabitants of the surrounding places, against the subjects of the Queen dwelling in Ireland in general, or against persons in the exercise of public authority.

---

[1] Chief-Justice Tindal.

IRISH PRISONERS BEFORE HOUSE OF LORDS. 71

In answer to a question whether there were any defects in the finding of the jury, the Judges were of opinion that the finding on the first, second, third, and fourth counts were not supportable in law, as they found the defendants guilty of several conspiracies on counts where only one conspiracy was charged. In reply to a question whether there was any sufficient ground for reversing the judgment on account of defects in the indictment, or in the finding of the jury, the majority of the Judges were of opinion that if the finding was good on one count, the judgment could not be reversed on the ground that the finding on other counts was bad. The judgment in the present case might be supported on the good counts. With respect to the Court in Dublin disallowing the challenge of the array, the Judges did not think this decision furnished a ground for reversing the judgment; for though it was stated that no less than seventy-nine names were omitted from the jurors' list, no unindifferency on the part of the sheriff was alleged, and this was the only ground allowed by law for a challenge of the array. They were of opinion therefore that the judgment of the Queen's Bench in Ireland ought to be confirmed.

But this conclusion, which fitted so imperfectly the premisses from which it was derived, had not the unanimous assent of the Judges. Baron Parke, whose reputation as a lawyer stood high, and Mr Justice Coltman thought the judgment ought to be reversed for reasons which still seem irresistible. There were confessedly defects in the indictment, defects in the finding of the jury, and defects in the verdict. Two counts of the indictment were bad, the finding of the jury on three other counts was bad, and the judgment passed on the defendants was that for "the offences aforesaid" they should be fined and imprisoned. It could not be known how much of the punishment was awarded for offences of which the parties were not legally convicted; how under such circumstances could the punishment be inflicted? For these reasons they were compelled to think that the judgment of the Irish Court ought to be reversed.

After the opinions of the Judges were read an adjournment took place, and there was a general impression that the case was practically decided. Lawyers and publicists did not hesitate to declare that it was contrary to a fundamental principle of English law to admit the existence of serious wrongs for which there was no remedy; but it was assumed that the opinion of the majority of the Judges in Westminster Hall, whether right or wrong, would be accepted by the Court of Appeal.

On the 4th of September, when the Traversers had been more than three months in Richmond Bridewell, the House of Lords met to determine whether or not they could be legally imprisoned. Such a question might seem fit only for the tribunals of Laputa : and the Court was constituted in a manner which would have suggested new illustrations of human folly to the cynical genius of Swift. It consisted of Lord Lyndhurst, Chief Law Adviser of the Government which would be defeated and humiliated by the reversal of the judgment; of Lord Brougham, who was the fierce and implacable enemy of O'Connell, from whom indeed he had received intolerable provocation ; of Lord Cottenham, ex-Whig Chancellor, who had political interests in the result diametrically opposed to those of Lord Lyndhurst ; and of Lord Campbell, ex-Whig Chancellor in Ireland, who owed his promotion in part to the patronage of the chief prisoner. The Lord Chief-Justice of the Queen's Bench, Lord Denman, who had been Brougham's colleague in the defence of Queen Caroline a quarter of a century earlier, completed the Court, and was perhaps as unbiassed by interest or sympathy as it is possible to find a man who is an active member of a political assembly in a free country.

The Lord Chancellor opened the business by moving that the judgment of the Court below be affirmed. An anxious observer of the proceedings on behalf of the Traversers described his manner on the occasion as dignified and impressive, and his voice as singularly penetrating and persuasive. But his speech would have furnished materials as suitable for the satire of Swift as the composition of the Court. It was an intrepid attempt to cheat the Traversers out of their legal rights. If there were any bad counts in the indictment, it did not by any means follow, he conceived, that the Court in Dublin in passing sentence had assigned any part of the punishment in respect to these counts. The contrary indeed might be inferred. With respect to the challenge of the array, all the Judges were of opinion that the decision of the Irish Court on that application was right. But was the case of an imperfect jurors' list therefore a case without a remedy? Undoubtedly not ; an appeal to the House of Lords, however, was not the remedy which the law provided. What the remedy might be was not before their lordships ; enough that it was not a writ of error. It was clear to him under these circumstances that the judgment of the Court below ought to be sustained.

Lord Brougham was willing to admit the technical informality of some counts, but was of opinion, nevertheless, that the judgment must stand. The question was, whether they would take the law from seven judges or from two. With respect to the challenge of the array, there had been no authority cited to show that there was any legal ground for such a proceeding.

Lord Denman replied on his noble friends with fatal effect. He began with the challenge of the array. If such practices as had prevailed in the present instance should continue, trial by jury in Ireland would become a mockery, a delusion, and a snare. The ground of challenge was that there was in fact no Jurors' Book for 1843 in existence. After the Recorder had determined in his judicial character what should constitute the list of jurors, somebody else had said, "That shall not be the jury list ; this shall be it," substituting a list of his own. If this person had added sixty unauthorised names instead of subtracting sixty which were sanctioned, was there to be no remedy? Had the law been complied with, the twelve jurors who tried the case might all have been shut out of the panel; the jury might have been taken wholly from the names improperly omitted. One of the learned Judges in Dublin was of opinion that the challenge should have been allowed, and with that opinion he entirely concurred. There was a confessed and serious wrong, and the only question was whether a challenge of the array was the proper remedy. If not, what was the remedy? The Lord Chancellor affirmed that the party was not without a remedy, but he had omitted to state what it was. If it could not be specified, what security was there for the Queen's subjects? The remedy was the challenge of the array, and no other; it ought to have been allowed; and not having been allowed the trial had erroneously proceeded.

With respect to the judgment, they were told they ought to assume that it was pronounced on the good counts only; but such a presumption would be in direct contradiction to a notorious fact. The sixth and seventh counts were now held to be bad; but the Judges in Dublin after argument had declared them to be good. The judgment was pronounced on all the counts; on counts stating no offence, and on other counts stating offences on which there had been erroneous findings; and therefore the judgment had been improperly passed. It was his duty under these circumstances to vote against the motion of the Lord Chancellor.

Lord Cottenham deplored the difficulty in which he was placed in differing from the majority of the judges, but having carefully weighed all that was said, he was driven to the conclusion that the opinion of the minority was right.

Lord Campbell, who, as Junior Law Lord, spoke last, broke new ground. He had been much struck with the objection to the validity of the judgment by reason of the form of the recognisances into which the defendants were required to enter. It might lead to perpetual imprisonment, for, if the required sureties were not found in the case of any one prisoner, they might all remain in custody for the rest of their lives. Adverting to another point, the bad counts contained the most serious charges in the indictment, including those for creating disaffection in the army; could their lordships concur in the incredible fiction that the Judges, in awarding punishment, had overlooked these grave charges? If they could not, the judgment was necessarily bad.

The Lord Chancellor then put the question—" Is it your lordships' pleasure that the judgment be reversed?" and the Law Lords having voted in accordance with their speeches, three declared themselves content, two non-content. It cannot fail to be noted that these eminent jurists voted as they would have done in a purely party division; but it has since been generally held that the decision was strictly in accordance with law.

In sitting as a Court of Appeal it is the practice of the House of Lords to leave the decision exclusively to peers who have held judicial office. The interest of the present case had attracted a number of lay peers, who, seeing that the decision was about to be unfavourable to their personal wishes, insisted on their right of voting. Lord Hawarden, the landlord who had cleared out his Tipperary estates as he might a rabbit-warren, was peculiarly demonstrative. The abstract right could not be denied, but they were exhorted to refrain on the ground of long practice, which confined to Law Lords the exercise of the appellate jurisdiction in the House; by the disastrous effect a violation of this practice would have on the character of the Chamber as a judicial tribunal; and for the irresistible reason that though they were all technically judges, no judge could decide a case which he had not heard, and they had not heard this case. They were at length induced to withdraw, and the decision of the House of Lords was announced by the Chancellor that the judgment of the Irish Court was reversed.

The result was a general surprise, but to no men in the Empire did the news come more unexpectedly than to the persons chiefly affected by it. After the opinion of the English Judges had been published, the prisoners in Richmond abandoned hope of a favourable judgment. There was no electric telegraph in those days, and on Friday, the 13th September, they were assembled for dinner, when the door of the dining-room was thrown open by a messenger of the Repeal Association, named Edmond Haggerty, who rushed in, exclaiming, "You're free, Liberator; you're free." Before he could fully explain himself he was followed by Mr William Ford, whom he had somewhat unfairly anticipated. Pale and panting, the aged attorney, who had posted night and day from London with the record of the Lords' judgment in his pocket, stumbled into the room, flung his arms round O'Connell, and thanked God that his friend and leader was entitled to walk out of prison. A private letter to friends in the country (written by a lady in the family of one of the prisoners) described the scene that ensued naturally and graphically:—

"There was nothing but shaking hands and embracing. Old General Clooney (one of the insurgent leaders in '98) sat down and cried like a child. When his sons, Dan and Morgan, came in, they could not speak for tears. There is a Governor and Deputy-Governor; the latter, after congratulating O'Connell, rushed out of the room weeping.¹ When the Governor came—a large fat man with a red face (Mr Purdon, whom the French newspapers called M. Pardon)—he was so much affected by the company cheering him that he almost fainted; he became ghastly pale and gasped for breath. We had to open the window and throw water upon him. . . . We got on the top of the prison and saw an immense crowd; and such a hurra I never heard."

Fresh arrivals came every minute till the great dining-room was

---

¹ This sentimental jailer was an Englishman and had been valet to Sir Robert Peel, who gave him his place many years before.

LEAVING RICHMOND JAIL

crowded, when a hasty conference was held on the best method of turning the victory to account for the public cause. The prisoners naturally wished to go home straight away, after three months' absence, but a public procession to accompany them had been already determined on by their friends in the city, and news came every quarter of an hour of the preparations which the Trades, the Repeal Association, and the citizens were engaged in making for it. It was finally agreed that they should go home that evening, and return next morning to the Penitentiary, to leave it in procession. The next morning proved unfavourable, it rained heavily till twelve o'clock; but the procession mustered as if the sky were radiant. Numberless vehicles and horsemen, the marshalled trades with banners and music, the equipages of the Lord Mayor and Corporation, of the Committee of the Repeal Association, and of the political and private friends of the prisoners, were with much pains distributed in the places assigned for them, and a triumphal car, drawn by six white horses, drew up at the prison door.

At two o'clock O'Connell and his late fellow-prisoners took their places; O'Connell and his son on the triumphal car, and the others, who declined that elevated position, in carriages. The rain had for some time ceased, and the autumn sun was shining pleasantly when the procession began to move. From front to rear it extended for nearly six miles, and it was computed that 200,000 men took part in it. It marched slowly into the city; past the Four Courts where the lists had been manipulated, the jury packed, and the illegal verdict found; past the Castle where the blundering and defeated conspirators against Irish nationality were hiding their heads; past the Parliament House which that great multitude confidently hoped to see restored to its original purpose; to the residence of O'Connell in Merrion Square, and then quietly separated.[1]

The public rejoicings extended over the island. Bonfires blazed

---

[1] A contemporary note from Dillon will show how complete was the surprise of the decision of the Lords among those who were most interested and most likely to be well informed:—

"For Heaven's sake, my dear Duffy, write three lines with your own hand saying that you are actually and *bona fide* out of jail. I am as incredulous as twenty St Thomases, and will not believe it until I see and feel you all. However, a line from you would go far to dispel my doubt, so in charity write.—Yours ever, J. DILLON."

Mr Ford's race home with the news gave birth to a story which amused people, who, being in good humour, were easily amused. On the journey he could not restrain his enthusiasm. When the train stopped at Chester he announced to the assembled passengers and porters at the top of his voice that O'Connell was going to get out. "Indeed, sir," said an imperturbable English porter; "did you say 'twas at this station the gentleman would get out?"

upon every historic hill in three provinces and throughout a great part of the fourth. In towns there were illuminations, and the popular bands summoned the people to rejoice; but north or south there was no complaint that any one had been insulted or injured. The Nationalists were proud of this unexampled spectacle of the whole people in a delirium of triumph maintaining moderation and courtesy.

The decision of the Lords was a bitter humiliation, not only to the Irish Law Officers whose indictment had broken down, but to the Minister whose policy was thwarted; and his antagonists were not disposed to make this catastrophe pleasant for him. There was a chorus of Whig recrimination. The *Morning Chronicle* declared that O'Connell came forth with redoubled power. "He trampled upon the Government as he left the prison walls, and after such an event Sir Robert Peel could not stand still; conciliation or coercion must be tried on some new and grand scale." "O'Connell," the *Examiner* remarked, "had first been made a martyr and then a conqueror. Peel had taken the wolf by the ears and was unable to hold it or let it go with safety. The Irish State trials might be placed next in infamy to the worst trials of the worst time of the Stuarts; and Peel was responsible because after the discovery of the fraud in the panel he had not stopped short." The *Globe* thought the integrity of the Union might still be preserved; but Sir Robert Peel could not accomplish this result; he had tried and failed. The Whig journal knew, however, where there were men fit for the emergency.

The first impulse of the Government Press was to treat the judgment of the Lords as a party plot to embarrass the Administration. But in truth the judgment was as much a surprise to the Whig party as to the Traversers.[1] Even the *Quarterly Review*, with leisure for deliberation, insisted that certain lay lords might properly have voted to forbid so great a wrong as the escape of O'Connell. Anyone called to the Bar was quite as good as Lord Campbell, and Lord Wharncliffe, as "one of the oldest and ablest chairmen of Quarter Sessions in England," was well entitled to rank himself in the select coterie of Law Lords. It was plain from the tone of the party Press on both sides that something more than the verdict of the jury had been reversed. An eminent Unionist, willing to improve the occasion, demanded of MacNevin in the Hall of the Four Courts if he must not admit now that justice was

---

[1] Lord Palmerston, writing to his brother at this date, says: "The ending of the O'Connell trial has surprised us all; but the man the most surprised is Chief-Justice Tindal" (who had delivered the answers of the Judges to the questions of the Lords).

to be had under the English system of jurisprudence. "Oh, certainly," MacNevin replied; "if your Court of Appeal be happily framed, justice may be had—after punishment has been inflicted, and at a cost of fifty thousand pounds." The entire defence had cost the Repeal Treasury this enormous sum, and had there been no Repeal Treasury there could have been no writ of error; and the bad law and foul practices of the Irish Courts would have remained in this case, as they commonly remained, without remedy.

A closer observer than the journalists, and one better informed of the facts, confirms the signal importance of the victory.

"Peel," says Mr Disraeli, "never recovered this blow. . . . . Resolute not to recur to his ancient Orangemen, yet desperate after his discomfiture of rallying a moderate party around his ministry, his practical mind, more clear-sighted than foreseeing, was alarmed at the absence of all influence for the government of Ireland."[1]

And the people of Ireland were not disposed to undervalue the victory. They had strictly obeyed the Leader's injunction to be tranquil, the popular organisation had been maintained in a high state of efficiency, funds had been plentifully supplied, new recruits of importance had been won, and now at length they expected to see some fruits of their patience and perseverance. The conditions, indeed, were singularly favourable for pushing on the cause another stage.

---

[1] "Life of Lord George Bentinck."

BOOK III.

BOOK III.

CHAPTER I.

IRISH PARTIES AFTER O'CONNELL'S DELIVERANCE.

THE conditions indeed were favourable to another move in advance —all except one essential condition: the Leader was no longer able to lead. O'Connell left Richmond Prison suffering under a mortal disease, aggravated by public and private troubles. The slow retreat before triumphant enemies from the Mallow Defiance to the sentence and the jail had tortured him. For a time he was disturbed by fears of a popular rising for which no preparations were made, and when these fears passed away, he had to bear the strain of a weightier responsibility in his new undertaking to conduct the cause to speedy success.

But in addition to these public grounds of anxiety there were private grounds. After the lapse of two generations history is entitled to become possessed of one fruitful cause of disquietude, without a knowledge of which the transactions of that day will be imperfectly understood. During the whole period of the imprisonment O'Connell was an unsuccessful wooer. He was labouring under the most distracting influence that can possess a man of his years—a passionate love for a gifted young girl, who might have been his granddaughter. His family were naturally alarmed by this incident, and the more so doubtless that the lady whom he proposed to place at the head of their house differed from them in race and religion, and their feverish anxiety could not fail to react upon him. Their fears were allayed in the end by the lady's persistent refusal to become his wife, but this result was not calculated to restore the composure of O'Connell. In truth, it left him discontented and perturbed in a high degree. Nor was this all; he was now suffering from the disease from which he died. A competent critic, with the best opportunities to form a correct judgment, has declared that even during the trial it was plain he was fatally invalided—"the old fervour had departed, the old mastery was no more."[1] And less than three years later the French physician who attended him at his death pronounced, after a post-mortem examination, that he died of softening of the brain, and that the disease had lasted for at least two years.[2] In such a condition, weakened by disease, depressed by a disappointment which turned the worldly wisdom of Henri Quatre to folly, stooping under the burthen of seventy years, no longer able to concentrate his faculties on a single point, his powerful will slackened, his great brain distraught, it is no wonder that he lost heart in the cause he loved. It was little suspected at the moment, but many of the ablest men familiar with the period came finally to believe, and they were justified in believing, that this time O'Connell had once more silently resolved to accept the largest concessions he could obtain from Parliament in lieu of Repeal of the Union. He was surrounded and solicited by men ready to make liberal promises on behalf of the Whigs, his life was drawing to a close, and he had little reliance on his probable successors. Compromise, which he named "the doctrine of instalments," was one of his favourite agencies, and at lowest the experiment seemed to be a safe one for the country. Had he taken the people into his confidence, he would probably have forfeited much of his popularity; he would certainly have lost his most devoted supporters, but he would have preserved his peace of mind. By not taking them into his confidence, he drifted by degrees, as we shall see, into a position where his secret purpose and his conduct were no longer in harmony, and his health and happiness were totally wrecked in the conflict. And the device which seemed so safe proved in the end to be charged with calamity and ruin. These were the causes which rendered abortive the

---

[1] "I believe that fatal disease was upon him during the trial. His brain had possibly been affected by the unexampled excitement he had undergone. When he spoke on his own behalf the old fervour had departed, the old mastery was no more, and he read to the jury an argument not void of high ability but wholly different from the appeal with which in other days he would have subdued them under the spell of his masterly advocacy."— Lord O'Hagan's Centenary Address, August 1875.

[2] Dr Lacour, of Lyons, who had been in attendance on O'Connell and accompanied him to Genoa, made a post-mortem examination, on which he read a paper before the Société Medicale of Lyons (copied into the *Lancet*, November 1847). Rammollissement of the brain, he declared, was the disease from which O'Connell had suffered during two years previous to his death, which produced the uncertain gait and failing intellect, and to which the fatal termination was entirely attributable.

opportunity for another move in advance. From the day he left Richmond Prison the leader of the people never took a step that was not in its design or in its result a step backwards.

The first meeting of the Association was eagerly expected. The business was fixed to begin an hour after noon, but before ten o'clock in the morning the hall was crowded from floor to ceiling, and multitudes continued to arrive for whom there was no place. O'Connell's reception may be conceived by those who recall the arrears of repressed wrath and indignation which furnished fuel for the present enthusiasm. Smith O'Brien opened the business by proposing as a member the Honourable Hely Hutchinson, brother of the Earl of Donoughmore, who had long thought that Irishmen ought to resume the undivided management of their own affairs, and who now joined the Association because he felt convinced that neither the people nor the leaders would give up the contest till success was achieved. Mr Henry Grattan followed him by proposing Captain John Mockler, an Irishman, an Orangeman, and a soldier, and Davis brought down in his hand a remarkable pamphlet in which Mr Grey Porter, High Sheriff of the Orange County Fermanagh, and grandson of a bishop of the Irish Establishment, had just declared for a Federal Union.

O'Connell spoke for more than two hours, and said many things natural and suitable to the occasion. But men missed what they chiefly expected—his programme of future action. The six months in which he had promised to carry Repeal, if public order were preserved, had nearly run their course, and though nobody thought of holding him to a literal performance of that rash undertaking, they desired to make sure that there was some relation between the means to be employed in the future and the end to be accomplished. The method of procedure symbolised in the Mallow Defiance was abandoned; but the need was more urgent that the substituted method should be intelligible and adequate. He began by recognising a providential character in the triumph of the last week.

"It was not by man's effort that they had achieved the victory over fraud and injustice, but as a blessing bestowed by Providence on the virtuous people of Ireland. But Providence acted through agents, and he owed some atonement to a class of men whom he had often assailed and sometimes supported—the Whigs. He had supported them mainly to keep out the Tories, and prevent them making partisan judges. Had there been no interruption of Tory rule, neither Cottenham, Denham, nor Campbell would ever have sat on the bench. Had the Whigs been recently in office, Pigot and Moore would have been judges in Ireland instead of Lefroy and Jackson."

He exhorted Mr Grey Porter in terms of hyperbole to take one step more, and join the Association. If he came among Repealers, he would command the position which his talents, his fortune, and his station entitled him to; the old leader would pull in the traces, and the new leader might hold the reins.

At length he turned to the topic for which his audience were impatient—the future policy of the national party.

"Three subjects were pressing on his mind. The first related to the Clontarf Meeting. It was legally summoned and illegally prohibited from assembling. The Repealers were bound to vindicate a great principle—the right of meeting; the question was whether it would be necessary to further assert it by still holding that meeting. The next subject was the plan which was under review when the State prosecution commenced of summoning three hundred gentlemen to act as a Preservative Society. The subject was full of legal difficulty and must be approached cautiously. His idea was that this Society should initiate nothing, but correct and control everything in the movement; that the Repeal Association should take no step without their sanction, and that they should be at perfect liberty to point out the course that appeared to them best adapted for carrying Repeal.

"The third subject was a plan to which he was greatly attached—to bring about an impeachment of the Attorney-General, the Judges of the Queen's Bench, and the Ministry. It was often said that the people of England were favourable to Ireland, though the aristocracy were not, and he was now about to try. He would go through England from town to town, and from county to county, and either they would insist upon this impeachment, or he would come back and say, 'Don't mind John Bull, look to your Parliament yourselves.' And were the Ministry to escape? That foul-mouthed letter-opener, Sir James Graham, had in his absence called him in the House of Commons a 'convicted conspirator.' And Peel had such unrivalled powers of face, such total disregard of truth, as to declare in the same place that the Traversers had a fair trial. He would have no faith in England if the English people did not join in hurling Peel from office, and send him adrift with the finger of scorn pointing to him as the monster liar of Parliament."

These were not hopeful devices for repealing the Union. The Council of Three Hundred, as originally projected, was a body designed to represent the constituencies from which an Irish Parliament would be derived; it was to assemble in evasion or defiance of the Convention Act, and O'Connell had suggested that it needed only a little sealing wax upon a piece of parchment to transform such an assembly into the Irish Parliament—which was true, doubtless, if only the sealing-wax were green and the seal, like Charlemagne's, the hilt of a conquering sword. The revival of the original project was impracticable; the national feeling had cooled down far below the point where such an enterprise would be fitting or well timed; but the men who had conducted the public business with vigilance and sincerity during the imprisonment would never have consented to substitute for it an abortion borrowed apparently from the mute voting machine which the first Bonaparte had bequeathed to the contempt of mankind. The Clontarf meeting might have been held in vindication of public right, but as it was certain that it would again recede before a proclamation, if Peel decided on issuing one, to hold it would be courting a new defeat. At best, since the change of policy, a Clontarf meeting had lost its original significance, and would be but a poor parody of the meetings of '43. Of the third proposal it was difficult to speak with gravity or patience. Impeachment, while it was still in use, was a State trial of the most solemn character, originated by command of the House of Commons and heard and adjudged by the House of Lords. It has been disused since the practice of responsible government has furnished a simpler and speedier method of punishing the great officers of state who lose the public confidence. To speak seriously of asking the House of Commons to revive this obsolete process against a Minister at the head of a compact majority, and to hold out a hope that the House of Lords, sitting, not as a court of appeal, but as a court of criminal jurisdiction, where every peer is entitled to vote, would afford the relief sought, was to affront the good sense of his audience. The most turbulent member of the Opposition in the House of Commons would no more vote for an impeachment than he would vote for sending the Wizard of the North to trial for witchcraft. But the futility of the project was not the feature that was most alarming at the moment. The appeal to the people of England to hurl Peel from power, and, failing their assistance, the promise to return and tell the Irish people not to mind John Bull but to look to their Parliament themselves, had a fatal resemblance to the former compact with the Whigs when Repeal was postponed to an experiment on English sympathy. Suppose the appeal were applauded by popular audiences in England, what, men naturally asked, would he come back and tell the Irish people to do under these circumstances?

The reception which these projects met in the councils of the party may be judged from the result. They were all abandoned either forthwith or after some courteous delay. At the next meeting of the Association O'Connell reported from the Committee that it was not considered necessary to hold the Clontarf meeting, as the right of the people to meet peaceably in any number had been recognised by the English Judges. And with respect to the Council of Three Hundred, further time was required, without any particular limit, to consider the question fully. The project of an appeal to the English people to insist upon an impeachment had not yet obtained the assent of his esteemed friend Smith O'Brien, who was of opinion that it would put the Irish Nationalists in a contradictory and undignified position. If he did not succeed in convincing Mr O'Brien that the project was right, he would manage to model it in such a manner that if it did not meet his approval it would at all events put an end to his opposition.

This was idle talk, painful to hear or read. A great opportunity seemed to be slipping away; and the austere gravity and veracity, as well as the methodical and practical work to which the public mind had been schooled during the previous three months, contrasted strangely with devices so lightly taken up and so lightly laid down. There was no public remonstrance, but much silent discontent and dismay. Davis advised patience; a few years or a few mistakes counted for little in the history of a nation which had made up its mind to succeed. The people must be taught that the way was long, but that it was sure if they were true to themselves. Some of his comrades answered that the cause was losing its moral dignity; it had been made ridiculous by threats which were not carried out; and now it was being made ridiculous by proposals which plainly led to nothing, unless they were to lead to a new alliance with the Whigs. But the bulk of the people did not detect much amiss, and the national spirit continued high and confident.

After a banquet in Dublin to the late prisoners, O'Connell returned to Darrynane to rest and recruit his health: and his tour through Leinster and Munster, from the British Channel to the shores of the Atlantic, was one long ovation. Smith O'Brien and Maurice O'Connell were left in charge of the public business in his absence, but no course of action had been agreed upon, and there was, as O'Connell afterwards notified, an intentional pause in the agitation—a pause as perilous as the torpor of a general who, when his enemy is routed, fails to push his advantage. Among those entitled to be consulted he excused his inaction by insisting that Peel would ask new powers of coercion if he got any pretence; but none of his counsellors shared his fear, which proved to be quite groundless.[1] Some politicians, accustomed to fetch and carry for the Whig peers, and who believed themselves able to guide counsels of which they were only the messengers, took occasion of the truce to whisper that a compact with the Whigs was at hand on a new platform; but few believed that they spoke with authority.

The national sentiment, however, had by this time found develop-

---

[1] See Mr Disraeli's "Life of Lord George Bentinck" and Mr Evelyn Ashley's "Life of Lord Palmerston."

ments which O'Connell did not originate and could not control. In Belfast there were private consultations between Mr Sharman Crawford, Mr Ross, and their friends, for the purpose of organising a Federal party on an independent basis. And throughout the Irish Conservatives there was the feverish anxiety for change which precedes definite action. Dr Maunsell, who was at that time a writer in the *Evening Mail*, of which he subsequently became editor, made a motion in the Dublin Corporation which attracted wide notice, less perhaps from its intrinsic interest than from the position of the mover and the motives to which he appealed. He proposed an humble address to the Queen, praying her to hold her Court and Parliament once at least in every three years in her loyal city of Dublin. Passing lightly over the economic and local reasons for desiring to bring the Imperial Parliament occasionally to Ireland, he addressed himself directly to his own party, and urged it upon them as a measure of self-defence.

"In determining his policy, and in distributing the public patronage, the Minister they had raised to power not only ceased to regard, but deliberately thwarted, their wishes. Only two institutions in which Protestants had a special interest, the University and the Church, were permitted to survive in Ireland. How long would they remain? Let no one hope that a Minister, expert in manœuvres for tiding over political shoals, would not let slip these remaining anchors of Irish Protestantism whenever he considered the sacrifice useful for his ends. When this catastrophe occurred they would find themselves a weakened, denationalised, and betrayed garrison of England. Let them come to terms before the breach in their bulwarks became indefensible. The time was suitable for the introduction of moderate measures such as he proposed ; for, strange as the assertion might sound to English ears, he never recollected a period when there was less party spirit or more general good-humour in Ireland. This measure would take Protestants out of the hands of place-hunting lawyers, who made barter and sale of their interest, and it would cut the unhappy ties that bound Irishmen to the tail of either English Whigs or English Tories."

The *Evening Mail* gave its unqualified approval to Dr Maunsell's proposal, and pressed it on the important party whom it represented.

This theory of the duties of Irish Protestants was considered worthy of an elaborate answer in the *Quarterly Review*. It enraged the party leaders to find a project which had been broached in the *Edinburgh*, and supported by the Christian Socialists,[1] and which was borrowed from the Radical scheme of William Cobbett, finding favour with an important section of the Conservative party. In Ireland the public applauded Dr Maunsell's arguments ; but if they were good arguments for a rotatory Parliament, it was felt they were still better arguments for

---

[1] See Rev. Charles Kingsley's "Politics for the People," p. 135.

a domestic Parliament. At worst they helped to shake the traditional Tory policy of an alliance with England in every contingency. Davis wrote to O'Brien:

"O'Connell's apprehension of a coercive policy is gone. It was absurd ever to have felt it. I look upon Maunsell's motion as a clear gain. He is an ultra Tory. Seeking an Imperial session in Ireland as a remedy for grievances may be illogical and is impracticable (so much the better), but it is a loosening of ideas, an abandonment of the old superstition that all was right, and good will come of it—if we are the men of the time. If not, it will be another event for history to scorn us for."[1]

Mr Porter went much further. He desired a Congress for the Empire, and local legislature for the Three Kingdoms. As an alternative, however, he proposed that no measure designed to be in force in Ireland, except army and navy bills, should be submitted to either House of Parliament without the previous sanction of the Irish members of the House where it was introduced. And he declared his object to be to raise his country to a full share in the honours, advantages, and management of the Hiberno-British Empire[2] or by slow and sure steps to the dignity of an independent nation.

The value of these recruits can be best measured perhaps at present by the impression produced on the most powerful and sensitive organ of opinion in England. In reply to a French journal which described the Irish movement as a Democratic one, the *Times* denied that it was Democratic, and pointed out that county magnates and professional men were falling into it: the identical class who had carried the American struggle to success.

"It is from these men that the Repeal ranks are recruited. Why? Because they are proud, aspiring, and ambitious. Because they think their position a false one and an ignominious one. They are nobodies out of their own counties ; and his own county each thinks has not its proper influence on the fate of the Empire. They seek what all men seek—to gain importance for themselves and theirs. They want, what all men are glad to obtain—power. They see no other means of doing this than by making Ireland a nation. A distinct nationality and a separate Parliament would give them opportunities of attaining eminence and rank, which are now only obtainable by a fortunate few among them. This would turn the squireen into a senator and give real value to the tinsel splendours of an Irish coronet."

---

[1] 25th Sept., '44.—Cahermoyle Correspondence.
[2] Bentham invented this phrase, to soothe national pride, irritated by having everything attributed to England. It anticipated the title of the Austro-Hungarian Empire.

Mr Porter's plan of a Congress found a certain measure of favour with the *Times*, for reasons which time has not robbed of their force.

"The idea of a Congress has occurred to other minds before this as a solution of many existing difficulties. We are becoming less of a nation and more of an Empire. The conduct of an Empire and the government of one's own people seem quite different and incongruous operations. The very ethical qualities necessary, perhaps, for keeping a barbaric continent in subjection don't do at home. One is shocked to see either Irish peasants or English labourers ruled with the same rod of iron as Mahrattas or Belochees —with the same suspicious discipline as a mutinous man-of-war crew or a black regiment at the Cape. There is, too, something absolutely ridiculous in the present mixture of Parliamentary subjects. An hour's talk on the balance of power between the Continental Empires is followed by three days' animated discussion on a personal squabble. The annexation of a great territory is passed over almost *sub silentio* in a storm of talk about some third-class official appointment. While Lord Lieutenants are called to speedy account Governor-Generals quietly accumulate transgressions. Parliament has too many irons in the fire."

The *Examiner*, which under the control of Mr Fonblanque exercised a decisive influence over English opinion, took nearly an identical view of the situation.

"In noting the monster misrepresentations about the nearness of success in the Repeal cause, we would not go into the opposite extreme in error of denying the progress of the question. We mark closely this stage of advance, that sensible men are disposed to agree that the Parliamentary organisation is not fitted to the exigencies of the Empire, and that some new arrangement is necessary to adjust the appropriate legislative capacity and attention to the peculiar wants of different parts of the country."

At home the *Warder* admitted that Protestant contributions were flowing into Conciliation Hall, and a Conservative journal well informed on the state of opinion in Ulster avowed that the national sentiment was spreading fast, "whole masses of nominal Protestants were preparing not to join the O'Connellite movement, in the first instance, but to adopt a system of organisation which without any effort on his part would enable the Agitator to carry his most ambitious schemes to an easy and triumphant issue."

The best assistance O'Connell could give these collateral movements was to let them alone; for the classes among whom they must find recruits could not forget the quarrels of thirty years or fall into the ranks of which he himself was the leader. But of all policies a policy of abstention was the one he was by nature and habit least able to adopt. And it is possible that his Whig friends saw in these moderate proposals a convenient opportunity of breaking with the monster meetings and the Mallow Defiance. What is certain is that through the agency of Mr William Murphy of Smithfield, a man of long purse and large brains, he opened negotiations with such of the Federalists as were disposed to listen to him to effect a coalition between them and the Repealers, with what disastrous results we shall presently see.

It was not convenient to interrupt the narrative of the State trials by completing the story of Lord Hawarden's action against Father Davern;[1] but it is necessary to revert to this transaction to complete the story of the contest in courts of law. Lord Hawarden, as one of the Queen's Household, was required to defend himself against charges of the gravest nature and of the most specific character; and he was expected at the same time to expose the libels of priests and popular writers against his class; but he was apparently in no hurry to undertake this duty. Before the proceedings against Father Davern had begun, the priest sickened and died of a fever caught in the discharge of his duty, and the case was supposed to have died with him. But when the proprietor of the *Nation* was entangled in the State Trial, Lord Hawarden apparently thought a suitable opportunity had at length come for renewing his operations. Mr Brewster mentioned the case in Court, and, to the public amazement, flatly denied that any promise had been made by the Lord-in-Waiting to abandon proceedings against the *Nation*, even if the manuscript and the author of the alleged libel were given up. He wished to know what course the defendant was prepared to take. I answered in the pages of the *Nation* that the Irish Land system wanted looking into, and that I was ready to proceed with the case. Upwards of sixty affidavits had been sworn, chiefly by ejected tenants, and an expense of nearly £800 incurred in preparing Father Davern's defence; and these materials were now available for a justification. A day was fixed for the long-postponed motion, and Mr Sheil appeared for the defence. Mr Brewster, however, asked further postponement, not having had time to read his brief. When he found time to read it, he made an offer which in an ordinary case would probably have been accepted: to stop the action on payment by the defendant of the costs already incurred. But this was not an ordinary case; it was the pitched battle of the ejected tenantry against the exterminating landlords, and I declined the offer. Mr Sheil was ready to proceed to trial; but Lord Hawarden's brother official, the Attorney-General, claimed precedence for the State Trial then pending, and the case was adjourned till the next term. When the next term arrived, this significant action at law, which was to justify not

---

[1] See *ante:* "Two Incidents," p. 102; note on Chapter VI., Book I.

only the particular landlord, but landlords in general against their libellers, was never carried a step farther. How the Lord-in-Waiting satisfied his leader I know not; but it is probable that his Irish advisers considered that further exposure was not convenient. Nor, indeed, was it. The duty of a people to go on for miserable years, and miserable generations, enduring chronic poverty and periodical famine, submitting to be driven from their homes like cattle to the shambles, for the benefit of a handful of absentees, is the sort of duty which will not bear too rigorous a scrutiny. The English landlords who had expressed such boisterous sympathy with their ill-used Irish brother never got the promised exposure of demagogues and libellers; and, if they knew the truth, had no more a common cause with the Irish exterminator and rack-renter than with a planter of South Carolina. Another libel case in which the *Nation* was defendant (these two being the only actions for private libel with which it was assailed, from its foundation in 1842 till its suppression in 1848) will be found in a note below.

NOTE ON CHAPTER I.

ACTION FOR LIBEL AGAINST THE *NATION*.

THE *Nation* was defendant in another libel case at this time, which curiously illustrates the spirit in which justice was administered in Ireland during that era.
 The result of the Writ of Error, it may be supposed, did not leave Chief-Justice Pennefather in a happy frame of mind. His law had been peremptorily overruled by the peers, his charge had found no cordial defender in the House of Commons, and the odium in which he was held by the bulk of the people was not compensated by the admiration or gratitude of the political party to which he belonged, for they commonly attributed the escape of O'Connell to the blunders of the Queen's Bench. His temper was further exasperated by the contemptuous and menacing tone of the National party. O'Connell reminded them that this functionary had a son-in-law who was made a bishop by Peel; but as the promotion took place in 1842, before the State Trial was foreseen, he took care to add that quite lately, since his achievements in the Queen's Bench, his nephew had got an excellent place in the Castle. The writers of the *Nation*, who thought it doubtful that a Minister of the cautious temper of Sir Robert Peel would consciously bestow patronage on a judge who had recently presided at a State Trial, took him to task on other grounds, and habitually treated him as one who had revived in the reign of Queen Victoria the prerogative law and the servile obedience which Chief-Justice Scroggs under Charles II., and Chief-Justice Jeffreys under his successor, had brought, with such disastrous results, to the servic of the Crown.

Under these circumstances an incident occurred which enabled the Chief-Justice to regain his good humour for a moment by bringing one of his opponents within the scope of his authority.

An apothecary, named Larkin, contrived to get inserted in the *Nation* an advertisement of certain pills, which he described as effecting an immediate cure in asthma, stomach, liver and bowel complaints, but above all, in consumption, " in all stages short of the actual gripe of death." This prodigious announcement was fortified by a statement that, to remove all doubts, Mr Larkin had exhibited testimonials of success to gentlemen in the *Nation* office, who, it might be assumed, would guarantee their authenticity. Puffs and medical advertisements were systematically excluded from the *Nation*, and on reading this one I wrote a paragraph to express my regret that a quack advertisement had accidentally escaped notice. The apothecary immediately commenced an action for malicious libel ; the libel consisting of the words " quack advertisement " applied to his announcement. I put in a plea of justification, and the action came on for trial before Chief-Justice Pennefather. The case turned upon the question whether the description of the cures Mr Larkin claimed to have effected was or was not a quack advertisement. This was the sole fact in controversy. If it were proved to the satisfaction of the jury that it was a quack advertisement, they had no option but to find a verdict for the newspaper. If it were not a quack advertisement, but a fair statement of fact, Mr Larkin was doubtlessly libelled, and might indeed be regarded as a great benefactor of his species. But in no case was it malicious, as I had merely guarded myself from being made responsible, under the guise of " gentlemen in the *Nation* office," for the truth of statements which I disbelieved. The plaintiff's witnesses, as it sometimes happens in dubious plaints, proved the defendant's case. A doctor, called to establish the fact that Mr Larkin was a qualified practitioner, swore on cross-examination that the pills could not perform the promised cures, and that the advertisement in question was in his belief a quack advertisement. A druggist was produced to prove that the plaintiff was in the habit of purchasing medicine from him, and that it was of the best quality—medicine presumably obtained for the manufacture of his panacea—but the witness admitted on cross-examination that these purchases occurred five or six years before, when Mr Larkin was an ordinary apothecary, and had not commenced the sale of his universal medicine. The advertisement clerk of the *Nation*, summoned to prove that certain testimonials had been exhibited to him by Larkin, swore that he had never read a line of them, and that he had strict instructions from Mr Gavan Duffy to refuse all advertisements of an indecent or immoral character. Three or four uneducated men, of the humblest condition, were then produced to prove that they had been restored to health by the use of Mr Larkin's pills. But of these perfect cures, Dr Corrigan (the late Sir Dominic Corrigan, since President of the College of Physicians), who was present in the Court during the examination, swore that he believed one of them was in a confirmed consumption and another in a hopeless asthma. Not a solitary witness was produced to swear that the advertisement in controversy was *not* a quack advertisement ; *quod erat demonstrandum.*

After such a case for the plaintiff a defence seemed superfluous, but a defence was made which would have been a sufficient answer to a case resting on stringent evidence.

Professor Kane—afterwards Sir Robert Kane, a chemist of European reputation, who within a few weeks of these events Sir Robert Peel in Parliament pronounced to be at the head of his profession—swore that he had analysed the pills, and could discern nothing in them but "crumbs of bread." Dr Corrigan swore that the statements in the advertisement could not be true, and that it was clearly a quack advertisement. Sir Henry Marsh, then President of the College of Physicians, swore that the promises to cure the disease specified under the circumstances stated were as false as the promise of the Philosopher's Stone, and that the advertisement was the very *beau idéal* of a quack advertisement. Mr Gunn, proprietor of the *General Advertiser*, swore that he had had twenty years' experience of advertisements, and that this was one of the worst quack advertisements he had ever met with. He added that an advertisement of a similar character had been brought by the plaintiff to his office, and rejected as a quack advertisement.

Then came the judge's charge. It was awaited with extraordinary interest. The *Nation* had criticised the judicial career of Chief-Justice Pennefather in a manner he was supposed not to have forgotten, and its editor was one of the State prisoners who had triumphed over his defective law. The charge, when it came, justified the curiosity it had excited. From beginning to end there was but one obscure reference to the fact that the question which the jury had to try was whether the advertisement was a quack advertisement. From beginning to end there was but a single allusion to the conclusive evidence delivered by Kane, Marsh, and Corrigan. He told the jury, indeed, that the case was so simple they could not require direction. But lest they should interpret this dictum as a suggestion to find for the defendant, he carefully warned them, twice over, that they could not give more damages than five hundred pounds. This was the amount claimed by the plaintiff, and this therefore was their limit. Thus far they might go, but no farther. After the jury left the box the defendant's counsel thought it necessary to insist upon having them called back to Court that they might be told "what they had to try."[1] They submitted that the Chief-Justice had not told them, as he was bound to do, that the substantial question they were put into the box to determine was whether or not the advertisement was a quack advertisement, and that they were not at liberty, in determining this question, to take into account whether the plaintiff was, or was not, injured by the publication. They were recalled accordingly, but the effect of the charge was not disturbed ; the jury found a verdict for the injured apothecary, forty shillings damages, to be supplemented by the costs of plaintiff and defendant. A provincial Medical Association immediately passed resolutions expressing their astonishment and disgust at a verdict against the editor of the *Nation* for asserting what "every respectable member of the medical profession and of society at large knew to be true," and proposing that the costs should be paid by a subscription from the profession. The Medical Association of Ireland, acting upon this suggestion, opened a fund for the purpose. As the bulk of the Association were Conservatives, there could not be a more significant proof of the effect the Chief-Justice's charge had produced. In this respect their movement was very welcome ; but I paid the costs myself, and thought the £100 well spent in exhibiting to the world the conditions under which liberty of the Press was maintained by Irish journalists. Perhaps the gentlemen of England, who live at home at ease, may understand, from transactions like these, why English law in Ireland, administered by Ascendancy judges, has not won all the veneration to which they esteem it entitled.

---

[1] Mr O'Hagan (afterwards a peer and Lord Chancellor) and Mr J. D. Fitzgerald (afterwards a peer and a law lord) were counsel for the defendant.

CHAPTER II.

RECREATIONS OF THE YOUNG IRELANDERS.

WE have seen the young men at work in the Council-room, on the platform, and in the newspaper office; the reader will scarce realise how gay and exuberant was the Irish nature that covered so much earnestness and assiduity without following them for a moment into their ordinary recreations.

Once a week, on Saturday evening, we still met at each other's houses in succession. Tea and serious debate occupied the time till ten o'clock; then a light supper, pleasant talk, fun and song till midnight. It was here the literary and political projects of the party were discussed, and the books and articles to be written, the plans to be proposed, and the places to be visited determined. A cordial friendship warmed and harmonised these pleasant meetings. Since that time I have lived in friendly social relations with several communities successively; but I have never seen anywhere such unaffected good fellowship and brotherly sympathy as existed among these young men. They escaped, I think, the chief danger of such reunions; they were far from being a mutual admiration society. Whoever laid himself fairly open to criticism during the week might confidently expect to be chaffed without mercy on Saturday night.

The Answers to Correspondents in the *Nation* were regarded as inflicting severe, and often savage, justice on contributors, and no doubt it was their purpose to repress nonsense; but sometimes the judgment which seemed to strike a recruit so hard was the verdict of his compeers upon one of the ordinary staff; and not infrequently it was the writer himself who reported the verdict. Sometimes an old contributor disguised himself as a new one to experiment upon the opinion of his *confrères*. I remember becoming impatient with one of my friends for the coldness with which he welcomed a genuine poet, whom I professed to have discovered under the blurred pot-hooks and fantastic signature of an illiterate woman; but by-and-by I discovered that "Carolina Wilhelmina," whom he would not be persuaded to admire, was my learned friend himself in masquerade. In the correspondence of the period I find some faint image of these meetings, which will exhibit at any rate the freedom of mutual criticism which prevailed. MacNevin wrote to me during the State Trial :—

"I never regretted your absence so much as last night. We had a most delightful evening. We talked some politics, but considerably of general philosophy—death, religion, and the State Trials ! We read Doheny's prodigious farce, 'Fate and the Florentine Picture'[1] (which, of course, not being in Italy, he never saw), whose voice (only think of a voice in oil colours and articulate canvas) speaks murmuringly in the low wind to Ireland, and tells her to be free. We unanimously agree that it was the worst thing that ever appeared in the *Nation*. We were forcibly struck, too, by your setting down Brewster among the flower of the Bar, one of those 'the least of whom had done something to make a name.' Oh, by the Law, that was too bad ! Altogether we had an extremely delightful evening, only marred by the often-expressed regret that you were not with us. You may judge we were in good trim when Davis was sentimental, and talked seriously of having speculated on death in his infancy. Lane not being here, we had none of the discussion on copperplate, line engraving, or generalities in art, which show how far a little knowledge can carry an adventurous spirit. Dillon got joyous over his water, and Cangley was profound over his ; both were supplied from the Basin (the Grand Canal Basin). Barry was epicurean and lauded my cook, and Davis and O'Neill and I were the only choice spirits of the night.

"Since I have taken to read Irish history, it clothes the landscape with new interest and beauty, and I have mooted your project of reading it *en costume*. Let us begin by making a party to visit Malahide Castle next week. There is a family portrait of Dick Talbot, I understand, and original portraits of Charles and James, his patrons, and several of the notabilities of that time ; worth seeing, I think—though

'Talbot's a dog and James is an ass
Lillibullero bullen a la.'

I am often disgusted with our history, though it is exhilarating reading ; not with the barbarities of England ; no, but with the factious frenzy and imbecility of our chiefs. Bah ! they might have ejected the marauders a thousand times. One of two things ought to have occurred : either Englishmen ought to have united and beaten us, or we ought to have united and beaten them. It was only lately I knew that Con of the Hundred Battles lost about two-thirds of the battles from which he obtained his tremendous title. It was granted him, it is to be presumed, as a compensation for his ill-luck."[2]

Some of the *bons mots* of that period will bear repeating, though it is generally a dreary task to pin down on paper those butterflies of the hour. M'Carthy wrote originally under the signature of " Desmond," which is the country of the M'Carthys. There is a story in mediæval

---

[1] Article in the *Nation*, Jan. 20, 1844.
[2] MacNevin to Duffy.

history (of which Maclise has made a striking picture) that when an Earl of Desmond fell wounded into the hands of his hereditary enemies (the Butlers of Ormond), his captors, as they carried him on their shoulders from the battle-field, demanded triumphantly, "Where's Desmond now?" and the stout old earl replied, "Where a Desmond ought to be—on the neck of the Butler." After a social Saturday night at Major Bryan's, of Raheny, the party returning to town missed M'Carthy, who had agreed to remain a few days with his host. "Where is 'Desmond'?" was demanded on all hands. "Don't expect him to-night," said Williams, "I saw him as we left Raheny, where a Desmond ought to be, on the neck of the butler!" It was a constant formula of O'Connell's, exhorting the people to pay the Repeal Rent, that it amounted only to a shilling a year, a penny a month, a farthing a week, and four weeks thrown in for nothing. After Clontarf, when it became a point of honour with the old agitators to repudiate all reference to arms or resistance, Barry wrote an historical song, the burthen of which was

"Charge for Erin and her flag of green."

"What do you mean by charging for Erin?" one of the old school demanded; "is that what you call peaceful and legal agitation?" "Certainly," replied Barry; "I mean 'charging' a shilling a year, a penny a month, a farthing a week, and four weeks thrown in for nothing." On some occasion MacNevin was recounting the friendly efforts he had made to induce one of his kinsmen, a Connaught squire, to become a Repealer, and ending by declaring that he despaired of him, and told him that he might go to the d——. "Did he go?" I demanded. "Well, yes," rejoined MacNevin, "he has gone the first stage; he has joined the Stephen's Green Club." Mr J. J. M'Carthy, the ecclesiastical architect, was a Young Irelander in those days, and his associates, to discriminate him from D. F. M'Carthy, sometimes called him "Jem." "Are you a relative of Jem M'Carthy's?" a visitor demanded of the former. "Oh, yes," replied the poet; "Jem and I[2] are twins." On the occasion of some popular movement in Tipperary, Doheny, on returning to town, described his labours. "For a fortnight I was constantly in the saddle or on Bianconi's car, or addressing meetings, or attending committees. For more than ten days I had not time to

---

[1] The Stephen's Green Club is the Whig Club of Dublin.
[2] Gemini.

WILLIAM CARLETON, 1845.
(From the portrait by CHARLES GREY, R.H.A.)

change my linen." "Not change your linen!" said McCarthy, with a shudder of disgust; "you're as bad as the fashionable ladies in the 'Song of a Shirt.'

"'Tis not linen you're wearing out,
But living creatures' lives.'"

Smith O'Brien's formal manners and English accent long proved non-conductors between him and some of the younger men. "What do you think of Smith O'Brien?" I asked one of them shortly after the former became a Repealer. "Well," he replied, "I think the amalgam is unskilfully made; there is too much of the Smith and too little of the O'Brien." Frank Dwyer, son of the secretary to the famous Catholic Association, was an official in Conciliation Hall, and used to compare his small income piteously with the liberal provisions made for the secretary, Mr Ray. He got some concession on this complaint, but renewed his claims. "Will nothing satisfy the fellow?" said Doheny; "what does he want now?" In reply, Lane hummed a couplet from Moore's Melodies—

"He longs to tread that golden path of Ray's,
And thinks 'twould lead to some bright isle of rest."[1]

While Mr Butt was still leader of the old Protestant Ascendancy party in Dublin, some one was lamenting the infatuation of citizens who abandoned the plain interest of the country at his bidding. One of our visitors, now a London journalist, suggested that it was the case of Othello,

"Who loved (not wisely) Butt too well."

Carleton, who never made puns, let fall occasionally a saying which exploded like a bomb charged with laughing gas. An occasional correspondent of the *Nation*, who had failed to secure domestic peace in his household, wrote a contemptuous letter against theories then beginning to be debated as the rights of women. "I think," says Carleton, "he is not past conversion; he would come round, I fancy, if some one offered his wife—a foreign appointment." Mr James Duffy, whose liberality contributed largely to create a national literature in Ireland, sometimes held his hand when it was too late to save judiciously. When

---

[1] "And as I watched the line of light that plays
Along the smooth wave tow'rd the burning West,
I long to tread that golden path of rays,
And think 'twould lead to some bright isle of rest."
MOORE'S MELODIES.

he issued an illustrated edition of "Valentine McClutchy," Carleton was of opinion that it was not duly advertised, or distributed for review, and remonstrated without result. I walked into Duffy's back shop one day about the time the second number appeared, and found the publisher and the author in high controversy on the subject. Carleton, on seeing me, took up a copy, and looking at me with a face mantling with suppressed fun, muttered, in a slow stage whisper, "'This, my friend, is an illustrated edition of 'Valentine McClutchy' that's coming out just now; but don't mention it to anyone, James Duffy does not wish it to be known."[1]

There were points upon which Davis found it impossible to influence more than a small section of his friends. When he proposed to form a class to study the Irish language, when he desired to revive the native names of historical men and places, there was vehement resistance. O'Brien seconded both projects energetically, if he did not originate them. "Accustom everyone," he wrote to Davis, "to write Irish words in the Irish character;"[2] and at forty years of age he became a student of Gaelic. A library edition of the "Spirit of the Nation," with music and illustrations was issued, and Davis procured the assistance of the Irish scholars O'Donovan and Curry to correct the proper names. But the first appearance of the genuine Gaelic patronymics created consternation like that which attended the introduction of Kalupso, Herakles, Hektor, and their associates into English literature, in the place of familiar favourites. Davis insisted that to understand history, topography, or romance, it was indispensable to study the native nomenclature. Fer-

---

[1] One evening when my house at Rathmines was the place of meeting, Barry, in passing the Canal at Portobello-bridge, slid accidentally into the water, and was drawn out with some difficulty by Lane. He returned to his residence to change his dress, and Lane reported the catastrophe to his friends. It was thought proper to assume that he was actually drowned, and his epitaph, his last will and testament, and an account of his premature death, were improvised, in various metres, by his comrades. Unfortunately the squibs have perished, and I can only recall a couplet from the mock heroic ballad on his death, on account of an allusion to a practice jocosely imputed to him, probably without any foundation—

"Pale, pale were his bonny cheeks and clammy as the clay,
Pale, pale were his whiskers twain, the dye was washed away."

In latter years, when Mr Barry renounced his early opinions, an indignant friend assured Denny Lane that all the good works of his life were counterbalanced by the sin of having saved a man from being drowned who proved in the end not worthy to be hanged ! The weekly supper never got any regular name fixed on it, though such an arrangement would obviously have been convenient. John Pigot tried hard, but unsuccessfully for Clan na Gael. At a much later period, when privacy was necessary, some one suggested the happy equivoque of the Invisible Greens.

[2] Davis Papers, Dec. 1844.

managh—to those who could interpret it—meant the land of lakes; Athenry, the ford of kings; Dunleary, the fort of the sea; Kildare spoke of wooded plains, and Clonmel of abundant fertility. But he pulled against a heavy current of resistance. A bantering letter of the period addressed to Thomas MacNevin, who was the peculiar enemy of the innovation, tells the story; with a little exaggeration, perhaps, designed to tease that anti-Gael.

"It was impossible to keep my appointment with you yesterday; I had a *sederunt* with Davis over a quarto edition (of the "Spirit of the Nation"), and it lasted long, because the moot points were various and troublesome. He wanted to strike out all the squibs—Mangan's, Williams', everybody's, in short; but I would not consent to this. 'Shall there be no cakes and ale because he is virtuous?' Yea, by St Anne, and banter shall be hot i' the mouth. I have yielded, however, about the native names, and I fear a new 'insurrection of the Bards' in consequence. The text of the ballads is to be larded with a Celtic nomenclature furnished by John O'Donovan, which sometimes consist of an aggregate meeting of consonants with scarcely a vowel to take the chair. They dislocate the metre, evaporate the melody, and often efface the rhyme itself. Since M'Carthy got back his revises he declares it is useless to rhyme any more; if he wrote

Let us go down
To pretty Kingstown,

Davis, he says, would turn it in the next edition into—

Let us go down
To pretty Dunleary,[1]

And Williams has sent back a bundle of proofs in which he was required to reconcile his verses to the Gaelic prosody, endorsed—

Lord save us
From Alaric Davis!

You will stare with all your eyes when you see what has become of some of your old acquaintances. What do you say to the Lee becoming the Laoi, and the Shannon the Sionàmn, Limerick Luimneach, and Sleive Donard Sliab Domangort? It seems to me this is going too fast: it would need the authority of an Irish Parliament, methinks, to get the present generation to call Glengariff Glengarbh? And how many men and women of our own age will be able to spell O'Shiadhail, which it seems is the correct name of your favourite orator in the Catholic Association? Pigot, in a fine frenzy, says, let them learn. But suppose (which is highly probable) they won't learn! My idea was to put the Irish names in notes, leaving the text as it was written, and await the possible future when the honourable members for Mallow and Fermoy will introduce a bill making the authentic spelling compulsory in official documents and national school-books. I am afraid to contemplate the effect on James Duffy's costly venture.

'Dear Tom, this green book, which once found a good sale,
I fear through these curs'd orthographics will fail.'

---

[1] Dunleary was the native name of Kingstown.

"I must tell you of a single combat we had in the course of the business, fought with broad-bladed sarcasms and short two-edged repartees. Davis demanded *apropos* of the line in the Muster of the North—

'Out from the stately woods of Truagh, M'Kenna's plundered home,'

who the deuce the M'Kennas were, of whom he professed never to have heard before. I told him they were Northern chiefs and kinsmen of mine. Could you conveniently, inquired my sarcastic gentleman, furnish as a note for the next edition, a list of the articles carried away by the invader from your kinsman's plundered home? 'Item,' one 'querin' for grinding corn 'item,' one stone pot for making whey; 'item,' six wooden 'methers' for drinking the same; 'item,' two rusty 'skians' and a set of bagpipes. But I gave him a Roland for his Oliver. He has written a fine resonant Cambrian march, and seems disposed to go extensively into Welsh nationality in honour of the Ap-Davises. I suggested that he was gilding refined gold, and otherwise indulging in wasteful and ridiculous excess, in writing national songs for a people so adequately provided already as his Cambrian kinsmen. 'How is that?' he said. 'Why,' I rejoined,' surely you cannot be ignorant of the great national anthem of the Principality—

'Taffy was a Welshman, Taffy was a ——'

By the way, what was the other illustrious thing besides a Welshman Taffy was? I have forgotten.'

"He was bent on spoiling his noble 'Owen Roe,' the finest effect of which is its dramatic opening ('Did they dare, did they dare?') by inserting an introductory verse. He did not quite yield to my vehement remonstrance; but I had a note from him since, saying Pigot agrees with him, but John O'Hagan agrees with me, and he submits to the majority."[1]

MacNevin replied that for his part he was not a man of the pagan or even mediæval period, but a mere modern, and that he would not allow himself to be turned into a Druid or a Brehon.

"I think"—he wrote in the gay, airy badinage which he loved—"I think our task is to work the virgin mine of nationality; but not, I submit, the nationality of Ollam Fodlah and other gentlemen before or immediately after the Flood. Or of Dathi (that antique hero whom Mr Holebrook depicts on the volunteer's card in a yeoman's uniform). Our task is to elevate the character of the people, raising up, in fact, their bump of self-esteem and suppressing the bumps of servility and fury. Drawing these fabulous heroes from their murky hiding-place is like Lane singing inane songs solely because they are older than Eman ac Knuc's hills.[2] We must be cosmopolitan, and deviate occasionally from our native bogs. We shall have a better chance of success by being less Irish, though not on that account less nice. James Duffy has agreed to publish a volume of biographical essays on the great men of European history; will you let us make it a joint book by you and me a little memorial of regard? Let us no longer

---

[1] Duffy to MacNevin.
[2] Eman ac Knuc, *i.e.* Ned of the Hills, a noted outlaw.

press poor Jacobo Duffei to the earth with records of centuries which no one will read, and, *O pessime!* which no one will buy. These pre-Adamite fictions are the Sabine bracelets and helmets which smother the Roman virgin of Wellington Quay."[1]

Excursions to memorable places was a favourite recreation in those days, and during the transactions which immediately followed the State Trials, I made a tour from Dublin to Darrynane, the home of O'Connell, with two friends, John O'Hagan and D. F. M'Carthy. We were all young and all Nationalists, and our course lay through some of the finest scenery and most memorable places in Ireland. Through Kilkenny, where the Confederation had sat two centuries before; where the hall of the Ormonds was still rich in portraits of memorable actors in Irish history, and where traditions of Grattan and Flood and young Tommy Moore, and of John Banim in a later day, had not died out. Through New Ross, where Martin Doyle, one of the survivors of '98, fought the battles over again on the very battlefields; along the Suir to Waterford, a land peopled with memories of every era of resistance to English supremacy, from the raid of Strongbow and the invasion of Cromwell down to the memorable election of 1826, which precipitated Catholic Emancipation. By Cappoquin and Lismore, through the divine valley of the Blackwater, with a detour to Mount Mellaray, where the Monks of La Trappe had established among the barren hills a model and museum of skilful industry, and, like Columbanus a thousand years before, were transforming the wilderness into cornfields and the people into docile pupils. Through Cork, dear to the young tourist, chiefly as the birthplace of Maclise, Barry, and Hogan, of Mahony, Maginn, and Forde, as the home in evil days of Arthur O'Leary, and still the home of Father Mathew and of some of their own associates in literature and politics. We had long known Father Mathew, but to see the great moral reformer, who was changing the character of a nation, living contentedly in a shabby little house, placarded outside and in with teetotal songs and broadsheets, with no attendant but one feeble old man, helping himself to whatever was wanted at table with an unaffected and cheerful simplicity, leaving his guests or his meals on the call of a peasant or a labourer who snatched a moment's leisure to take the pledge, was to comprehend the lives of the saints as we had never done before. Our way lay also by the Lakes of Killarney, Inistioge, and lone Gougaune Barra, where the dream of Callanan was realised by the students of

---

[1] MacNevin to Duffy.

another generation praying for his memory in a scene which he had made poetic ground. Through the gloomy pass of Ceimaneich and over the sombre mountains of Kerry, to the home of O'Connell on the shore of the Atlantic, where a cordial welcome awaited us.

During the journey, after a day's travel or sight-seeing, tea, seclusion, a volume of poetry, and a talk prolonged beyond midnight, made a feast which had no need to envy the luxury of chateaux. But the privacy was hard to obtain for a state prisoner fresh from Richmond; and deputations, addresses, bands, and the endless good cheer of a hospitable race, drew us constantly back from the world of poetry and dreams. To win a few hours' privacy was a triumph sometimes bought too dear. In Waterford, the birthplace of Richard Sheil, whilst we were hastily visiting the historic places, the "son of the Mayor" was reported at various points to be in search of us, but we exulted in escaping his pursuit; and only came to know him two years later as Thomas Francis Meagher, who will be longer remembered in Waterford and in Ireland than the orator whose birthplace was an object of such interest to us that day. O'Hagan suggested it was now my Repeal martyrdom commenced. When we reached Darrynane we found O'Connell and a number of visitors in his mountain home. He looked an Irish chieftain nowhere so thoroughly as in his own house. Whoever has seen him conducting his guests on an autumn noon through the picturesque defiles above Darrynane, or out with his beagles enjoying the primitive sport of a mountain district, and sitting at the head of his board a gracious and watchful host, will have a series of pleasant pictures in his memory.

At Darrynane I found letters from Davis which throw some light on current events, and on his own generous character. He was doing my work to ensure me a holiday, and he was chiefly anxious that it should not be too short a one, as I desired to return and relieve him from his post.

"My Dear D——,—You must not come back here till the middle of October. I cannot leave town, as one of my brothers is going to be married about the middle of next month. The *Nation* is easy to me, and will grow easier. Send 'Laurence O'Toole' within a week, or leave it to number six of the revised 'Spirit of the Nation' [then in course of publication]. I am proud of my own dear, dear Munster having pleased you so much. I love it almost to tears at the thought. Maddyn has puffed me frightfully in the third part [of 'Ireland and its Rulers']. You forgot the literary materials [materials for the literary pages of the *Nation*]. O'Connell holds out against any rule on the Reading-Rooms [a rule to grant a subsidy on certain conditions], but is practically liberal in voting money for them, so we must make the best of it. I wrote to William Griffin [brother of Gerald Griffin,

THOMAS FRANCIS MEAGHER.
Ireland, 1847.

GENERAL T. F. MEAGHER.
Commanding Irish Brigade U.S. Army, 1862.

author of the 'Collegians'], he will gladly guide you in Limerick. Tell M'Carthy to write words to M'Carthy's March in the *Citizen*. Give him my respects, and my best regards to John O'Hagan. E. B. Roche wants much to meet you and to get you to Trabolgan.

"So you really think you met my sweet girl [the girl of Dunbuie, the heroine of a song]. Vanity of vanities. She appeared only to me; even Lane who was by my side did not see her. I again pray for 'St Larry O'Toole,' or for his postponement to number six. Do answer me about it. The *Belfast News-Letter* [a Conservative journal] has by far the most able and flattering review of the 'Spirit' I have seen. *The Northern Standard* [organ of the Orangemen in my native town] is beginning to quote our poet's corner wholesale. Tell O'Connell that the first news Robert Tighe [an Irish barrister] had of the liberation was from the shouting of the Frankfort mob! What other man since Napoleon could have produced such an effect? Present my respects to the O'Connells, and believe me as busy as a swallow."

A couple of days later there came another hasty note—

"Dear D——,—Here are some letters which you can leisurely answer at Darrynane. I reviewed the 'Memorandum on Irish Matters' on September 14. Get John Pigot to play the 'Bouchaleen Buidhe' and 'The Marriage' for you [airs to which Davis had recently written songs]. 'Tis as sweet as your 'Mina Mumhain.'

"For God's sake get O'Connell to undertake, or to allow others to undertake, a plenipotentiary mission to establish Repeal Reading-rooms, and give them books and good advice. Damn the ignorance of the people; but for that we should be lords of our own future; without that, much is insecure."

A letter written to Davis by one of the tourists will illustrate the character of the pleasures and studies he had encouraged his friends to relish.

"I send you a handful of hasty memoranda. At Kilkenny the hall where the Confederation of 1644 met is used as a coach-house; only the Gothic windows remain. The Franciscan Abbey is a ball-court. Of Rothe's house there is enough to enable one to comprehend what sort of a residence belonged to a prince-merchant two hundred years ago, who coined money and levied troops; but the tomb of the best of the Rothes, the Bishop, in the Cathedral has the inscription barbarously scratched out; tradition says by order of one of his English successors. Doctor Scott has a banner of the Confederation era with the head of the Virgin, of exquisite beauty, brought over by Rinuccini, I fancy. Did Michael Banim ever tell you the romantic story of John Banim's early courtship, during which he caught the disease that finally killed him? You know the wonderful portrait of Black Tom [Charles the First's Earl of Strafford] at Ormond Castle—a human panther, lithe, beautiful, and terrible; there is another head of him at Lismore Castle, no more like the first than I to Hercules or the Head Pacificator. Have you ever visited Mount Mellaray? Do. The monks show what industry and security could

---

[1] 21st September, '44. Davis to Duffy.

make of the waste lands of Ireland. It is very solemn up yonder in the mountains, and the organ in the little church, playing a 'Te Deum' for our victory, moved me as music never did before. It was like a chorus of exulting angels. We were delighted to find the 'Voice' [of the *Nation*] in their library, and when we reached Cappoquin celebrated our visit by six-and-thirty rhymes on Mellaray, which are duly recorded in O'H.'s journal.[1]

"We visited Schools, Reading-rooms, Teetotal Societies, and bookshops everywhere, and made notes. The books are detestably English; no Irish novels, poems, or plays, except by accident. There are six-and-thirty teetotal bands in Cork, set up at a cost of from fifty to a hundred pounds each, but the Teetotal Reading-rooms are a melancholy spectacle. We inspected them with Father Mathew, and he laments the bookless shelves, so much that I count on an improvement. We promised some books, and I suppose Hudson and you will aid us. Compared to the peasantry in Waterford and Kilkenny, who are fine vigorous and masculine fellows, your compatriots in Cork are an inferior race. In the beautiful city the Sleive[2] insists that the young men look like mice. I hope they are mice fit to gnaw the net that has trapped the wolf-dog. One of Hogan's earliest works, a Britannia done for an insurance office, was shown us, and it struck me as weak and spiritless; and Desmond insists that his bust of Father Mathew is a likeness neither of body nor soul. We had bands, bonfires, arches, addresses, 'sound the loud timbrel,' etc., till we were aweary and longed for a little quiet. At Roche's Hotel (Killarney) the waiter informed us that Mr

---

[1] Duffy to Davis. — The students of another generation will perhaps like a specimen of these versicles. Somebody started the idea of finding a rhyme for that puzzling noun proper, Mellaray. It was at first assumed that there was no English rhyme but celery; the travellers, however, soon hit upon others, and agreed to fabricate a couplet in turn till ore of them broke down. They succeeded in turning out three dozen jingles, and each new success was welcomed with a chorus of huzzas and laughter, louder and heartier of course when the success was only won by a hair's breadth. After the lapse of a generation some of the couplets linger in my memory with other reminiscences of that pleasant time. This was the first and the worst:—
" From O'Connell and Steele and that jolly good fellow Ray
I've scampered away to the monks of Mount Mellaray."
And this, perhaps the most audacious, when one of the competitors was driven to extremity for the six-and-thirtieth rhyme:—
" They tunnelled a road would have puzzled Brunel, R. E.,
Such adroit engineers are the monks of Mount Mellaray."
Long before each man had completed his round dozen it became necessary to shift the accent from the antepenultimate syllable, *ex. gr.*
" I met a young maiden, but straightway down fell her eye,
She took me for one of the monks of Mount Mellaray."
Since the first edition of this book was published I have seen the diary of that day of one of the tourists, and select from it a couple more of the jingles which, it seems to me, a discriminating critic might easily attribute to their respective writers:—
" Say, shall we muster the people in fell array,
Or sleep in seclusion and sackcloth in Mellaray?"

" *Diabolum semper memento repellere*—
Such is the maxim of life at Mount Mellaray."
[2] Sleive Cuillen was the *nom de plume* of one of the tourists.

D——, the martyr, had been in Killarney yesterday ! We expressed our regret that we had not the pleasure of an introduction to that eminent person, and Sleive Cuillen read us the 'Lord of the Isles' in peace. Orange handkerchiefs are the common head-dress of the women in Kerry, who have no idea of the significance of that colour in the North. There is a charming library at Darrynane, looking over the Atlantic, and rich in presentation copies : but better than the library is the kennel. The dogs are the noblest I ever saw. Some of the old ones have a dignity that is superhuman. One venerable beagle ought to have been a Chief-Justice as far as wisdom and authority are concerned ; only he looks too honest for the office.

"Talk of a Highland breakfast ; but give me a Darrynane breakfast, and O propitious gods, give me an appetite to enjoy it. 'Tis Homeric, or rather let me say Ossianic. A hot roast or two, grilled fowl, smoking potatoes, slim-cake, delicious fresh honey, home-made bread and baker's ditto, and added to these all the ordinary edibles and drinkables of a metropolitan table. John went out fishing to give us another dish, but only caught turbot, which were reserved for dinner. 'Tis a fishful bay ; he tells me that the local fishermen have sometimes brought home forty thousand mackerel and the like in a single haul. Desmond says : 'Conciliation Hall is nothing compared to a Darrynane hawl.' O'Connell ate like a chieftain— if the table was abundant and varied, the great man had stomach for it all. Let no puny nibblers of toast or sippers of tea pretend to resist a Titan like this. The O'Connells have a stock-farm on an island called Scariff, which rises perpendicularly out of the Bay, and breaks the wave from Labrador ; of which you have perhaps heard ! [it was a constant allusion in O'Connell's speeches] which wave, by the way, your three friends got up at peep of day to see, but did not altogether identify.

"Before reaching Darrynane we visited Staigefort. You have never seen it, I fancy ; though you know it perhaps from the model in the Dublin Society. 'Tis an Irish Colosseum—the grandest and most extensive Pagan monument in the island ; and sitting in the midst of circling hills which seem a gigantic copy of it. The walls are nearly twenty feet thick, built of dry stone—but I am not going to write a bad antiquarian essay.

"I was struck by a saying of Father Mathew's the other day, at Cork, that Orphan Societies rear a bad and dangerous progeny—without home or social affections. He prefers the good old practice of fosterage, and thinks it ought to replace those societies. He wishes to see fruit-trees planted on the highways and in domains, which travellers should have an unquestioned right to pluck. He says they would be an agreeable offering to the poor. Are not these the thoughts of a genuine Apostle?

"At Cappoquin a vigorous young priest (Father Meany) addressed the people in Irish by the light of a bonfire, and I have seldom witnessed a scene fitter for an Irish Wilkie to paint. We sailed down the river to Youghal and had Dominick Ronayne's house pointed out to us. Poor Dominick, whose squibs were so popular in the first Repeal movement, is now nearly forgotten. It was he, his friends insist, who prompted O'Connell with the 'Derby Dilly, carrying six insides,' and the comparison of 'The Last Rose of Summer,' for Walter of the *Times. Sic vos non vobis.*"

A second letter from the same correspondent finishes the account of this southern excursion.

"You are an infidel in the case of 'the Girl'; I swear we saw her twice.

The second time was in the evening of the same day; there was a bonfire opposite the hotel for 'the Martyr' and a dance by its light, and who should reappear but 'the Girl'? We were tempted to join the crowd and trip a measure, but we thought it would not become the austerity of martyrs and confessors.

"I do not care about having 'Laurence O'Toole' or anything else of mine in the sixth number [of the 'Spirit'], but pray put two or three things of M'Carthy's and Fraser's; and I think you ought to put in O'Callaghan's song. We found it in the country in several places where we did not expect it. O'H. and M'C. are brimming over with poetry, begotten of the beauties of Munster (animate and inanimate); expect great results by-and-by.

"I am impatient to see Maddyn's third part. We got the *Tablet* at Father Mathew's and read Dormer [a sketch of Davis] there, which we thought clever and generous, but not graphic. As O'H. says, an acquaintance recognises its truth, but it would give a stranger no clear notion of the original. It is a sin to complain, however, where there was so much good feeling and manliness.

"From Darrynane we will go to Limerick, where I will call on your friend Griffin, and home immediately, making a month in all—the pleasantest I can recall, always excepting my honeymoon. *Apropos* of honeymoons, I wish it was your brother's brother that was getting married—I fancy it would promote his happiness, and put a strait waistcoat upon discontents which shake the peace of Jupiter in his seclusion."[1]

---

[1] Davis's Papers, Duffy to Davis.

CHAPTER III.

THE FEDERAL CONTROVERSY.

AFTER a month's retirement at Darrynane, O'Connell broke silence in a letter to the Association on a long-postponed topic—the future policy of the National party. The letter reached the proportions of a President's Message, and touched on so many subjects, that for a moment its main purpose was not understood. The projects recently announced were tacitly or openly abandoned. There was no reference to the Council of Three Hundred; the monster meetings were declared to be at an end—"it would be insulting braggadocio to revive them"; and as respects the impeachment, there was merely a passing allusion to the incidents of the State Trial as furnishing materials for Parliamentary inquiry. In lieu of these proposals O'Connell entered on an elaborate comparison between the demands of the Repealers, that the Constitution of '82 should be restored, and the proposals of the Federalists to create a subordinate legislature for strictly local purposes; and this comparison closed with a declaration which it was the main purpose of the letter to make.

"For my own part," he said, "I will own that, since I have come to contemplate the specific differences, such as they are, between simple Repeal and Federalism, I do at present feel a preference for the Federative plan, as tending more to the utility of Ireland and the maintenance of the connection with England than the proposal of simple Repeal. But I must either deliberately propose, or deliberately adopt from some other person, a plan of Federative Union, before I bind myself to the opinion I now entertain."[1] This sudden preference, it was intimated, would explain his motive for not improving the decisive victory obtained on the Writ of Error. "The Federalists cannot but perceive that there has been on my part a pause in the agitation for Repeal since our liberation from unjust captivity."

It was not surprise these confessions created so much as dismay. A year had elapsed since the suppression of the Clontarf meeting, and

---

[1] Repeal Association, October 14, 1844.

during that year we had become familiar with retrograde movements. The language of the defence in the Queen's Bench bore slight resemblance to the language of the Mallow defiance. The relinquishment of the Arbitration Courts and the disratement of the Repeal Wardens fell even below the tone of the defence. The projects announced on the release of the State prisoners, such as they were, had disappeared; and now, as it seemed, he meditated retreating at one stride from the demand for legislative independence to the suggestion of a subordinate Parliament. One other backward step would bring us, as in 1834, to "Justice to Ireland" and alliance with the Whigs.

What was fitting to be done in such a contingency? Hitherto the Young Irelanders had acquiesced silently in his public proposals, or merely dissented as far as was necessary to save their honour. But here was counsel to abandon the specific demand to which the country was pledged in the face of Europe and America, and to abandon it in favour of a scheme whose chief merit was that, as a *tertium quid*, differing from O'Connell's proposal, and suggested by men not in alliance with him, it began to get listened to by Irish Protestants and English Radicals. Once adopted by O'Connell, it would have to encounter the same hostility as his original demand; and it would gain no counterbalancing support; for nothing was more certain than that the men who gave Federalism its chief importance would not enlist under his leadership. Federalism as it was then generally understood meant little more than the creation of a Legislative Council with fiscal powers somewhat in excess of the fiscal powers of a grand jury, but not authorised to deal with the greatest concerns of a nation—domestic and international trade, the land code, education, national defences, and the subsidies to religious denominations.

Looking back now with a knowledge of subsequent events, it is difficult to doubt that if the Repeal Association had retreated on Federalism it would have committed suicide. The most capable and public-spirited members would have left it, as they did subsequently leave it in 1846; the sympathies of foreign countries would have been withdrawn from a people so fickle in their aims; and at the same time the original Federalists, who naturally desired to retain the control of their own cause, would have held aloof; the Association would have dwindled into the condition of the nameless and forgotten societies which had preceded it, and the National movement would have ended in '44 as it ended ten years earlier.

I had returned to the *Nation* office from the Munster tour before this event, but my colleagues had scattered on similar excursions—Davis to the North, Dillon to the West, Barry and Lane to Cork, MacNevin to Gort, and others elsewhere. There were none of them in the Association when the letter was read, and there were none of them in the *Nation* office when the letter came to be reviewed. I had to act without the benefit of their advice, or to take the responsibility of maintaining silence before so cardinal an event. None of us distrusted the Federalists; on the contrary, we had close friends among them, and watched their progress with constant interest. Davis had defeated an attempt to exclude them from Parliament as Anti-Repealers; we were in habitual communication with the chief Federalists in Dublin and Belfast, and they had been treated nowhere with more respect than in the *Nation*. But we were all persuaded, and I, who knew them of old, felt certain that Mr Crawford or Mr Ross would never act with O'Connell, that Mr Wyse or Colonel Caulfield would probably never act with him, and that if he attempted to force a junction the result would be alienation and hostility.

The duty of the *Nation* under the circumstances seemed clear to me. At any risk it must hoist the danger signal. Otherwise, not only the present fortune of the public cause, but its prospects in the coming time, might be wrecked. The writers in the *Nation* had won the confidence of their own generation to an unexampled degree; if they forfeited it by want of courage or independence, the effect on the character of the generation would be disastrous. The best recruits who joined the Association had joined it because they believed there were now men in its ranks who would resist any arbitrary stroke of authority, even from O'Connell. They would not long remain if this belief were destroyed. The Protestants of the middle classes who still held aloof justified themselves on the ground that to join O'Connell was to abandon all individual discretion; and the Unionists had jeeringly warned the young men, from time to time, that they were the marionettes of a showman who when it suited his purpose would ring the bell and announce that the performance was at an end.[1] It was about to be seen whether this description was just either to him or to them. With respect to the people, the duty of the *Nation* was still clearer. The aim of the journal had been to so educate and discipline them that it would be impossible to retain them in subjection to England; but if they were passive in the hands of their leaders they would never be formidable before their

---

[1] "Voice of the Nation," p. 35.

enemies. Liberty does not reside in institutions but in habits of thought and action; nor is there any mode of winning it compatible with retaining in pupilage the nation who are to be liberated. In truth, at this time the Irish people were far from being passive; how far was exhibited significantly two or three years later. They were eager that the movement should be kept in the right path, but unwilling that O'Connell's authority should be rudely questioned, even when they believed him to be in the wrong. It might be said of the masses of the people, and said with equal truth of the cabinet of the movement, that they often desired a change of policy but never a change of leaders.

My only difficulty was consideration for my colleagues. The *Nation* habitually spoke in behalf of men who had refrained from direct controversy with O'Connell whenever it was practicable, and I was unwilling to commit them, even in this serious contingency, to a conflict which they might still see some honourable method of avoiding. But, after all, the responsibility lay mainly with me; for if O'Connell could ruin the *Nation* for resisting his new policy, I would be the chief sufferer. I determined, therefore, after anxious reflection, to address a remonstrance to him in my own name, printed in the place ordinarily occupied by the chief leading article, but practically speaking only for myself. As it produced important results, it will be necessary to give some extracts from this document.

After excusing myself for addressing him in a public letter because I was no longer a member of the Association where the subject ought properly to be debated, and because a letter seemed a more friendly and respectful method of remonstrance than a leading article, I proceeded to combat his proposition that Federalism was better than Repeal as a national settlement, and contended that it was not better but worse:

"In the first place, the Imperial Representation on which it is based is calculated to perpetuate our moral and intellectual subjection to England. It will teach the aristocracy still to turn their eyes to London as the scene of their ambition. It will continue to train them in English manners, feelings, and prejudices, and establish permanently a centre of action apart from their native country. By the same process it will plant deeper the evil of absenteeism. It will compel Lords and Commons to reside out of the country, and continue the drain upon our resources in which you found so strong an argument for Repeal. In this respect it is, I think, a worse cure for absenteeism than Dr Maunsell's Teetotum Parliament."

A share in the control of the Empire I contended was an inadequate compensation for accepting an Irish legislature with shorn authority, for our minority in the Imperial Parliament would be as powerless hereafter as it was powerless at present to determine the policy of the Empire. It was, moreover, a settlement not less difficult to obtain; for while Repeal only contemplated the restoration of a Constitution which formerly existed in Ireland, Federalism raised a new and serious difficulty by necessitating a reconstruction of the Empire on a new basis, with local legislatures in each of the three kingdoms.

I then urged, as courteously as I could, the delicate objection that Federalism, whatever were its merits, would not be promoted by his adopting it.

"Federalism has undoubtedly the advantage of Repeal in one point—it is less hated. Unionists have not been trained to regard it as a raw head and bloody bones. They look upon it with comparative calmness, and are certainly more likely to become reconciled to it than to Repeal. But it would not be in a better, but in a worse, condition for effecting this purpose if the national party adopted it to a man. The Lords used to think it an excellent reason for rejecting measures that they were countenanced by O'Connell; and I fear party prejudice at home would treat Federalism in the same way. To be misunderstood and misrepresented is the progressive tax upon greatness, and since you are a millionaire you cannot complain of paying in proportion."

I warned him that, even if Federalism were desirable, the way to create a party for it was not by identifying it with Repeal. The men mooting the question were men who always kept a day's march behind the people. If he had begun three years before by asking Federalism they would be now speculating on "Justice to Ireland" and the restoration of the Whigs; and if ever he fell back on their ground he would inevitably find it deserted: Federalism was the shadow of Repeal, he could not get nearer to it or farther from it.

In conclusion I intimated in studiously courteous language that his unexpected change of opinion did not involve, and must not be supposed to involve, any corresponding change in the opinions of the National party.

"I do not gather from your letter that if you settled down into a preference for Federalism you contemplate proposing the adoption of that principle by the Association. I earnestly hope you do not. Either the adoption or rejection of it would be an evil; the rejection as a breach of discipline towards the leader of the movement; the adoption on many serious grounds. The overwhelming majority of the members joined as Repealers; it would be all but impossible to collect their individual suffrages on the proposed change, and no chance meeting at Conciliation Hall would be entitled to alter the fundamental principle upon which the body was organised and supported. The Committee of the Association is no more entitled to abrogate its constitution than the Irish Parliament was entitled to surrender its own functions. The great constituency outside in both cases is the body in whom the power resides. Such a change would fatally weaken the moral weight of the Association. In an individual a deliberate preference of a new opinion over an old one may argue candour and courage; in a nation it is generally a sign of weakness; and in our case, surrounded by enemies at home and abroad, it is sure to receive the worst interpretation."

A shrewd critic at the time summarised my remonstrance in a single sentence:—"Your proposal, if it be not checked, will ruin Federalism and ruin Repeal; and though you are the leader you shall not lead us to destruction."

The letter was universally reproduced and commented upon by the Press. O'Connell occupied a position in which he was sure to find writers to justify him, however flat a contradiction existed between his opinions to-day and his opinions yesterday; but it is creditable to the bulk of the Repeal journals that the prestige of his name, and the long and wholesome habit of awaiting his counsel, did not prevent them from declaring their dissent with sufficient plainness. They were divided between surprise that after nearly half a century's familiarity with the question he should still be in doubt upon the character and powers of the legislature he desired to establish, and a tacit conviction that he must have some worthy, though unknown and incomprehensible, motive for the course he adopted. Nearly half of the leading journals declared or implied that they were not ready to welcome the projected change; a few pronounced it to be the height of wisdom, and the rest proposed to wait for further developments, which from the sagacity and experience of O'Connell they did not doubt would justify his course. Only one writer complained that I had submitted the question to public scrutiny. The *Pilot* could not conceive why a journalist need trouble himself with fantastic notions and crotchety objections when the leader had spoken; if any publicist took so unwarrantable a course it must—it was manifest to Mr Barrett—be for some unworthy motive.[1]

The Whig and Tory Press in Ireland pounced upon O'Connell's confession with shrieks of exultation. The latter saw in it the disruption of the National party; the former the beginning of an alliance between the Repealers and the Whigs. There was an end, the Ministerial journals declared, of Repeal. Federalism was the device of

---

[1] A *précis* of the opinions of journals which spoke with some special authority or responsibility on the question at issue will help to realise the state of mind in which the controversy found the country; and such a *précis* will be found in the Appendix.

a defeated demagogue to escape from an untenable position. It was the first symptom of a foul compact with the Parliamentary Opposition to displace the Government and barter Irish votes anew for concessions and patronage. They quoted his declaration at Tara in August '43, that twelve months would not pass before an Irish Parliament was sitting in College Green, and his announcement before entering Richmond that it would come in six months, if peace were preserved; and scornfully demanded where was his Parliament, now that the promised time had arrived. They reminded the *Nation* that no newspaper on the popular side had opposed him and lived, and they predicted that he would first destroy the men who were in earnest, and then make over the *débris* of the Repeal party to the Whigs.

The tone of the Whig journals was calculated to strengthen the suspicion which the Tories sought to sow. The *Evening Post* was then edited by a man who had apparently been a serviceable ally of O'Connell in the Catholic Association, but had passed over to the Whigs when they came into power in 1830, and openly occupied the position he had long secretly held, of a stipendiary writer for the Castle.[1] He had assailed O'Connell with the foulest ribaldry during the first Repeal Agitation. "Paid Patriot," "Big Beggarman," and a host of similar amenities were of his invention; and it was well understood that his journal existed on the secret service money with which it was fed when his patrons were in power. This gentleman was enthusiastic for O'Connell's new proposal, and indignant that it should be subjected to criticism. He demanded triumphantly whether, if O'Connell asked the Association to substitute Federalism for Repeal, Mr Duffy contemplated the possibility of its rejection. The *Monitor*, also a Whig journal, but understood to be free from official influence, and, if controlled at all, to be only controlled by Mr Purcell, aimed to become the organ of Federalism, and treated O'Connell's advance towards that safe and practical doctrine as a new point of departure in Irish politics. The bulk of the Whigs held the same language. Mr Crawford and his associates desired a Federal Union because it embodied their idea of a permanent connection between England and Ireland. But as always happens in political parties, there were others who desired that Federalism should be proposed whatever might finally become of it, because it was a party convenience of the hour. In truth, it was a question of political existence with the Irish Whigs. A general election

---

[1] Frederick William Conway. See M'Carthy's "Early Days of Shelley."

was expected; and if they faced a general election without coming to an understanding with the National party, it might be doubted whether a single Whig would remain in Parliament for an Irish constituency. But this was far from being their only motive. Living under the influence of Irish opinion, which they could not avoid sharing, familiar with the contemptuous and empirical treatment of Irish questions in Parliament, they longed for some arrangement which would satisfy their conscience and honour as Irish gentlemen, without forfeiting their party relations at headquarters.

The Whig leaders in England, who have been charged with secretly abetting the hopes of the Federal party, gave no colour for this belief by the tone of their party organs. They not merely repudiated the policy of the Irish section, but mercilessly unveiled its motives. The *Morning Chronicle* declared that no sensible observer of Irish politics would be more taken in by the delusion of Federalism than by the defiance of Repeal; but with a view to a general election, an agitation for electoral purposes might be carried on with greater effect than in the name of Repeal, especially if any Liberals of weight could be induced to head it. Mr O'Connell was a more safe and more liberal guide than Mr Duffy; but much good would ensue from the discussion of Federalism, which could not fail to show the evil and absurd results not only of that theory but of Repeal. The Whig journals in Ulster sided with the English rather than the Irish leaders. They lent no aid to the Federal movement, although it was known that a private conference was being held in Belfast at that time between Mr Crawford and some of his political friends to launch the question. The *Northern Whig* was neither for Repeal nor Federalism; but a public mind was the great want of Ireland, and the independence exhibited in the manifesto of the Young Ireland party in the *Nation* was therefore a subject of no ordinary satisfaction. The *Banner of Ulster*, organ of the General Assembly of the Presbyterian Church, was persuaded that Mr O'Connell would carry the Association to any course he might suggest, and that the Young Irelanders could offer no effectual resistance.

The controversy was taken up by the French Press. *Le National*, as might be expected, was indignant at any backward movement; but even the cautious *Journal des Débats* declared that O'Connell's letter was the funeral oration of Repeal. The controversy also extended to America, but before the American journals reached Ireland the question was disposed of in an unexpected manner.

While this controversy raged in the Press, an absolute silence on the

THE FEDERAL CONTROVERSY. 115

subject was maintained in the Association, where the public business was managed by Maurice O'Connell in the absence of his father and Smith O'Brien. I thought it prudent in the interest of the National cause, and courteous towards O'Connell, to exhibit a similiar reticence in the *Nation* till the question had ripened for some decision. For two numbers, which in the feverish state of the public mind covered a period that seemed interminable, the question was not revived, except by copying the comments of leading journals on both sides of the controversy. In the meantime most of my colleagues had returned to town and unanimously approved of the course I had taken.[1] Tory journals in Ireland, and Chartist journals in England, conducted by men who hated O'Connell with personal malignity, shrieked that the *Nation* was dumb, that it was cowed, that O'Connell had threatened it with extinction and privately whipped it into submission. It was not necessary to notice these pleasant inventions, but when the *Pilot*, so long the personal organ of Mr O'Connell, chuckled over some insinuation of the same character, the time to speak had come. The next *Nation* contained two articles on the state of public affairs. In one of them Davis said :—

"But, then, O'Connell is a Federalist! Well, if he be, as his letter seems to say, what reason is that for discouragement? Ireland is for Repeal; the Association is and will remain the Repeal Association; and if the people go on organising and educating they can carry Repeal. The

---

[1] It is probable that Davis would have confined himself to private remonstrance; but when the resistance was publicly made he triumphed in its success. On reading O'Connell's letter he wrote to O'Brien from the North, where he was at the moment : —"O'Connell's letter is very able of its kind, but it is bad policy, if not worse, to suddenly read his recantation. He insulted the Federalists, then patronised them, then refused to tolerate them in Parliament unless they joined the Association, and now he discovers they are right all out, and of course they were right all through. My opinion is, you know, what I have always avowed in the *Nation*—namely, that Federalism is not, and cannot be, a final settlement, though it deserves a fair trial and perfect toleration. I believe there would be no limit to our nationality in twenty years whether we pass through Federalism or—[a blank in the original letter]. I write by this post to John O'Connell, urging his father not to repeat his opinions at least till Federalists do something." (Cahermoyle Correspondence.) Barry, who had great authority on practical questions, wrote his immediate assent to the course taken. "I was greatly gratified at the stand made by you against Federalism in the *Nation*. . . . I have of late been considering in every way the project of a Federal Union, and I conceive it to be an entire and absolute delusion. I am delighted with the latter part of your letter—your suggestion that the Association may reject the proposition if laid before it for adoption, that the great 'leader may not find it a mere machine to turn to whatever purpose may suit his notion at the moment. One thing I am resolved on, that is, that if the Association passes any vote changing its character to a Federalist body, I will at once resign as a member of it, and wait till better and more honest men arise in the country to seek Repeal, or something more, in a more independent fashion.— M. J. Barry, Cork, 23rd October 1844."

Federalists have put out no plan. . . . It is doubtful if they will. They are amiable and able men, but they are agreed on nothing. Some are for a House of Peers—some against it; some, whom O'Connell perhaps was thinking of, would make the Irish Parliament supreme in purely Irish affairs; many of them would deprive it of all commercial, ecclesiastical, and constitutional power—most probably they will do nothing. The aspiration of Ireland is for unbounded nationality. To the policy of this we are sure O'Connell will return. God grant that he soon may."

In the other article I answered briefly some criticisms on my letter; and with respect to the imputed motive of the silence maintained in the *Nation* for the previous fortnight, I said:

"The legitimate leader of the movement was not more willing to lead than we to follow; we proclaimed strict obedience and discipline as essential to success, and we practised them; for where there are many captains the ship sinks. But at all times, and now not less than any other time, we stood prepared to hold our own opinion against him upon a vital question (such as the present) as freely as against the meanest man of the party. We do not run all risks with a hostile Government, in proclaiming day by day weighty and dangerous truths, to abandon the same right under any other apprehension. O'Connell is incapable of playing the tyrant in the fashion these gentlemen suppose, and if he were not, we are incapable of submitting to tyranny. Let it be understood, then, that our opinions are unchanged, and unchangeable for personal motives, or under personal influence."

One member required to have his name withdrawn from the Association; he could not, he said, hope to stem the current of public opinion guided by Mr O'Connell, but, remembering how fatally a compromise on the tithe question had paralysed public opinion, he would not by remaining lend any countenance to a new compromise. One seceder was not much; but it might be that he was only the first; in the Alpine regions the fall of a fragment of frozen snow no bigger than a musket ball threatens an avalanche.

In the following week the silence of the Association was broken by letters from Smith O'Brien and O'Connell. O'Brien, who had scrupulously withheld himself from all party relations and preached forbearance and conciliation on all sides, avowed his personal preference for Repeal, as more easily attainable and more useful when attained than any Federal constitution which could be devised. But he was not prepared to reject any plan for repealing the Union which should appear to be more practicable and more satisfactory to all who might fairly claim to be parties to the adjustment of the question.

O'Connell's letter took a shape which gave his enemies an excuse for bantering him, which they were not slow to use. The remonstrance in the *Nation* had been the subject of comment in nearly every journal of political importance in the three kingdoms; but none of these comments apparently attracted his notice. His letter was addressed to the local paper published in his county town, and on its objections his attention was concentrated. The editor of the *Kerry Examiner* had misapprehended the precise nature of the Constitution of Eighty-two, and O'Connell read him a lecture on the danger of treating subjects on which he was imperfectly informed. The occasion, however, enabled him to offer some general observations to the country which were well timed.

"I have read," he said, "your article headed 'Federalism,' and I feel very much obliged to you for the civil and kind things which you have said of me in that article. To be sure, I have been working for upwards of forty years in the popular cause, and though I have often opposed the popular sentiment for a time, one way or the other the people have come round to my opinion, and such temporary disagreement has only tended to augment the public confidence. If there be any difference of opinion between me and the people at large on the present occasion—which I am not disposed to believe—yet the time is not come when any explanations can be given or any received, for this simple reason that up to the present moment there is no plan of Federalism before the public."

It was for the "federative plan" he had expressed the preference out of which the controversy arose; and if it were sufficiently developed to be approved of, it might be assumed that it was sufficiently developed to be disapproved of. But the last sentence of his letter gave so much satisfaction that all disposition to criticise its details was lost. "Whatever," he said, "shall be the result (of an investigation of the Federal plan when proposed), you may easily venture to believe that I for one will never consent to receive less for Ireland than she had before. I am ready to accept as much more for her as I can possibly get."

The writers of the *Nation*, who hated dissension as the worst evil short of dishonour, promptly accepted this declaration as putting an end to all differences: Federalism was all along "an open question," and so let it remain; but the object of the Association was the re-establishment of the Constitution of '82.

"We shall," Davis said, "rejoice at the progress of the Federalists because they advocate national principles and local government. Compared with Unionists, they deserve our warm support; but not an inch further shall we go; principle and policy alike forbid it. Let who will taunt or succumb, we will hold our course. No anti-Irish organ shall stimulate us into a quarrel with any national party; no popular man or influence shall carry us into a compromise. Let the Federalists be an independent and respected party, the Repealers an unbroken league—our stand is with the latter."[1]

Meanwhile the Federalists showed no disposition to accept O'Connell's overtures. Mr Crawford, in a confidential and affectionate letter to O'Brien, passed the harshest judgment on them.

"He wants," he said, referring to a former transaction, "he wants to take the same undignified course, humbugging both Repealers and Federalists; trying to make the Repealers believe they are Federalists and the Federalists that they are Repealers; and keeping a delusive joint agitation, knowing right well that whenever particulars came to be discussed they would split up like a rope of sand. I conceive that the principles of '82 and those of a Federal constitution are so essentially different that it is impossible for the supporters of each to work together, unless one gives way to the other."[2]

But Mr Crawford did not confine himself to the confidential expression of his dissatisfaction. In a series of letters describing his plan of a Federal Union, he permitted himself to be drawn aside by the taunts of Tory journals, that he was playing the game of a man whom he had recently condemned. "It was true," he said, "that he had condemned the course taken in the Tithe question, and he should still condemn it. He considered the junction of Mr O'Connell and some of the Irish members under his influence with the Whigs on that occasion a stain on the records of Irish proceedings." If sensible men are striving for a common end, they dwell upon points of agreement, not on points of difference; but this indiscretion was what any one who knew Sharman Crawford might have foreseen. The weak and strong parts of his

---

[1] I find by a letter in the Davis Papers that I had to go to London to keep a term as a law student at this date, and thus the controversy which I opened was taken up by Davis. Before starting I wrote to him :—" Dillon and J. O'H. have been here to counsel two things, the suppression of MacNevin's letter (on Young Ireland) as a pamphlet, and the receiving of O'Connell's last letter as a full declaration for Repeal, as the *Freeman* has done. Dillon, who is anxious, will speak to you about this himself. I am inclined to agree with him. All we can hope from O'Connell is a *practical* return to Repeal; a verbal confession of error is out of the question. Dillon justly argues that if we treat him captiously we will have no sympathy from the people, who want to see him right, but don't want to see him scolded. . . . I wrote to MacNevin to suppress his pamphlet, if it be printed, and that I would pay any expense incurred. You ought to see that he does this for prudence' sake, . . . I don't think it would be wise to make the letter the subject of the leading article—it would be helping to cut off his retreat, which is not our object. Treat him to a brevier sub-leader. I send you some materials for 'Answers,' and I sent several to the printer. I sent also poetry enough for the number, and Dr Madden's sketch for a literary leader. Pray read the proofs. I will finish 'Tow row row' on my way to London, as so popular an air ought not to be missing."—Davis Papers. Duffy to Davis.

[2] Nov. 1844, Crawford to O'Brien.—Cahermoyle Correspondence.

character alike forbade any cordial union with O'Connell. He was proud, punctilious, and angular, unlikely to forget past affronts, and more solicitous to be conspicuously right than to be successful. O'Connell was not implacable, and could even be magnanimous in personal controversy; but this maladroit revival of an old quarrel affronted him. In a letter to the Association he regretted that Mr Crawford should, as usual, have gone out of his way to attack him, but he heartily forgave him, and only lamented that the Federalism described in his letter should be so wholly worthless.

"I may be greatly mistaken, but, as far as I can form a hasty opinion, Mr Crawford's plan seems to me to be an elaborate scheme to make matters worse than they are at present, and to reduce Ireland from a nominal equality with England to a real and vexatious provincial degradation."

O'Connell's return from Darrynane was celebrated by public entertainments in Tipperary and Limerick, to which I was invited; and Doheny, who lived on the route, was anxious on grounds of public policy that I should attend.

"Will Duffy come down to our festival?" he wrote to Davis. "I think he ought, if it be at all possible. There is no doubt of there being sedulous attempts made to persuade the people that we are distrusted by O'Connell. I invited Dan here to dine and sleep, not without some hope that you and Duffy would be able to come and meet him. Could ye do so? Besides the pleasure it would give myself, I am sure it would be useful to our friends and the country. There seems to be a public estrangement between ourselves and O'Connell. But without reasoning the thing, I am sure of its value. Say you'll come, and let me hear where Duffy is?"[1]

Doheny reported later that the Federal controversy had produced a fermentation of opinion in the district. Immediately after the Limerick dinner he wrote to me:—

"Your name was received with the loudest cheers; to such a degree indeed as, in my mind, to rouse the great man's wrath. But although the reception was most flattering, still there is a strong feeling that the *Nation* was wrong in intimating that Dan had abandoned the cause. To be sure, most men who entertain that feeling have not inquired into the justice or the value of the argument in the *Nation;* they content themselves with saying that it is necessary to preserve the inviolability of his character."

On 25th November O'Connell returned to the Association. His first task was to assert and justify himself. He replied to the critics who had discussed his Federal letter, passing lightly over the objections of Irish writers, but falling with intense bitterness on English and

---

[1] Doheny to Davis, Cashel, September 10, 1845.

French journals. The Whigs were never, he affirmed, so hated in Ireland as now, and the reason was to be found in the conduct of their newspapers.

"It was to be found in the solemn insolence of the *Morning Chronicle*, the slanderous mummery of the *Examiner*, and the stupidity of Lord Palmerston's paltry *Globe*, which turned the just aspirations of the Irish people into unholy mockery. Even the Press of Louis Philippe took up the cry. Odillon Barrot's *National* began; but the Repealers were lovers of monarchical government and were Christians, two unpardonable offences in the eyes of the *National*. Thiers' paper, the *Constitutionnel*, joined the cry. He was glad to have the animosity of such a man. Next came the *Journal des Débats*, which said, 'Let not O'Connell and Ireland imagine that in case of a war with England they would get assistance from France.' He hurled his contempt on the paltry usurper Louis Philippe and his newspapers. He would not accept Repeal at the hands of France. Sooner than owe anything to France, he would surrender the cause of the country he loved best in the world. It was likely the *National*, the *Constitutionnel*, and the *Débats* were not scoundrels for nothing. They gave money's worth to England, and they probably got money value in return."

But though O'Connell reprimanded his critics, he amended as far as possible the blunders they had exposed. He broke decidedly, and even rudely, with the Federalists.

"After the liberation of the State prisoners," he said, "advances had been made to him by men of large influence and large property, who talked of seeking Repeal on what they called the Federal plan. He inquired what the Federal plan was, but nobody could tell him. He called upon them to propose their plan; the view in his own mind being that Federalism could not commence till Ireland had a Parliament of her own, because she would not be on a footing with England till possessed of a Parliament to arrange her own terms. The Federalists were bound to declare their plan, and he had conjectured that there was something advantageous in it, but he did not go any further; he expressly said he would not bind himself to any plan. Yet a cry was raised, a shout was sent forth, by men who doubtless thought themselves fitter to be leaders than he was, and several young gentlemen began to exclaim against him, instead of reading his letter for explanation. It was not that they read his letter and made a mistake, but they made the mistake and did not read the letter. He had expected the assistance of the Federalists, and opened the door as wide as he could without letting out Irish liberty. But," he continued, "let me tell you a secret: Federalism is not worth that (snapping his fingers). Federalists, I am told, are still talking and meeting—much good may it do them; I wish them all manner of happiness; but I don't expect any good from it. I saw a little trickery on the part of their 'aide-de-camp,' but I don't care for that; I have a great respect for them. I wish them well. Let them work as well as they can, but they are none of my children; I have nothing to do with them."

If the writers of the *Nation* desired controversy, here was a tempting thesis. If they desired a personal triumph, here was a signal victory. It might have been asked: If no one could tell him what their plan was,

["HB." Sketches, No. 822.]

THE POKER TRICK.

O'CONNELL, SHARMAN CRAWFORD AND GAVAN DUFFY.

how came he to give the "Federal plan" a preference over simple Repeal, which he had been discussing for thirty years? It might have been easily shown that these young men, of whose rashness he complained, asked to have no more done than he himself now found it necessary to do, to satisfy public opinion. They asked even less, for they did not want to have the Federalists treated with levity or incivility. The suggestion that he expected the Union to be first repealed, and an Irish Parliament established, before Federalism came to be mooted between the countries, was a text upon which they could have scarcely trusted themselves to write; for it was cynical experiments like this which had reduced O'Connell's influence over the educated classes so low. But instead of having recourse to any of these themes, they uttered no personal complaint and no note of triumph, but urged the whole party on to a campaign of renewed hope and restored confidence.

The contest was celebrated by an H.B. caricature, the substitute in that day for Mr Punch and his numerous family. It represented O'Connell dropping a poker inscribed "Federalism," which had become suddenly red-hot by a touch from the sword of Harlequin, whose cap is made from a copy of the *Nation*, and whose sword is inscribed "Young Ireland"

Looking back at these events, it cannot be concealed that O'Connell's treatment of the Federalists was a series of mistakes throughout. They were doing important work by leavening new classes with the national sentiment; they should have been encouraged, applauded, and left unmolested. His proposal to unite with them, and even to subordinate his opinions to theirs, was made without having taken the obvious precaution of ascertaining their wishes. Their aversion to such a union arose, perhaps, in some cases, from personal feelings; but in the main it sprung from the belief that the great Tribune would frighten away the very recruits whom they hoped to win. Had he quietly withdrawn from his negotiations at this point, the Federalists would still have done useful work for the national cause. But he withdrew in a tempest of wrath and scorn, and from that hour the hope of assistance from the Northern Federalists was at an end. It is the task of men of genius to show the people its own wishes, often imperfectly understood, and the way to realise them. The movements which have changed the fate of nations have always been the work of a man, or of a few men, in the first instance. But these men cannot undo their own work. Whenever they have attempted to do so, they have fallen like Mirabeau and Dumouriez.

Hampden could not have turned back the people of England, nor Washington the people of America, nor Kosciusko the people of Poland, from the goal to which he was their leader; nor could O'Connell have turned back the people of Ireland.

And we now know beyond controversy what was little suspected at the time, that the plan he had under consideration was the meanest and feeblest form of Federalism anywhere seriously proposed. In a confidential letter to O'Brien, full of exaggerated professions of confidence, which have borne the test of time but indifferently, he sent him the plan in question, and urged him, on a variety of grounds, to give it a favourable consideration. This letter was written a week after he had opened the subject to the Association, and a day or two after the newspaper containing my remonstrance had reached Darrynane. After a quarter of a century it has become historic, and I leave it without comment to justify the alarm-bell rung in the *Nation*.[1]

Simple persons have sometimes inquired in latter times, "Why did you reject Federalism? Was it not better than nothing? Wasn't it a good beginning of all you hoped to win?" No doubt; but what we rejected was not Federalism, which no one proffered, but the first step in a retreat upon a new Whig alliance. The combination O'Connell suggested was a moral impossibility. The very suggestion that he and the Repeal party would become Federalists gave Federalism a blow from which it never rallied. An eminent Whig barrister, since a judge,[2] who was asked later, "What has become of the Federal party?" described their fate graphically and accurately. "O'Connell," he said, "jumped on board our boat and swamped it."

The Federal episode thus ended, men became eager to hear what was to be done to carry forward the national cause. At the succeeding meeting of the Association[3] O'Connell spoke at great length, but the only practical measures on which he touched were two originated by the General Committee while he was in prison. He recommended attention to the registry with a view to a general election, and the systematic extension of Repeal Reading-rooms. It is impossible to doubt that at this time the luminous intellect, which for more than a generation had been like a lamp to the feet of his people, was clouded by disease. The

---

[1] O'Connell's letter to Smith O'Brien will be found in the Appendix.
[2] Baron Deasy.
[3] Repeal Association, Dec. 2, 1844.

time when he was resourceful and electric with ideas was quite gone. He took up lightly the suggestions of others, and contributed none of his own. A week later, he again spoke at great length, retorting bitterly on the English newspapers which had assailed him for breaking with the Federalists, but making no reference to any policy for advancing the cause. Among the English journals his chief complaint was against the *Examiner*, then edited by Mr Fonblanque, whom he charged in language of extravagant censure with being indifferent to truth when it served his purpose to lie.

"The bribed wretch who made this truculent attack upon him complained, forsooth, of the violence of his language, because he had called him a liar and a miscreant. Yet the scoundrel had neither proved his charge nor withdrawn it, when time for mature reflection had been granted him."

These were not the opinions which any of his educated audience entertained of Mr Fonblanque or of the French journals. But it was not desirable to begin a new controversy on a subject so far removed from the business of the Association. Controversy was sure to come without seeking it; for invectives so unmeasured against critics at a distance, accompanied by singular forbearance towards the critics at home who had begun the controversy, was not natural: and no one of any foresight could doubt that the punishment of the latter was only postponed. One thing at any rate was plain, the opportunity afforded by the defeat of the Government on the writ of error was lost. We had won the battle, but we had not known how to improve the victory. The precious opportunity which does not return was lost in a barren negotiation with suspicious allies. The movement began to lag, for the lassitude of a leader soon communicates itself to the cause. The English Press exaggerated the check, and insisted that it amounted to a disaster. But the people of Ireland had not changed their mind. They were still resolved to obtain the control of their own affairs, and though they were distressed and perhaps dismayed at the recent turn of events, their determination to succeed in the end had not slackened. The Young Irelanders uttered no complaint, but applied themselves to make the best of existing circumstances. Whatever O'Connell might do, or leave undone, their duty was the same; and some of them might hope to outlive him a quarter of a century.

The Federal movement languished under the hostility of the Whig leaders and the controversy between Crawford and O'Connell. To Smith O'Brien, who was at Cahermoyle, Davis wrote at this time:—

"All chance of a Federal movement is gone at present, and mainly because of O'Connell's public and private letters; yet I am still doing all in my power to procure it, for I wish to cover O'Connell's retreat. He is too closely bound up with Ireland for me ever to feel less than the deepest concern for his welfare and reputation."[1]

---

[1] Cahermoyle Correspondence. The students of history will find the opinions of the Irish Press on O'Connell's Federal proposal an interesting and essential part of the narrative, as illustrating the condition and character of public opinion in Ireland at that time. They are printed in the Appendix.

CHAPTER IV.

RELIGIOUS INTRIGUES, AT HOME AND ABROAD.

THE punishment of the Young Irelanders came in a shape no one had foreseen. Subsequent events show that at this time it was determined to render them odious to the people and drive them out of the Association. They were to be represented as "the secret enemies of the Church and the Liberator." Mr John O'Connell was probably the author; he was at any rate an active agent of this project. His father, who in feeble health and hopes had fallen under his influence, permitted, and in the end abetted, the scheme. What was best as well as what was worst in the nature of O'Connell was easily enlisted in a design like this. He was above all things the Catholic champion, and an imputation of secret hostility to the Church naturally called him to arms; he was very jealous of his personal authority; he had often encountered turbulent and envious spirits during forty years of agitation, and sometimes found himself pressed hard by honest rivalry, and he was never scrupulous of the means to be employed in freeing himself of such embarrassment. With Mr John O'Connell, who united a stealthy ambition to a narrow intellect, the motive was different. He was "the Young Liberator"—so his flatterers were accustomed to style him—predestined to inherit the Tribune's wreath. The human mind is so prompt to deceive itself that it is impossible to affirm that he had no faith in the stories he propagated; but I am persuaded, from a close observation of his career, that his main motive was dislike of the brilliant young men whose gifts made his feebleness and mediocrity painfully conspicuous, and a conviction that he could not rule where they were his competitors. At a later period, as we shall see, his more generous brother pronounced that "John had done it all." Had these young men been assailed in the Association, they were very certain to defend themselves; and the most distinguished of the recent recruits would have taken part with them. Had they been assailed for their real sin, the share they took in the recent controversy on Federalism, the bulk of the Association and the country had already ranged themselves on their side. But there were other methods by which they might be more securely and effectually attacked. Whispers began to circulate against them in various parts of the country at the same time, so uniform in their character as to bespeak a common origin. These young men, it was said, with sad shakes of the head, were unfortunately quite indifferent to religion; nay more, they were the enemies of religion, and in fine, they wanted to introduce the license of French principles into Irish politics. They were jealous of the Liberator; then, they were the enemies of the Liberator; and, after a while, they wanted to displace the Liberator and throw the country into confusion. It is often the curse of a distinguished man to be surrounded by slaves and sycophants who exaggerate his prejudices, and this class was not wanting about O'Connell, who had lent his countenance to some of the least reputable men in Parliament and at the Press. To these men the unstained lives of the Young Irelanders were a constant reproach, and they took up the new device *con amore*. The staff of professional agitators, the veterans who were receiving salaries for nominal services, and the ill-used gentlemen whose sinecures had been threatened, swelled the chorus. The Press threw out mysterious hints of danger. The honest *Pilot* was alarmed to think that there were persons prominent in the national movement whose religious opinions were not sound; and various local "Pilots" echoed the warning. It is not wonderful that a serious impression was made upon many pious and upright men, especially among the senior clergy, by charges so skilfully and authoritatively circulated. The main body of the young priests rejected them with scorn, and among laymen under thirty they had no partisans. The young men felt in the first instance a mixture of amazement and contempt. Davis was the person chiefly pointed at, and they refused to believe that doubts could arise in any honest mind respecting the intentions of one so transparently pure and upright, so free from all taint of *finesse* or double-dealing, and whom they knew to be among the most unselfish of God's creatures. But Davis himself did not regard the danger lightly. At the beginning of the Federal controversy a professor of Maynooth, who certainly had no share in the conspiracy, for he was open and bold and quite incapable of baseness of any sort, wrote a letter to one of the national journals[1] complaining of a dangerously uncatholic tone in the writings of the *Nation*. In his case the alarm was honestly entertained,

---

[1] To the *Weekly Register* (which had outlived the *Morning Register*, of which it was an offshoot). He wrote under the signature of "An Irish Priest."

but it was founded on complete ignorance of the men, and was stimulated at the moment, half unconsciously, by criticisms on writings in the *Dublin Review* in which he had peculiar interest. I answered him in the same journal, not unsuccessfully, and the controversy left us personal friends. He proved, indeed, in later difficulty and peril a friend worthy to have been won on a generous field of battle. Father Meehan, as one who shared our principles and aims, and knew the men concerned, repudiated the charge publicly, and other young priests made light of it. But Davis feared the influence of such debates on the uneducated people, and in another sense on the educated class who still held aloof. He wrote to O'Brien indicating the danger and the remedy:—

"I entreat of you," he said, "to write to O'Connell requiring some disavowal, or at least a stop to the bigoted attacks on the *Nation*. I wrote that a man had as good a right to change from Catholicity to Protestantism as from Protestantism to Catholicity, and called the State Trial miracle 'mock,' and censured the Italian censorship. I shall do so again; and I shall never act with a party that quarrel with such opinions. I will not be the conscious tool of bigots. I will not strive to beat down political, in order to set up religious ascendancy. You, unless I have much mistaken you, will subscribe to what I now say. The Federalist leaders here go entirely with me, and, in fact, now or never, we Protestants must ascertain whether we are to have religious liberty. I have written to J. O'C. on this. My defence of D. O. Maddyn ("Ireland and its Rulers," Part III.) against the *Dublin Review* seems to have called out this attack. Is this to be endured? Is it even politic to endure it?"[1]

On the same day he wrote to me on the same subject:—

"I have written to J. O'Connell, O'Brien, etc., by this post to stop the lies of the bigot journals. I have done so less even on account of the *Nation* (which can be steered out of the difficulty in three weeks without any concession) than to ascertain whether the lay Catholics can and will prevent bigots from interfering with religious liberty. If they cannot, or will not, I shall withdraw from politics, as I am determined not to be the tool of a Catholic ascendancy, while apparently the enemy of British domination. Your Lawrence O'Toole is very strong and original, though I am not quite reconciled to the metre yet. The last *Nation* is excellent, and is another proof that after March next you will be able to let me retreat for a year on my History [of Ireland]. I have given up verses since I left Dublin, and feel as if I could not write them again; so leave plenty (for publication in the *Nation*) when you are going to London. I shall be up by the end of the week. Hudson and I took a sly trip through Monaghan, Leitrim, Roscommon, etc. I am tolerably well in body and in good spirits."

---

[1] Dated Belfast, October 27th, 1844.—Cahermoyle Correspondence. He had gone to Belfast with Mr Eliot Hudson to confer with the Northern Federalists.

By this time the Federal controversy was at its height, and O'Connell was probably in no humour to reassure Davis. His answer to O'Brien's representation was general and vague. The upshot of it was that no harm would be done to the public cause. "I do not believe," he wrote, "that there is the least danger of bigotry tainting the Association. Not the least. I am thoroughly convinced that any sentiment of that kind would be scouted with unanimous execration."[1] Meanwhile warnings came from many quarters that the influence of the young men was being systematically undermined, and their speeches and writings misrepresented. In the beginning of November, Davis wrote to O'Brien, sending him country journals in which the attack had been reiterated, and others in which it was rebutted.

"All this might pass for newspaper hubbub, to be frowned at and forgotten, but I know that it is part of a system for stopping the growth of secular education and free discussion, and that it has been, and is again likely to be within this month, a subject of serious debate, whether the *Nation* and 'promiscuous education' and independent lay opinion should not be formally denounced by authority. I am not to a shilling's value proprietor of the *Nation*, and would be a much greater gainer by other literary pursuits, to say nothing of my profession, than writing for it, nor do I think its property would be much injured by such a denunciation were it met, as I trust it would be, with decent firmness and increased ability in the journal assailed. But I do fear that such an event would ruin Repeal. The Federalists to a man would stand by us in such a quarrel, and the desire now entertained by some of them to leave all ecclesiastical matters to an Imperial Parliament would become the fixed principle of all of them. . . . The same feeling prevails amongst the men represented by the *Warder*, and the least hint of what I have told you about the denunciation will at once change their tone. How far the separation of the individuals connected with the *Nation*, and those who would go with us in such a quarrel, from personal co-operation with O'Connell, would serve or hurt Repeal, deserves consideration. Finally, the question at issue is religious liberty. I for one will not sacrifice my right to it for any consideration. We are assailed for condemning the Roman Censorship, for praising the simplicity of Presbyterian tenets, for not believing 'O'Connell's miracle,' for appreciating William Carleton's genius while we condemned his early offences against the Roman Catholics, and finally for resisting all sorts of religious persecution, from brickbats to defamation. If I am to be set upon for these things, and the *Nation* officially denounced, or systematically run down for them, I pause ere I give any more help to put power into the hands of men with such intolerant principles. . . . Mr Hutchinson during my absence wrote to me to say he had spoken to Maurice O'Connell, who professed to agree with him as to the impolicy and injustice of these attacks ; but in order to bring this matter to an end, and to enable Protestant Repealers to know where they are drifting, I would entreat of you to write without delay to O'Connell before worse things

---

[1] Cahermoyle Correspondence.

happen. . . . O'C.'s Federalism is self-contradictory. Two Supreme Parliaments! Bah!—that is not Federalism, or Porterism, nor anything but an apology for a guilty blunder.
"Of course you heard of his letter to Pierce Mahony to get up a Federalist declaration. This converted Pierce, who showed the letter all over Dublin. Not one influential Federalist would go into the same room with him; so between O'Connell's letter and his agent a Federalist declaration is very doubtful."[1]

Looking back on the facts in the perspective of over half a century, I do not insist that nothing was written in the *Nation* to which a censor might take legitimate exception. The writers were of various creeds; they were engrossed with political, not theological, questions; they aimed to unite the people, and naturally dwelt upon points of agreement rather than on points of controversy. But I do insist, with full knowledge of the circumstances, that there was not the faintest truth in the charges made against them of a design or desire to reject religious authority. In a community fed for generations on mutual prejudice they preached "a truce of the Lord," and it was because they did so that the cause had won so many important recruits. To discuss the tendency of writings is to embark in an interminable dispute, but I can speak confidently of motives and intentions. The passion for liberty, which had burned up the trivialities of youth and cleared their lives of foppery and licentiousness, left no room for sectarian animosities. But it would have been easier, I am persuaded, to have found among them, than among any group of their contemporaries, men who would have laid down their lives for their religious convictions. The influence of their writings has confessedly been to make the young men of their race for two generations more upright, truthful, and generous; if they have lessened the reverence of any one for the obligations of conscience or religion, I have never heard of such a case. The orthodoxy of a man, however, is like the chastity of a woman; a nod, a shrug, will bring it into question, and what can a modest woman or a pious man do to remove such a doubt? We can measure the morbid susceptibility of the religious sentiment when we remember that Montalembert was denounced from the pulpit of Notre Dame as a bad Catholic, and Walter Scott charged by the Evangelical Press of Edinburgh with promulgating Atheism.

O'Brien replied to Davis in terms which, read a generation later, must be recognised as just and reasonable in their general scope; but at the moment they were probably not a little exasperating, as an answer

---

[1] Cahermoyle Correspondence, Nov. 3, 1844.

to the warning of a danger which was imminent, and which might lay the national cause prostrate at the feet of its enemies.

"In compliance with your request," he said, "I have written to O'Connell requesting his intervention to put a stop to the discussions arising amongst the national party. I have read the letter of an Irish priest. It is very clever, very Catholic, and if unity were not essential, it would be a fair manifestation of opinion adverse to those promulgated by the *Nation*. I need not say I agree much more with the opinions of the writers in the *Nation* than with those of the Irish priest; but then you and I should remember that we are Protestants, and that the bulk of the Irish nation are Catholics. I foresee, however, that unless O'Connell is able and willing to act as a mediator on the present occasion we shall have a PRIEST and an ANTI-PRIEST party among the Catholics of Ireland. This I should much deplore. Unity is essential to our success, and therefore division at present would be madness; but even if Repeal were won, I should deeply regret such encroachments on the part of the clergy as would justify organised resistance, or, what is quite as bad, infidel hostility to all those feelings and opinions upon which religion rests. I make these observations without professing any sort of propagandism in regard of the matter of Faith, and as an uncompromising advocate of civil and religious liberty in its most unlimited sense."[1]

John O'Connell replied to similar remonstrances, and to a note on the Federal controversy, by some unctuous generalities which left the business where he found it.

"I need not in any way discuss the question of the letters of the 'Irish priest,' as my father has written to you on that subject; and I think I had better not interfere. Neither will I discuss the Federalist affair. My father is gone to town to show what his ideas, plans, and hopes are; and you have there the opportunity of discussing them with him, while I, in these remote parts, remain in waiting for his words to influence my opinions and acts. I am very sorry indeed to gather from your letter that neither your bodily health nor spirits are what I sincerely wish them. Take care you do not overwork both, as I strongly think you have done; especially the physical vigour. To judge from your sweet poetry, the powers of the mind in no way fail under their fatigue."[2]

But his father was sufficiently precise and specific. He wrote ten days after the Federal controversy had commenced, and the tone of his letter indicates how deeply he was offended. The writers in the *Nation* were, of course, entitled to disbelieve the State Trial Miracle and "every other miracle from the days of the Apostles to the present"; but Catholics must be left free to believe them, if they saw reason to do so. As to his using his influence to prevent the newspaper war, he had no

---

[1] Davis Papers. Cahermoyle, Nov. 5, 1884. O'Brien to Davis.
[2] Davis Papers. John O'Connell to Davis, Darrynane, Nov. 16, 1844.

such influence. The *Nation* was wrong in the controversy with the *Review;* but he was only anxious that it should escape the possible consequences, and be lucrative and successful. As for his correspondent, he had a great regard for him and heartily forgave him the unfair insinuations which his note contained. "You are really an exceedingly clever fellow, and I should most bitterly regret that we lost you by reason of any Protestant monomania."[1]

No public notice was taken by the young men of these underhand proceedings; some faint echo of the subterranean controversy, however, appeared in the Conservative Press, which affirmed that for their success in the Federal controversy the Young Irelanders were about to be sacrificed.[2] But this was a result not so easily attained. The young men gathered round Davis with prompt loyalty. They insisted on his taking some part in the public business of the Association, that the people might come to know him; and his name for the first time began to appear in reports and speeches connected with some of the work he had done, which they would not consent any longer to ignore. MacNevin, who was deficient in reticence and easily moved with generous impatience, broke out in the Association and in the provincial Press in his direct defence;[3] but his other friends maintained a haughty but watchful silence. O'Brien insisted, however, on his taking the chair of the Association at one of the weekly meetings,[4] and the use he made of the occasion was characteristic. Instead of flattering the pride or the hopes of the people, he told them the stern truth that they would fail

---

[1] This remarkable letter will be found in a note at the end of the chapter. By some Post Office accident it did not reach Davis for several weeks after its date, and has since lain hid for a whole generation.

[2] "Mr Duffy has already declared that he will not follow Mr O'Connell in his tergiversation, and the enthusiasts whose writings in his journal have given to the cause whatever dignity belongs to it will abide by him. Already, we are informed, have the engines of intolerance been set in motion to crush the *Nation*. The cry of infidelity has been raised. . . . The underlings of the faction are now denouncing its independence and prophesying its downfall; and we shall not be surprised if a few days bring us accounts that an open war is waged upon a journal that but a few months ago commanded a popularity unprecedented in Ireland."—*Morning Herald*. Mr Butt was at this time a contributor to the *Morning Herald*, and was presumably the writer of this article.

[3] "Woe to the country wherein could be found a single tongue to slander so pure, so upright, so earnest a man; one whose indomitable labour, whose wonderful information, and whose glorious enthusiasm are devoted without one thought of ambition or self to the elevation of Ireland; to the arduous task of doing what Mr Grey Porter calls raising our country."—Letter of MacNevin to *Belfast Vindicator*.

[4] "I must positively insist on your taking the chair next Monday. The time is come when you ought to act a prominent part in Irish affairs."—Davis Papers. O'Brien to Davis, Jan. 7, 1845.

ignominiously if they did not cultivate the qualities essential to success. No enrolment of members or collection of funds would win national liberty except on this condition.

"Trust me," he said, "that no men in the country have more clearly considered the greatness of English power and the animosity of English feeling towards Ireland than the men who are now in that box (the box reserved for the Committee), and who in the Committee-room upstairs laboured day after day to remove English rule from Ireland. Have you, before embarking in this great contest, looked to the magnitude of it? Have you clearly weighed that this power which you seek to get rid of has now ruled your country for six centuries; that it is an Empire with hundreds of thousands of soldiers in India, and with an extent of Canadian territory so large that from its face the whole surface of England and Ireland would not be missed; or are you men who have rashly entered perchance a quarrel—certainly a serious moral struggle—with such a power as this? If you are, and you are now looking upon these things for the first time, you will be beaten, and will deserve to be beaten; you will be trampled on by the British Minister. If you are cowards—if you are rash—if you are capricious men who shrink from long labour—I tell you you will be beaten and put down amidst the scorn of Europe, and you will deserve it. But if you have clearly considered the cost of what you are doing, if you are resolved that you will succeed, from this spot, in the name of my friends, in your name, I may tell the British minister to give up a contest in which he must eventually be beaten."

But events intervened which made any immediate conflict between the parties ill-timed and dangerous; the Association itself was in peril of losing its authority.

Before the meeting of Parliament political gossip was usually busy in forecasting the business of the session. It had leaked out in the great party clubs that something quite new would be attempted; something, it was mysteriously hinted, which would take Ireland out of the hands of O'Connell and the Repealers. The Whigs had jeeringly recommended Peel to try concession instead of coercion, and the whisper grew that he would improve on their hint; concessions of a large and practical character, addressed respectively to every great interest in the country, being in preparation. But this was not his only device for taking Ireland out of the hands of the Repealers; there were at the same time sinister rumours that he had prevailed on the Propaganda, through a confidential agent at Rome, to forbid the Catholic clergy from taking any further part in the national movement. Since the reign of Elizabeth the Government of England was forbidden by a penal law to hold direct communication with the Holy See; but the Stuarts openly or secretly—William III. through his continental allies, and the House of Brunswick by the agency of Hanover—had maintained a representative near the

Pope. A newspaper ordinarily well informed on Catholic interests [1] published correspondence from Rome strengthening these reports; and the Press which called itself Protestant repeated them, with malicious triumph over the discomforture of the Repealers.

The *Nation* met the double project promptly and frankly.

"If Peel, it was said, hoped to denationalise the Irish people by making them prosperous and contented, let him try, and he should have thanks and applause for every good measure, whatever was his motive in proposing it. If he hoped to coerce or trick Ireland by any arrangement with the See of Rome, as if the Irish were a handful of prisoners whom the Pope could surrender in chains to English vengeance, he was laying up for himself disappointment and disaster. The Court of Rome had learned a bitter lesson from the working of concordats granted to Protestant Governments, and were unlikely to concede another. But though all the parchment of Rome were granted to Downing Street, the Irish clergy would maintain that faith in Irish freedom which the sword of Cromwell and the gibbet and scourge of his successors had failed to extirpate. The story of a concordat was doubtful; let the truth be probed, let two delegates from the clergy, and two from the laity of Ireland, go to Rome and ascertain whether the English Minister sought to make the Vatican an ally of St James's against Ireland. If the story proved to be false, the lie might be flung in the face of the baffled intriguers; if it be proved to be true, if the Ministers, not content with trying to repeal the absurd statute of Premunire, and to open a Christian diplomacy at Rome, had frightened or deceived the Holy See into measures injurious to the independence of the Irish Church, the course of the people would be plain, and their blow decisive."

Mr O'Neill Daunt, whose presumed relations with O'Connell gave his action significance, opened the subject in the Association.

"A conspiracy," he believed, "was on foot to induce the Pope to prohibit the Catholic clergy from taking part in the Repeal movement. With what shameful inconsistency English statesmen acted! They required Catholics to swear that the Pope neither had nor ought to have any temporal authority in Ireland; and they were labouring underhand to induce him to exercise the very authority, the existence of which Catholics were required to deny upon oath.

"He did not believe that his Holiness would be induced to forget the just distinction between his temporal and spiritual power; but even supposing that improbable case, the people of Ireland would not forget it. Nor would the clergy of Ireland. If a rescript emanated from Rome denouncing the national movement, the Catholics of Ireland would treat it as so much waste paper."[2]

---

[1] The *Freeman's Journal*. The information was understood to have come from Dr (afterwards Cardinal) Cullen, who represented many of the Irish bishops in their business with the Propaganda.

[2] Repeal Association, January 13th, 1845.

These rumours obtained unexpected confirmation by a letter from O'Connell to the Catholic Bishop of Meath.

"He warned the prelates of Ireland that Mr Petre, an English Catholic, was employed by Peel at Rome to negotiate a concordat which would give the English Government control over the Catholic hierarchy, in return for great concessions and liberal pecuniary assistance to the Catholics in British possessions abroad. Mr Petre was aided by an agent of the Austrian Government. This bait, he affirmed, had taken, and had already produced a letter from the Propaganda to Archbishop Crolly unfavourable to the Repeal Association. The strength of the English envoy consisted in the support of Austria, whose assistance was needed to repress insurrection in the Papal States and throughout Italy. Thus the British agent, backed by the Austrian, was almost irresistible with the politicians of the Court of Rome. To meet this intrigue, he recommended a deputation to Rome. The laity ought to send two delegates to insist that the Irish Catholics, in their struggle along with liberal Protestants for liberty, ought not to be impeded by any species of ecclesiastical censure or intervention whatever. He hoped some of the bishops might be sent on a similar deputation. They must meet the conspiracy and crush it for ever."

A deputation to Rome was the course previously recommended by the *Nation ;* but O'Connell was no longer fruitful in device, even where he was greatly moved.

That some negotiations had been opened at Rome is certain, but they had not taken the precise shape which rumour attributed to them. The Lord Lieutenant was able to address a letter to Archbishop Murray, denying on the part of the Government that there ever had existed the intention of negotiating a concordat; and Archbishop Crolly, who published the letter he had received from the Prefect of the Propaganda,[1] declared at the same time that he would resist by every influence in his power the project of a concordat if any such project was meditated. The Prefect's letter restricted itself to questions of ecclesiastical discipline and conduct. It appeared by newspapers brought under the notice of the Holy See that speeches were made to the people at meetings and banquets, and even in churches, by certain of the priesthood, and by some of the bishops, which did not show them to be solely intent on the salvation of souls, and strangers to the strife of political parties or temporal engrossments. The Primate was directed to counsel ecclesiastics, especially those holding the episcopal office, whom he perceived in any degree wandering from these precepts.

Here were the specific orders of the Holy See speaking through the Propaganda; and a political philosopher, who made no allowance for

---

[1] Cardinal Fransoni.

the influence of human nature on human action, might infer from the discipline of the Catholic Church a prompt and strict submission. But the Irish bishops knew their countrymen much better than Peel or the Propaganda did. Had the policy of this rescript been peremptorily enforced it is certain, in the temper of the people at that time, that it would have been met by a storm of wrath and resistance. The majority of the bishops with commendable prudence evaded this catastrophe. They interpreted the letter of the Cardinal Prefect as censuring only the use of violent and intemperate language. They did not consider it incompatible with taking a moderate and prudent part in public affairs, and they continued to correspond with, and contribute to, the Repeal Association as before. The end it was designed to accomplish may be surmised from the conduct of the minority of the bishops, who accepted it as conveying a complete prohibition of attending any meeting or banquet for political purposes.[1]

The Duke of Wellington, who, in civil affairs at any rate, knew when he was beaten, admitted that this diplomatic stroke had failed. "O'Connell and his 'democracy,'" he said, "are too strong for the Roman Catholic nobility, gentry, and hierarchy, with or without the Pope."[2]

---

[1] Letter of the Right Reverend Dr Cantwell, Bishop of Meath, to O'Connell.—*Nation*, January 18th, 1845.

[2] Conversation with Mr Raikes, September 1843.—*Raikes's Journal*. Negotiation with the Pope was a Whig not less than a Tory practice. Lord Palmerston a few years later wrote to Lord Minto (then at Rome, "not as a minister accredited to the Pope, but as an authentic organ of the British Government"): "We wish to make to the Pope the plain, simple, and reasonable request that he would exert his influence over the Irish priesthood to induce them to abstain from meddling in politics." And again, *apropos* of the provincial colleges, "You must say (to the Pope) that if he expects the English Government to be of any use to him, and to take any interest in his affairs, he must not strike blows at our interior."—Mr Evelyn Ashley's "Life of Lord Palmerston," vol. i., pp. 38 and 40.

CHAPTER V.

PEEL'S CONCESSIONS TO IRELAND.

To prepare for Peel's proposals now became necessary. O'Brien urged O'Connell to resume his place in the Association before Parliament met, and O'Connell assented with an effusion of confidence and gratitude. "*Aux ordres*, as they say in France. I cheerfully obey your commands, for your wish is to me a command. . . . Reckon, therefore, on my meeting you at the Association on Monday, and returning you thanks for your inestimable services. You literally are a living treasure to the cause." And again, on the question of attending Parliament: "Are we to go over? Decide for me, as well as for yourself, and if that decision be in favour of action—I mean, of course, of going over—I will leave this for Dublin immediately after I get your answer."[1] But when he arrived it was noted with dismay that he had nothing to propose, except the formal abandonment of the projects with which he had opened the renewed agitation.

"The Irish members would not bring the question of the State Trials before Parliament. The Whigs advised them to do so, but if the Whigs thought the experiment a good one let them make it themselves. What inducement was there to appeal to England? The Tory Press had, of course, attacked him, but the Whig Press had assailed him in a more truculent manner, and, so far from inciting the people of England to demand the impeachment of those who took part in the trial, they dissipated whatever feeling there might exist on the subject."[2]

At a subsequent meeting he submitted resolutions affirming that the hopelessness of obtaining redress from the Imperial Parliament made it useless to appeal to it; and that the Irish members by attending in

---

[1] Cahermoyle Correspondence.—O'Connell to O'Brien, Jan. 1845.
[2] Repeal Association, Jan. 27.

Conciliation Hall would best further the restoration of a domestic legislature. O'Brien concurred in thinking the Repeal members would be more useful at home; but though he had originated this policy, he was not willing to push it to irrational extremes. Having Peel's new measures in view, they must, he said, be prepared to go to London whenever the exigencies of the country required it.

Parliament met, and the English minister's proposals became known. They were practical and substantial measures of relief. The education of the Catholic priesthood at St. Patrick's College, Maynooth, was conducted with sordid economy, on a small annual grant, which at each renewal was made the subject of offensive controversy in the House of Commons. He proposed to increase the grant to a sum more adequate to the service, and to withdraw it from annual controversy by making it a permanent appropriation. The education of the middle classes in Ireland was in a shameful condition. The Protestants were in exclusive enjoyment of such endowed schools as existed; and they were few and ill regulated. The Catholic laity did not possess a single school subsidised by the State. He proposed to create colleges for the middle classes which would remove this reproach. In the previous year, as we have seen, he had appointed a Royal Commission to enquire into the condition of land tenure in Ireland; and it was intimated that a bill was in preparation founded on their report.

The *Nation* gave the promised reforms a frank welcome. The men whom it represented were not afraid of prosperity. It is not a prosperous people, they said, who bend their knees to subjection. On the contrary, out of wealth and leisure come the longing for nationality and the ambition to rule. The full yeoman and the successful merchant would not accept a domination which the shivering pauper and the ruined shopkeeper had spurned. Thrice welcome then was everything, great or small, which enriched the people or made them skilful and wise.

These concessions, and especially the Maynooth Grant, were very offensive to Irish Tories. Was Peel, they asked, again going to play the traitor? for to concede anything to the race they had so long wronged was treason to them. When an English minister was to be intimidated the stock resource with the Irish gentry was to murmur nationality, and there was now to be heard in unaccustomed places allusions to 1782, and the memory of Flood and Charlemont. Among the Protestant artisans, who were too simple and downright for diplomacy, and who had no interest to divide them from their fellow-countrymen, these allusions began to be repeated with an emphasis the sincerity of which could not be mistaken. They were distracted by a painful struggle between the bigotry in which they had been bred and the nationality which was becoming so attractive, and they could not determine on a clear course. But it was plain they were on the move. Early in February a meeting was held in the Royal Exchange to devise means for encouraging Irish manufactures. In that hall, vacant because Irish trade was in decay, but where the statues of Grattan and Lucas forbade it to be forgotten that under its dome the business of a prosperous nation had once been transacted, a number of needy artisans and a few of the popular leaders assembled. O'Connell, O'Brien, Davis, and MacNevin came from the Repeal Association; Sir James Murray, and James Haughton, Dr Maunsell, and the Lord Mayor from the general body of citizens. Before the business commenced the Rev. Tresham Gregg, Grand Chaplain of the Orangemen, and the leader and idol of the "Protestant Operatives," entered the Exchange, and announced his intention of taking part in the proceedings. His speech was a curious image of the conflicting sentiments by which his party was agitated. The new sympathy for nationality found voice first. He came there, he said, with a heart glowing with affection for his country. Though he was popularly regarded as a man actuated solely by bigotry, he had no doubt that the meeting would give him a fair hearing and judge for themselves whether he was not as anxious as the most jealous among them to forward the interests of Ireland.

"He had heard it said that the Orange and Green must be combined together. He was identified with the Orange, but he dearly loved the Green. He believed in his conscience that Ireland was an ill-treated and ill-governed country. She had resources second to scarcely any State in Europe. He never visited England without being struck by the marked and painful contrast between the two countries. When he considered the great men who had made Ireland illustrious; when he remembered the patriotism of Grattan, the science of Berkeley, the noble intrepidity of Swift, the admirable gifts of Moore, and, coming to our own day, when he contemplated the genius and eloquence which week after week were displayed in the *Nation*, he found everywhere emanations of the Irish mind so marked by power that other countries might envy it. Looking from north to south, from east to west, he saw a people patient to suffer, active to labour, quick to conceive, bold to dare, a people second to none in the world whether for physical prowess or the more sublime attributes of the mind. Blessed with such advantages, inhabited by such a people, what was Ireland? A wagging of the head among the nations, a distracted, ill-used land, as noted for her sufferings as she was distinguished by her gifts. Ireland, instead of being a submissive province, might, if it so pleased the Almighty Ruler of things, stretch her sceptre over wide dominions."

This was speaking a language which found a joyful reception from his audience. But to remedy these evils Mr Gregg fell back upon his traditional opinions. Protestantism, being the established religion in Ireland, ought to be sustained; it was absurd of the Government, who, to his thinking, were a contemptible crew, to encourage systems opposed to it.

Out of this hybrid harangue each party took what suited it. O'Connell declared he had never listened to a better speech, and that for the rest of his life, let Mr Gregg do what he might, he would never utter a reproach. His own party recognised the old note of "Protestant Ascendancy," but missed the blare of "No Surrender," and were not altogether content. Mr Maxwell, a scion of the Farnham family, who probably saw with dismay the fictitious nationality of the gentry echoed in good faith by their retainers, refused to fulfil an engagement to preside at Mr Gregg's Protestant "Operative Society," because that gentleman had been guilty of the crime of associating with Repealers and Papists.

Early in April there was a most important evidence of the change in Protestant sentiment. Mr Grey Porter authorised Smith O'Brien to propose him a member of the Association, stipulating, however, for the strange condition that he should be at liberty to advocate an alternative to Repeal. His fine natural abilities, frank generous character, social position, and manly bearing (he was a handsome young squire in those days) would have rendered him a very important recruit, had these gifts been ballasted by a more solid judgment. But he wanted patience, and the habit of forecasting his course, and could not be counted on for a persistent policy. His first speech in the Association made an immediate impression by its openness and unreserve. He joined, he said, from no feeling of animosity towards the English people, but, on the contrary, with the strongest desire to promote union and intercourse of every sort between the two nations.

"Ireland had outgrown the treaty of Union made at a time when England treated the Irish as an inferior people; but a new Union might be framed which would recognise the independence of Ireland as a voluntary partner in the Hiberno-British Empire. This plan would be supported by many persons in England and Ireland who would never join the Repeal party. An unfair proportion of the public burden was thrown upon Ireland, and she could get no redress, because while in population she was as forty-five to a hundred and in territory as thirty-nine to a hundred, her members were only in the proportion of nineteen to every hundred and forty British members. And she was governed in a widely different spirit. The other day Sir Thomas Freemantle, on assuming the office of Chief Secretary, confessed that he was unacquainted with the country he came to rule, but announced as his policy that Ireland must be governed like Yorkshire or Cornwall. How many votes would a candidate for Yorkshire get if he proposed that Yorkshire must be governed like Ireland? The inveterate prejudices which separated the Protestant gentlemen and yeomen of Ulster from their Catholic countrymen were in rapid process of dissolution. The Act of 1800 was daily losing favour in the eyes of the men of Ulster, and in the end, like their ancestors the volunteers of '82, they would follow the generous impulses of their hearts and stand up for Ireland."

Having secured the sympathy of his audience by this skilful exordium, he invited them to consider the difficulties of the position.

"The first and greatest difficulty was the unwillingness of many sensible men in Ulster and elsewhere to commit themselves to the national movement. They held back under the belief that the Association was a mere instrument in the hands of Mr O'Connell. But this was not the fact. Though the Duke of Leinster became a member, Mr O'Connell would still be the first man; he was the captain, they were his army; but that the Association was O'Connellite in the sense that he could turn it as he pleased to his own purpose, they utterly denied. It was the Council Chamber, where men of all creeds and classes could express their individual opinions frankly. The second reason why men of education and rank still kept aloof was because they only desired an Irish Parliament as a last alternative in case of the continued refusal of the London Parliament to redress the grievances of the country."

The third reason was quite different from the others, but it was the most important of all: it was the non-publication of the Repeal accounts. "He could not have joined the Association," he said, "but that Mr O'Connell gave him a distinct promise that the accounts should be published."

Such a frank and manly criticism, had it been followed up by corresponding action, might have produced important and even decisive results. But it was destined to have a different issue; after a few weeks Mr Porter retired from the Association as precipitately as he had joined it, and the engagement made to him was never carried out.

Before his coming, and after he left, the Repeal fund was a topic of constant uneasiness to the best men in the movement. O'Connell retained in his own hand the exclusive control of the immense receipts, on the ground that it was necessary to provide secretly for expenditure which the courts might pronounce illegal. The bulk of the people who contributed the money would probably have authorised him to take this course had they been appealed to. But they were not apprised of the arrangement, and this was the fatal weakness of his position. He had broken with Mr Purcell, however, on the same question, and he could not be moved from his policy. He disposed of the funds doubtless in the manner which he considered most serviceable to the public cause, but the practice had the effect Mr Porter attributed to it, of sowing suspicion and sapping confidence. And it tortured men like O'Brien, Davis, and his comrades, none of whom would accept so much as a postage stamp from the fund. But they could not remedy the wrong except at the cost of destroying the Association. Some pious partisans of O'Connell, indeed, declared that their morbid anxiety on the subject was no better than Judas's hypocritical lamentation over Mary Magdalen's wastefulness when the precious ointment was poured at the feet of her Master.

A more stringent stimulus than Mr Porter's speech was applied to public opinion by the report of the Devon Commission.[1] The Commissioners were landed proprietors and Unionists, who had no sympathy or interest in popular agitation; but, half unconsciously, they unveiled a series of social phenomena like those which in Arthur Young's pages explain and palliate the subsequent horrors of the French Revolution. The destitute poor amounted to one-third of the entire population. Agriculture was the national pursuit, but the men employed in it were steeped in poverty and misery; and this poverty and misery were traceable to English law and the English connection as its fountainhead. Much of the land was held in principalities by absentees, mainly English peers, who were described as "regardless and neglectful of their properties in Ireland." The effect of the laws under which the bulk of the people had lived since the Revolution—laws framed or sanctioned by the English Privy Council—was "to create a feeling of insecurity which directly checked industry." The landowners, it was confessed, had trafficked mercilessly in the happiness and lives of the tenantry. To create votes, when votes were a saleable property, and to increase produce when prices were high, they had multiplied small tenancies; and when prices fell and votes became precarious, they had cleared out tenants with the same indifference that a man thins his warrens or diminishes his grazing stock. Tenancy-at-will had produced a condition of national existence the like of which was to be found nowhere under the sky of heaven. The farm labourers, depending on casual employment for

---

[1] The Commissioners were the Earl of Devon, the chairman from whom it took its name, Sir Robert Ferguson, M.P., Mr George Alexander Hamilton, M.P., Mr (afterwards Sir Thomas) Redington, and Mr Wynne; with Captain Pitt Kennedy as secretary.

daily bread, were badly housed, badly clothed, and badly paid. In many districts their only food was the potato, their only drink the running stream; their cabin was seldom a shelter against weather; a bed or blanket was a rare luxury among them; and, commonly, a pig and manure heap constituted their sole property. They were generally holders of small farms till the practice of systematic ejectment had commenced. When they were ejected, they flocked to the towns and carried disease and death in their train.

"It would be impossible," say the Commissioners, "for language to convey an idea of the state of distress to which the ejected tenantry have been reduced, or of the disease, misery, and even vice which they have propagated in the towns wherein they have settled; so that not only they who have been ejected have been rendered miserable, but they have carried with them and propagated that misery. They have increased the stock of labour; they have rendered the habitations of those who received them more crowded; they have given occasion to the dissemination of disease; they have been obliged to resort to theft and all manner of vice and iniquity to procure subsistence, but, what is the most painful of all, a vast number of them perished from want."[1]

This population has been habitually described as violent and revengeful in newspapers supported by their oppressors, in order to misrepresent them, but the Commission bore different testimony. The labouring population, they admitted, had generally exhibited a patient endurance under sufferings greater than the people of any other country in Europe had to sustain.

With the report was published the evidence of the principal witnesses. Many Englishmen, well disposed towards Ireland, were long perplexed by the fact that agrarian outrages commonly occurred in the south or west, and were seldom heard of in Ulster; and they saw no escape from the explanation tendered by the No-Popery Press, that this contrast was referable to the Scotch descent or the Protestant creed of the population. The agents of great proprietors in Ulster set this difficulty effectually at rest. There were few agrarian outrages in Ulster because there were few agrarian grievances; wherever the grievances appeared the outrages speedily followed. From the time of the Plantation a custom existed to allow the tenant, when he desired to quit his holding, to sell the goodwill or right of possession, and it was sometimes worth twenty years' purchase. This practice of selling the goodwill, which was at first a concession to the tenantry, was found to be equally beneficial to the landlords. It caused estates to be improved with-

---

[1] Devon Report, page 21.

out any expenditure of capital by the owner, and it secured the payment of arrears of rent; for an occupier could only sell his tenant-right on condition of discharging his liability to the landlord. Some attempts had recently been made on certain estates to disallow tenant-right, and the attempt had been immediately followed by offences of the same character complained of in the south; the incoming tenant's house was burned, his cattle houghed (the tendons of the hind leg cut), or his crops trodden down by night. "The disallowance of tenant-right," said Lord Lurgan's agent, "is always attended by outrage." The witnesses were asked what would be the effect of treating the Ulster tenantry as the Munster tenantry were habitually treated. "You would," said the agent of the Marquis of Londonderry, "have a Tipperary in Down if it were attempted." "I do not believe," said the agent of another great proprietor, "there is force at the disposal of the Horse Guards sufficient to keep the peace of the province in such a contingency."[1] The peace of the province was kept by a simpler method; but it had not hitherto dawned on the mind of English statesmen that, if injustice would create a Tipperary in Down, justice, it might be surmised, would create a Down in Tipperary.

If this penetrating light had been thrown upon the condition of Russian serfs or Indian ryots, opinion in England would have speedily adjusted itself to the new facts. But there is still, I fear, an Englishman here and there who does not quite understand the simple problem why there is peace in Down and war in Tipperary.

The first of the Irish projects submitted to Parliament was the bill to endow Maynooth. It was a measure of generous statesmanship, and its character was promptly recognised in Ireland. "Peel has been just, it was said, why should not we?"[2] Thirty thousand pounds were granted to enlarge the college, and the annual endowment to pay professors and maintain free students was raised from £9,000 to £26,000. And, what was rare in Parliamentary boons to Ireland, the measure was not fettered by any provisions offensive to the feelings of Catholics. This expenditure was not an extravagant one to educate the clergy of eight millions of the people in a country where one of the richest universities in Europe provided for the education of the clergy of the minority; but it was too liberal for England, and a frenzy of

---

[1] Evidence of Mr Hancock, agent to Lord Lurgan.
[2] See note in Appendix on Peel's Concessions and Young Ireland.

resistance rose against it. Peel once more, as in 1829, was reproached as a new Iscariot. Cities and towns and villages competed for priority in denouncing the measure. Three thousand petitions were presented against it, embracing all classes, from the citizens of London, headed by their chief magistrate, down to the Methodists' congregation in the remotest hamlet, who were enjoying the religious equality which Catholics had helped them to obtain. The petitioners were computed at a million and a quarter. The Protestant minority in Ireland, laden with spoil reft from the Irish nation, were among the loudest objectors.

Mr Shaw, who represented the exclusive University of Dublin, threatened Peel with a Protestant movement for Repeal if he persisted in improving the condition of the Catholic college. Ireland, he insisted, had of late been treated rather as a colonial dependency than as an integral portion of the Empire.

In the same key the *Evening Mail* assured Irish Protestants that they were about to be utterly betrayed; and forewarned them that when the Church was destroyed and Repeal accomplished they would have bitter cause to remember that they allowed the guardianship of their religion and their liberties to pass from their own hands.

There were two sentiments struggling for mastery in the breasts of the young men at this time; horror of the existing land question, and the hope of a compact with the gentry which would at once secure justice to the tenantry and restore the country to its rights. The junction of Smith O'Brien, Lord Cloncurry, Grey Porter, and other landed proprietors naturally encouraged this hope.

John Dillon, who was impatient of the slow progress of opinion among the gentry while the tenantry endured poverty and ruin, had urged a little earlier a combination to compel concessions. It was a forecast of much which has since befallen.

"What is the course," he wrote, "which the people of Ireland ought to pursue? They ought to join together, and call with one voice for a complete remodelling of the laws affecting landed property. Instead of committing unmeaning murders, which every good man must condemn, however he may pity the unhappy wretches who are driven to these dreadful deeds—instead of breaking out into partial insurrections, which only expose them to the vengeance of their oppressors, let them unite and work with a common purpose, and their combined strength cannot be resisted. What have the aristocracy to oppose to the united strength of the people? Their power is based upon force, and that force is derived from the people; let the people withhold that force to-morrow, and the power of their tyrants is at an end. Let them demand a valuation of the land, and perpetuity for the tenant—let them be faithful, united, and bold, and this demand, founded as it is in justice, will not, must not, be refused."

And on another occasion he painted with vivid power a specimen of the worst landlords in his native province ;—

"A Connaught landlord sees but one object in creation, and that is himself. He alone is made for enjoyment—all things else are made for him. He counts the potatoes on which the poor man lives. His horses are better lodged and his hounds better fed than the most comfortable tenant on his estate. Even his own interest is sacrificed to the gratification of his shortsighted avarice. If any man should be so desperate as to expend his money or his labour in improving his land, he raises the rent or turns him out. He is without even the more vulgar sort of benevolence ; he squanders the patrimony of his own children in ostentation and luxury, and leaves them beggars. As for patriotism, he either fears or laughs at it. A Connaught landlord has no country."

But Davis and the majority of his comrades thought a truce with the gentry would produce such important results that we must patiently work out the experiment of gaining them, even when their motives were narrow and ungenerous. And Dillon acted on this opinion.

MacNevin, to whom a conviction often came as it comes to a woman of genius rather by intuition than by any process of reasoning, thought the experiment would fail. But like Camille Desmoulin, he threw out his thoughts disguised as pleasantries, and could not always get men to accept them seriously. "The Protestant gentry were excellent patriots, he said, "when they had everything their own way in the country ; and perhaps they will be excellent patriots again when they have nothing their own way ; but if you expect them in a fit of enthusiasm to make such a surrender of privileges and monopolies as their class made in France, you must first bring them, like the French *seigneurs*, face to face with Revolution."

It was pleasant to note among the hubbub of alarmed monopolists some creditable instances of fairness and sympathy. The Remonstrant Synod of Ulster, remembering the recent assistance they had received from the Catholics, petitioned in favour of the measure. They enjoyed liberal aid, they said, for the education and support of their ecclesiastical students out of the public taxes, and they wished the same advantages to be extended to the Catholics. And the Methodists of Barnstaple in Devonshire prayed Parliament that no more public money might be advanced to the Church of England or her universities or schools unless the College of Maynooth were allowed to participate. The resistance to the endowment, though bitter and frequently malevolent, was not altogether bigoted. It is impossible to doubt that it sprung in some considerable degree from preference to the voluntary system, when Mr Bright and Mr Sharman Crawford felt themselves constrained to support it.

On the second reading of the Bill the Prime Minister explained and justified his new policy. There was then pending a dispute with the United States respecting England's claim to the Oregon territory, a claim which, as first minister of England, he had shortly before intimated his intention of supporting by force. It was his design to make peace at home before entering upon a foreign contest; and for this purpose he was ready to face serious difficulties, and to make painful sacrifices. He would state his object plainly. In 1843 there was formidable and dangerous excitement in Ireland; the Government had resorted to the courts of law, which pronounced the condemnation of the persons engaged in these demonstrations; a calm ensued, and then he thought it was the duty of the Government to take into consideration the condition of that country.

"You must break up," he said, "the formidable conspiracy which exists against the British Government and the British connection. I do not believe you can break it by force; but you may break it up by acting in a spirit of kindness, forbearance, and generosity."

The Whigs had been the first to exhort Peel to try concessions, but when their advice was adopted they were not overjoyed at their success. Mr Macaulay, in those days one of the chief spokesmen of the Opposition, fell foul of the Government for their sudden change of front. He supported their proposal, but he complained that it should have been made by such unfitting agents. The minister, he said, had taught one immortal lesson to Ireland—a lesson rulers should be slow to teach, for it is a lesson nations were not slow to learn. He had long told Ireland by his acts, and now told her in express words, that the way to obtain concessions from him was by agitation. "They were granted, because Mr O'Connell and Mr Polk had made the Government uneasy; and it seemed that the best and most effectual place for an Irish representative to serve his country was in Conciliation Hall."

It was perhaps an effective stroke of Parliamentary fence to smite the minister for his inconsistency; but as Ireland was looking on, it was the stroke of a party gladiator, not of an Imperial statesman. In what followed the Whig rhetorician more plainly subordinated the interest of his country to the interests of his party. Peel was bidding against O'Connell for the control of Ireland; he was not making concessions to Repeal, but concessions which he hoped might mitigate the desire for

Repeal. Mr Macaulay was coerced to vote with him, but he did his best to disparage his policy. He demanded why, after having goaded Ireland to madness for the purpose of ingratiating himself with England, the minister was setting England on fire for the purpose of ingratiating himself with the Irish. He invited the Conservative party to consider where a policy would lead them which gave nothing to justice and everything to fear. But whoever might coquette with Irish sedition, he and his friends would never do so. They would not concede Repeal :—

"Never, though the country should be surrounded by dangers as great as those which threatened her when her American colonies and France and Spain and Holland were leagued against her, and when the armed neutrality of the Baltic disputed her maritime rights ; never, though another Bonaparte should pitch his camp in sight of Dover Castle ; never, till all things had been staked and lost ; never, till the four quarters of the world have been convulsed by the last struggle of the great English people for their place amongst nations."

Challenged in this manner, Sir James Graham, on behalf of the Government, hastened to echo the war whoop. He, too, would uphold the Union, though the foundations of the Empire should be shaken in the struggle.

When these declarations reached Ireland they were met in language of dignified rebuke which Irishmen may still read with cordial assent. Smith O'Brien spoke in terms well becoming an Irish gentleman, and expressing his exact opinions and intentions. If the question was to be treated as one in which the interests of England alone were consulted, and the interests of Ireland ignored, he was persuaded the Union could not be sustained on this basis. Though he was not fond of holding out promises, he did not hesitate to declare that if the North joined with the South the Union would be repealed without striking a blow.

" I tell Mr Macaulay," he said in conclusion, " that if the contingency which he contemplates were to happen, it would then be too late to negotiate with the people of Ireland. I tell him that if fifty thousand French stood on the strand of Normandy ready to pass over by steam to the undefended shores of Britain, if an American fleet swept the Irish Channel and carried on board regiments of Irish emigrants enrolled, armed, and disciplined, ready to land on Irish soil to defend the rights of their native land ; if the Irish soldiers in the British army, forming one-third of that entire force, should refuse, as I believe they unquestionably would refuse, to shed the blood of their fellow-countrymen ; if one million of the natives of Ireland resident in England and Scotland were prepared, as I am of opinion they would be prepared, to co-operate with the firm resolve of the people of this country; if such a state of things should come to pass, why, then, the consummation which Mr Macaulay appears to contemplate would take place—the British Empire would be broken up, and thenceforward the history of Ireland would be written as that of a separate and independent country."

Mr Grey Porter, like Mr Macaulay, appealed to history. Sixty years before, English politicians employed similar language. When they were asked to redress the grievances of America, they declared that heaven and earth would come together before they would concede what was asked; and yet three years later the treaty was signed that recognised the independence of the United States. And MacNevin bade Repealers remember that the party who, by the mouth of Mr Macaulay, offered the Irish people the Jacobin alternative of fraternity or death, were the same party who, under the Rockingham administration, had solemnly pledged themselves to the legislative independence of Ireland as a final adjustment of the controversy between the countries, and carried through the English Parliament an act renouncing for ever all legislative control over Ireland.

O'Brien's speech was undoubtedly seditious, more seditious than the language for which O'Connell had been prosecuted in 1833 or 1844. But it was received with nearly universal applause by the gentlemen of Ireland. Their pride was wounded by the Whig rhetorician's appeal to brute force, which in essence did not differ from the language of Nicholas to the Poles or of Metternich to the Italians. Had the speech been prosecuted O'Brien would have reiterated and justified it. And he would have had the sympathy of his order; for if Ireland was living under the British Constitution it was felt to be as improper to answer her demand for local government in these brutal terms, as to make such an answer to the contemporary demands of the Anti-Corn Law League. But if she was not living under the British Constitution, if this foolhardy warning that she must not expect relief except when her neighbour was in the last extremity expressed the settled purpose of the Empire, Irish gentlemen foresaw with consternation the consequences which would flow from such a fact. With what certainty men would desire that that last extremity, in which only they would expect fair play, would speedily arise? It is the duty of a statesman to teach nations that the claim of justice cannot honourably, and in the long run cannot safely, be resisted. To republican America and philosophic Germany, to France which had formulated the doctrines of public liberty, and Belgium which had fought for them, the proposal to reconsider the relations of two united countries and rearrange them more conveniently, was a very moderate and rational project. But the mass of the English people have never been able to recognise any equity which countervails their interests or alarms their pride. And this blind doltish obstinacy Mr Macaulay clothed in the vesture of rhetoric and eloquence. Like Peel, he taught a lesson which rulers ought to be slow to teach, for nations are not slow to learn, the bitter lesson that the Irish people had a vital interest in the calamity and discomfiture of England.[1]

The second reading of the bill was carried by a large majority, and it passed through its subsequent stages and became law.[2]

The Repeal members still attended Conciliation Hall in lieu of Palace Yard, and this preference was regarded with grave displeasure and alarm by the Whigs and by many of the Radicals. Mr Hume, after having privately remonstrated with O'Connell and O'Brien in vain,[3] gave notice of a call of the House to compel the attendance of the Irish members. The General Committee took this menace into consideration, and after careful deliberation, resolved that the call ought to be disobeyed. Smith O'Brien, who was absent in the country, sent a prompt adhesion to this policy. "I will not," he wrote, "attend the call of the House with which Mr Hume menaces us." Mr John O'Connell echoed this language, and O'Connell went the length of contending that the House of Commons under the Act of Union had no power to enforce its orders in Ireland. For a moment a dangerous contest between an authority which claimed to be supreme in the Empire, and the Association which swayed opinion in Ireland, seemed imminent. But the Government did not choose to have their concessions embarrassed by this Opposition escapade, and on the day fixed for Mr

---

[1] Mr Macaulay seems always to have proceeded upon the assumption that God's justice is a luxury, like Bass's beer and Holloway's ointment, intended specially for British enjoyment. In his article on Milton in the *Edinburgh Review*, he says: "One part of the Empire was so unhappily circumstanced that, at that time, its misery was necessary to our happiness, and its slavery to our freedom." This maxim describes his own policy in the reign of Queen Victoria as accurately as Cromwell's in the Commonwealth. It is as base a rule of conduct at bottom as any that can be picked out of Machiavelli. It may be noted that whereas O'Connell has been assailed for teaching that "England's difficulty is Ireland's opportunity," Mr Macaulay taught in this debate that England's greatest difficulty is Ireland's only opportunity. Peel gallantly facing the prejudice of his partisans on that occasion to accomplish a public good, and Macaulay stimulating their blind rage for the benefit of party, is not a picture men of letters will recall with pleasure.

[2] The majority was 328 votes to 176.

[3] Cahermoyle Correspondence.

Hume's motion there was no House, and it fell ignominiously to the ground.[1]

---

[1] Mr Hume was much censured in Ireland for becoming the cat's-paw of the Whigs upon this occasion. In 1837, when he was rejected by Middlesex and could not obtain a seat in his native country, he was elected for the city of Kilkenny without a penny of expense, beyond the postage of a letter announcing the fact, which in those days amounted to tenpence. It was always supposed in England that this seat had been procured for him by O'Connell, but in fact it was the spontaneous compliment of the reformers of Kilkenny, led by Dr Cane, to a prominent English reformer. His new constituents sent a deputation to London at their own cost to announce his election, and one of them afterwards assured me that Mr Hume, after listening to an address of congratulation with which they were charged, excused himself for a brief reply by informing them that his luncheon was waiting, and bowed out his new friends without ceremony. This was the last deputation Kilkenny sent to a financial reformer.

CHAPTER VI.

THE WORKSHOP OF YOUNG IRELAND.

As Peel's second proposal led to serious controversy, which in the end compelled the young men to confront the greatest tribune of modern times in the arena where he had long been supreme, it will be convenient, before describing it, to take note of the work in which they were engaged at that time. Notwithstanding the stealthy attempts to injure them, they pursued their policy with unflagging industry. The Eighty-Two Club, projected during the imprisonment, was now founded. The design was to bring the intelligence, rank, and wealth of the National party into one centre, and to open a door to adherents who on various grounds held aloof from the Association.[1] Lord Cloncurry was the first recruit of this class who justified their hopes. The express object was to encourage Irish art and literature, and to diffuse a national feeling through society, and its chief means to accustom Catholics and Protestants to act together. An expensive uniform and a strict ballot rendered it somewhat too exclusive in its character, but in the end it answered its purpose by becoming practically a muster of the National leaders of the present and the future. O'Connell was president, and of the five vice-presidents three were Protestants; of the two secretaries, one was a Protestant; and at its public meetings the resolutions were generally proposed and seconded by a Protestant and a Catholic. Its first public banquet was held at the Rotunda on the 16th of April, the sixty-third anniversary of the day upon which Grattan moved the Declaration of Independence. Upwards of a hundred gentlemen, many of them men of name and mark, arrayed in native green, destined, as they believed, some day to become the official uniform of a national Government, and

---

[1] O'Connell did not conceal from himself the necessity of offering this alternative. In the Association (Jan. 25th), speaking of the Club, he said: "The prejudice which existed against the Repeal Association would not exist against it."

a national army, sat round the board. They included the most conspicuous Nationalists in Parliament, at the Bar, among the gentry, and in the municipalities, and some who were destined to become conspicuous in the approaching future. Among the latter were Thomas Francis Meagher, John Mitchel, T. B. M'Manus, John Martin, and P. J. Smyth, who had not yet written, spoken, or acted under the public eye; who, except in one or two instances, did not know each other, or the comrades with whom they were to be associated in life and death; but who were drawn by an irresistible gravitation to the new centre of action. Only one member was excused from appearing in uniform, the venerable Cornelius M'Loughlen, who had borne arms among the volunteers when the historic events occurred which the Club was founded to commemorate. Over the president's chair hung Kenny's picture of the Irish Parliament on the night when Grattan rose to proclaim it a free and sovereign legislature, crowded with the portraits of the men of Eighty-two. Flags symbolising the past and the future of Ireland were distributed throughout the hall, and the presence of nearly three hundred ladies gave to the striking scene its final grace and triumph. Among the toasts was " The Memory of Grattan and Flood," angry rivals in life, but reunited in the love of the people whom they served; and it was pleasant to hear the son and namesake of Henry Grattan declare that his father had drunk the divine draught of liberty from the fountain of living water of which Flood was the guardian. Molyneux, Swift, and Lucas, the forerunners of Flood and Grattan, were fitly commemorated. MacNevin, who proposed their memory, read from their career the lesson that persecution or defeat does not render the life of the patriot useless; at worst he sows the seed of happier days. As the midnight hour approached, and the company began to separate, Davis was called upon to propose a toast connected with the Arts in Ireland. He had rarely made a set speech in public. The late hour, the exhaustion of the company after an exciting day, and the triteness of the topic, made his friends who had pressed him into the position anxious and nervous. But a voice vibrating with sincerity and conviction arrested the company already beginning to separate; they gathered round him with the silent rapt attention which is the orator's greatest triumph, and remained to the close impatient at missing a word. Next day one of his friends who had watched the scene with critical care assured him that he might count on success as an orator as authentic as that which he had won as a poet and a thinker.

But the new organisation involved one grave danger, which no

THE WORKSHOP OF YOUNG IRELAND. 153

prudence could altogether evade. If it opened its doors to the disreputable tail of the old Association it would plainly miss its aim, for it was they who frightened away the class whom it was founded to enlist; and if it refused to admit them, the refusal was sure to create bitter and deadly enmities. Lane, who was then in Cork, wrote to Davis insisting on this latter danger:—

"I'm sorry that I can't have a talk with you on the subject, as I must confess I do not at all understand the Eighty-Two Club. I fancied at first that I had some glimmering of its meaning, but I thought that the means adopted were altogether inadequate and inappropriate to secure the end in view. I fancied it was to make Repeal genteel—which I do not consider of any value, even if it were possible; to turn Hercules into an Antinous, and teach him to wield his club gracefully, is, I think, an idle task. Let Repealers be strong and earnest and they may be as ungraceful as they will—it is better have them clench their teeth and knit their brows than smile with elegance. It would be impossible to form a large body of Repealers who have what may be called 'position in society.' If you can form a star of them so much the better, but where do you draw the line of distinction between the nucleus of aristocracy and the nebulous mass of shabby gentility which surrounds it? Begin with Lord French, Sir Richard Musgrave, Smith O'Brien, and the members of Parliament—exclude (M. N.)—he is indignant; admit him—well, exclude (O. P.) and he is outrageous; or admit him and you must admit (X. Y. Z.)[1] and so on until you include every man who can borrow a guinea and get tick from his tailor—or else you cause dissension. You must either miss your proposed object, or do worse, divide your party. No! You should have got up a good club, like the Kildare Street, where a man could not complain if he were rejected; or you should have had a society of some sort like what you once proposed to Lefanu for the Young Ireland of both parties, into which men of all opinions would be admitted; or you should deluge Royal Irish Academies, and Royal Dublin Societies, and every old institution with Repealers. You may make the great body of the Protestants at present swallow nationality, but you cannot make them gulp down Repeal, or, as they believe it to be, O'Connellism. If they become national 'tis all we want; the rest will follow as sure as the fruit follows the flower; you must have a spring and a summer before you have an autumn.

"In Cork the people in general have a great hatred of uniforms; the Town Councillors and Aldermen here could not be got to wear robes. This I think principally arises from the morbidly keen sense of the ludicrous which Cork men generally possess. Tom Steele could not live a week in Cork."

Searching criticism like this from observant friends generally came to temper whatever project the party undertook. The attempt to nationalise art had been only moderately successful. From the beginning some of us held that all we could accomplish was to replace the rude and sometimes indecent daubs which were to be found in the humblest lodging and in the poorest cabin by lithographs and wood

---

[1] In the original letter, names, not symbols, are employed.

engravings carefully drawn, and presenting scenes of historic or traditional interest.[1] Davis had hoped for much more, but one of his personal friends, the most gifted of the resident artists in Ireland, who loved the man more than he shared his opinions, dissipated this hope.[2]

"How to answer your question regarding the nationalising of art," he wrote, "I hardly know, but I fear certain hundreds of pounds will never produce either art or nationality. Indeed the measure of success the Parliamentary Committee have attained in their praiseworthy endeavours in England is a sufficient commentary upon such a mode of attempting the end sought. You should give Ireland first a decided national school of poetry—that is song—and the other phases will soon show themselves. This I must allow is being done—but the effect is not complete. You know that this mode is the only possible one as well as I do, but you have lurking hopes that things can be forced. Ah, my dear friend, free, spiritual, high-aiming art cannot be forced. Some great passion—some earnest and all unworldly feeling—some profound state of thought—something that, whilst making this material universe the scene, and its material offspring the actors, shall yet reach at what is far above and beyond it all—something of this kind alone will extricate the lightning flash 'from the black cloud that bound it.' And would you seek any less than the highest? But I blunder, for I cannot admit anything less to be art at all. . . . The Germans have a school of art—but they have one of poetry—eminently German too, therefore eminently original. The English have no truly English school of poetry (although they have had great—the greatest poets), consequently no truly English art, at least beyond a certain reach in landscapes. Why is all this? The Germans have, to go back further, a school of philosophy, even as the Greeks had, and the mediæval Italians—mingled in all three with their deepest religious faith. It is from this that issued all the rays that, combining, made one brilliant and consistent flow of vivifying light. When England can unveil such a sun—when Ireland can rub her eyes clear of short-sighted, mean, and petty, and too often selfish, ends, then shall the irresistible influence, the welcomed law of art, proceed also from them as from new centres."

But it is through the discipline of failure that success is oftenest won,

---

[1] "I wish much that you could get something done by the Repeal Association towards providing good prints, very cheap, for the poor. I observe in almost every cottage where absolute destitution does not exist a disposition to hang up prints on the walls. Generally they are wretched productions, having neither grace nor truth. Could we not induce some competent artist to give us lithograph sketches, which could be circulated through hawkers and pedlars at a low price? Religious subjects appear to be the most popular—military come next. Temperance prints also are not uncommon. It would be well to invite proposals, with a view to see what sort of artists we should be able to get. I wish that the Reformed Corporations would take upon themselves to found picture galleries in the Town Halls of the several towns. If each Corporation in the kingdom would order from some Irish artist one picture each year, what great and immediate encouragement would be given to Irish art! So also with sculpture. The present appears to me to be a very favourable moment for such a suggestion."—Davis Papers. O'Brien to Davis, Aug. 3, '45.

[2] Mr, afterwards Sir, Frederick Burton.

and the young men undertook other work which had a speedy and complete success; work by which they are most affectionately remembered at present, and will probably be longest remembered in the future. They determined to make a careful attempt to fill up certain obvious gaps in the national literature. The most urgent want was an adequate history of Ireland. Among a library of books labelled "histories" there was not one which could be put with credit into the hands of a stranger or a student. Jeffrey Keating's big volume, which is a congeries of dull fables relieved by some glimmering of traditional truth, only comes down to the period of the English Invasion. Dr Leland is prejudiced and meagre, relieved by such stinted fairness as a professor of Trinity College and viceregal chaplain in the reign of George III. might venture to exhibit, and he only comes down to the Treaty of Limerick. Plowden is Leland rewritten, compressed, liberalised, and supplemented by original documents. Moore stops at the Commonwealth, and his first volume is overloaded with worthless antiquarian essays. MacGeoghegan's history, a faithful and honest book, was written in France, and in French; was clumsily translated, and closes at the termination of the Williamite wars. O'Connell's "Memoir of Ireland" did not pretend to be a history, but only a skilful brief of the case against England; and Moore's "Captain Rock" (a pleasant *jeu d'esprit*) is not a narrative, but a commentary, and a commentary not free from the *soupçon* of contempt for Ireland, which, after the fashion of Sydney Smith and the *Edinburgh Review*, was considered essential to get justice and common-sense on the subject a hearing in England. A generation earlier Shelley, then a boyish enthusiast, went on a mission to Dublin to preach the policy of Ireland breaking away from the Union, and this want struck him so painfully that he contributed a liberal sum to procure the publication of a national history; but unfortunately the result was a rhetorical pamphlet of no weight or authority.[1] And now (in 1844) another generous Englishman, Dr Smiles, wrote a serviceable handbook of Irish transactions, marred only by a stranger's necessary ignorance of the relative importance and historical perspective of events. The void still remained to be filled, and the Repeal Association offered a prize for a competent book for schools and students. Davis, who had only moderate trust in the effect of prizes, was disposed to relinquish his work in the *Nation* for twelve months, and write a history himself.

---

[1] D. F. McCarthy's "Early Days of Shelley." The book he promoted is known as Lawless's "History of Ireland," John Lawless being a fluent and effective popular orator in those days.

MacNevin was fired with the same ambition, and began to study the materials; but it was a task for which he had no natural aptitude, and he had to learn laboriously facts which were as familiar to Davis as the days of the week. Davis sought to enlist a friend, to whom he had recourse in every literary emergency; he besought Maddyn to do the work :—

"I undertook to write a History of Ireland from the Treaty of Limerick to 1829, or such other period (earlier or later) in this century as I thought fit. The work was to be issued in parts, and then in a volume of six or seven hundred octavo pages. For this I was offered £300, and £100 more if it succeeded. Now, I have not written a page of this. I could not write it well without leaving to other men political duties which are every day becoming more weighty and solemn. You would write the history of such a time, abounding in civil events, parties, and characters, infinitely better than I could, even had I the utmost leisure. It is most desirable for Ireland that you should live in and write for it. Will you then seriously deliberate on this? If the authorship of 'Ireland and its Rulers' do not interfere with the success of the Grattan [he had edited Grattan's speeches], I assume James Duffy will give you at least £300 for a book which will be better than I *could* have given him, and which your literary repute will serve more than my political connections could. Consider, then, whether this sum would pay you, and whether your mind would not be better and happier at home here than in the brick desert of London. As, however, the British Museum has many materials, you might write most, or all, in London, if you preferred it."

In the end the design was put on a more practical footing; it was agreed to write the history in eras, and entrust it to as many competent writers as could be procured. The success of the shilling volumes issued by Lord Brougham suggested the application of the same method and machinery to the diffusion of Irish books, and I proposed to my friends a series of shilling volumes of biography, poetry, and criticism, to be called the "Library of Ireland," in which the historical design might be carried out. They took up the project eagerly. MacNevin wrote the first volume, the "Irish Volunteers," and Davis, in the midst of a hundred engagements, set to work upon a memoir of "Wolfe Tone," whom he esteemed one of the greatest Irishmen of the eighteenth century; Father Meehan wrote the tragic story of the "Confederation of Kilkenny"; other friends followed, and a volume issued every month for nearly two years, till a fatal conflict with O'Connell diverted their energy into fresh channels. The little books had an immediate success, and after the lapse of half a century, when the writers are dead, new editions constantly issue from the press in Ireland and America. In the year 1890 the forty-second edition of some of the volumes is current, and more than a quarter of a million of copies of

C. P. Meehan

MEMORANDUM.

With the portrait now reproduced Father Meehan sent me some dates in his life which ought to be preserved till his memoir is written : —" Born in Great Britain Street, Dublin, July 12th, 1812. Schooled in Ballymahon, Co. Longford, where I learned the first rudiments in a hedge-school kept by one Peter MacCabe of drunken memory. 1828 saw me in Rome, whence I returned in 1836 and had my first mission in Rathdrum, Co. Wicklow. Early in 1842 for the first time saw C. G. D., with whom I dined in Leinster Square, Rathmines, where I saw a gathering such as I may never hope to see again. *Voilà tout* about a very insignificant individual. The photo does resemble, but *un portrait ne doit être regardé que de loin.*"

C.G.D.

the more popular books have been circulated wherever the English tongue is spoken. The Memoirs of Francis Jeffrey and of Miss Mitford and the miscellanies of Leigh Hunt enable us to estimate the impression they created among the critical class in England, never too friendly to Irish experiments. Scholars and critics have followed who may smile at the hasty generalities and ill-digested facts which sometimes passed for history in these little books; but it must always be confessed that the writers opened a mine shut up for two centuries and a half, and taught their successors where the precious ore might be found.[1] And one at least of the workmen has never relinquished his task.[2] When his friends were dead or exiled, and the country torpid, he still bestowed upon Ireland books which in happier days will class him with MacGeoghegan, Lanigan, and O'Connor, the patriot priests who continued in adverse times the pious work begun in the Monastery of Donegal.

I find among the letters addressed to MacNevin at this time one which will exhibit the sort of discipline to which the young men subjected each other, that they might become skilful soldiers, and be able to stand fire before the enemy.

"Three editions of the 'Volunteers' in a few weeks, and a fourth on the stocks, is a great triumph. I have read the last as carefully as you wished, and I set down suggestions for the next edition as they occured to me :—

"1. Take your name from the preface. It is in the two preceding pages (viz. the title page and the dedication), and, in the new edition, to the new preface. The four Thomas MacNevins in four consecutive pages constitute an aggregate meeting which in my opinion ought to be dispersed.

"2. Page 28. For 'Tyrone' write 'Hugh O'Neill'; and put in a note 'The great Earl of Tyrone, properly Aodh O'Neill.' It is so he is spoken of in Irish annals, and thus people will be able to identify him with Mitchel's hero when Mitchel's book appears.

"3. Page 29. 'O'Neill was attainted.' Which O'Neill? There were several rather eminent men of the name at that time. Shane, I presume, is intended ; but you must specify."

"4. Same page. 'His *inherited* territories of Down and Antrim.' No Irish chief of that period inherited his territories ; he was elected to them ; and one of our complaints against the English is that they dealt with the property of the clan by forfeiture as if it were inherited by the chief; which it was not any more than the Lord Mayor inherits the Mansion House.

---

[1] The "Library of Ireland" has often, and very naturally, been attributed to Davis, who originated so much. But this design and the conduct of it to the end belonged wholly to one far less capable of turning it to account.
[2] The late Rev. Charles P. Meehan.

Moreover, Down and Antrim certainly were not *his* territories inherited or acquired. You must have fallen into some error here.

"5. Page 43. 'There was no virtue too pure, no patriotism too generous. Are these fitting terms to apply to the opposition in question? Is it wholly improbable that he would have lauded the Wood scheme to the skies if it had been proposed by St John or Harley?

"6. Page 74. 'Now for the *first* time a people sprung to life.' Was it the first time, my friend? and were the volunteers the Irish people? Shade of Roger O'Moore and Patrick Sarsfield forgive you!

"7. At page 115 you determine the number of the volunteers to be fifty thousand, yet you afterwards repeatedly speak of them as a hundred thousand — for example at p. 146, and p. 153, and p. 191.

"8. Page 128. 'Rebellion and conspiracy.' Pray transpose the words. Don't men conspire first and rebel afterwards?

"9. Page 192. Where you mention Lord Kenmare you ought to state that he was a Catholic peer, without which intimation English readers will be slow to understand what follows.

"These suggestions are worth little or nothing, but they give me a claim upon you to read my volume next month as assiduously, with a similar purpose. Davis will be busy for three weeks on 'Wolfe Tone,' during which time pray send me a literary paper in addition to your political article as often as you can."[1]

Sir Colman O'Loghlen promised me his aid, and projected two books, neither of which unfortunately was afterwards written. But his design may stimulate some lawyer of a later generation to undertake the relinquished task.

"We propose to begin with the first volume of the Bench and the Bar of Ireland. The series will probably run to two or three volumes. We of course exclude all living men, and have divided the subject between us. I take the earlier and O'Donohue the later portion. The series includes sketches of Sir John Davies, Sir Richard Bolton, Patrick Darcy, C. J. Keatinge, Sir Toby Butler, C. J. Whitshed, Anthony Malone, Lord Avonmore, Hussey Burgh, Lord Clonmel, Curran, etc.

"With respect to the work in which I have no fellow-labourer — the 'Legal History of Ireland'—I cannot promise a volume till September 1846. I propose to go back to the remotest times—to that of the Brehon law, and the customs and tenures of ancient Ireland—the introduction and gradual progress of the Anglo-Norman law—the legislation of the Parliaments of the Pale—the rise and history of the present Courts of Justice—the history of the Castle Chamber—of the Courts of Presidency of Munster and Connaught, etc., and to bring down the history of Irish legislation, social, political, and commercial (as far as can be done in an historical and not a technical work), to the Revolution of 1800. This will consequently give me a great deal to do."[2]

Though a knowledge of Ireland was first insisted upon, the teaching of the young men was not narrow or insular. Among work begun at

---

[1] Duffy to MacNevin.
[2] O'Loghlen to Duffy.

this time were a series of critical papers on the English poets, and on continental literature, accounts of colonial and foreign legislatures, historical essays on obscure or misunderstood eras, popular summaries of political science, essays on national sports, and retrospective reviews of the best Irish books in history, fiction, and the drama. The number of books published in Dublin coloured with the new national sentiment continued to excite the wonder of English critics. Many of them were poor and temporary, but some were of permanent interest. Carleton wrote, as a *feuilleton* for the *Nation*, a story of landlord tyranny which outgrew the limits of a newspaper and became the most successful of his novels. Dr Madden in his "Connection between the Kingdom of Ireland and the Crown of England" furnished original and important materials for Irish history; and even Lever made the experiment of a story founded on the wrongs and sufferings of the peasantry ; the first and last of its class in all his writings.[1]

---

[1] Carleton's story was "Valentine M'Clutchy," Lever's "St Patrick's Eve." In London, Mr Marmion Savage, Clerk of the Privy Council, and a writer in the *Examiner*, published a novel entitled "The Falcon Family ; or, Young Ireland," John Pigot, under the title of "Tigernach MacMorris," being the hero of the story, which was a long and rather feeble pasquinade. The books projected by the Young Irelanders were nearly all published by Mr James Duffy. He was originally a bookseller on a small scale in an obscure street, dealing chiefly in reprints of religious publications, but his enterprise and liberality carried him into a wider field, and ultimately created a trade extending to India, America, and Australia. The "Spirit of the Nation" was issued in the first instance from the *Nation* office, but as the demand for it became embarrassing I looked out for a publisher, and fixed upon Mr James Duffy. This was the beginning of his connection with the Young Ireland party. He was a man of shrewd sense and sly humour, but without cultivation or judgment in literature, and it was a subject of constant vexation to the men who were making his name familiar to the world that, side by side with books of eminent merit, he would issue some dreadful abortion of an Irish story or an Irish pamphlet which was certain to be treated at a distance as the latest production of Young Ireland ! It is impossible to read even now without mingled amusement and sympathy the explosions of wrath over these shortcomings, which found vent in their private correspondence at that time. On one occasion the writer of a book of careful thought and great research had promised an early copy to an eminent English critic, to be sent through one of Duffy's London agents. It did not arrive in due course, and the critic caused an application to be made to the agent in question. The agent was a woman, keeping a newspaper shop near a Catholic chapel—for the regular trade did not circulate Duffy's books till he established, in later years, a branch in Paternoster Row—and she sent the critic back his own note refolded and unstamped, with a notification on the blank sheet that she knew nothing of Mr So-and-So or his book. The critic sent his note and its endorsement to the author, with what result I may leave to the imagination of readers familiar with the *irritabile genus*. It was a standing joke somewhat later that the publisher had made a just and successful criticism at the expense of D'Arcy M'Gee. M'Gee described the hero of some national legend as having hair black and glossy as the wing of a young raven. "Why," says Mr Duffy, with a sly smile, "when I was a boy the wing of a young raven was grey ; but 'tis long ago, and I suppose they have altered since then."

Davis was an indefatigable worker on a settled plan of work, and did not waste an atom of his power on show of any sort. His notes to his friends bear the same relation to his published writings that hasty scratches in a painter's note-book bear to the glowing canvas. With his comrades, whom he saw daily, there was little need for correspondence, but to Smith O'Brien, who resided much in the country, he wrote often, and in his brief notes we get not only an insight into his own life, but a striking picture of the energy and diligence of the party. It was proposed to erect in Limerick an equestrian statue of the skilful soldier who defended the city against William III., and Davis was eager that the work might be entrusted to a competent artist.

"What of Sarsfield's statue?" (he writes to O'Brien). "I think Moore would like to do it. [Christopher Moore, who had made effective busts of Curran and Plunket, but proved on trial to be unequal to statues.] Kirk is not competent. The Ballad Poetry [second volume of the new Library of Ireland][1] has reached a third edition, and cannot be printed fast enough for the sale. It is every way good. Not an Irish Conservative of education but will read it, and be brought nearer to Ireland by it. That is a propagandism worth a thousand harangues such as you ask me to make. We are going to print (Torrens) M'Cullagh's Lecture on History and O'Donovan's Essays on Irish Names and Families in the series. Hugh O'Neill's life is written, and is admirably done. One of the volumes will be 'Thomond and the O'Briens,' dedicated to a living member of that clan, written by a Clare man of Conservative family, but this is a secret known only to you, to the author, and to myself. I have little chance of getting from town. Still I am in iron health. Many thanks for your kind invitation to Cahermoyle. Grey Porter is here; he is unchanged."[2]

And again—

"Grey Porter is here, full of projects and ambition. . . . . Here are two projects for you to digest. First and nearest, is to put you, John O'Connell, Duffy, and five or six more on the committee of the library in D'Olier Street (the Dublin library) at the coming election in February. It has thirteen thousand volumes, a noble and well-situated house, and only wants vigour and control to be a great civic library and literary institute. Porter is at work for his Polytechnic in connection with the Mechanics' Institutes, but that will be for mechanics and practical science. Secondly, a solemn meeting of Irish M.P.'s, corporators, etc., to discuss and issue a Declaration of Irish grievances, rights, and remedies. By a little diplomacy we might get through this without quarrel or illegality. . . . But these things should be considered and done by three or four men, and not spoken of till all was ripe."[3]

---

[1] Ballad Poetry of Ireland. Edited by Charles Gavan Duffy.
[2] Cahermoyle Correspondence.
[3] Cahermoyle Correspondence. This latter project became in the end a Levée held on the anniversary of the Richmond imprisonment.

THE WORKSHOP OF YOUNG IRELAND.

To the first note O'Brien replied:—

"I cannot but hope that the publication of the monthly volume will be of infinite value to the national cause if the intellectual and moral standard of the work can be kept as high as it ought to be. I like the two first numbers very much—I could not lay down the "Ballads" until I had read the whole volume. I am delighted with the article in yesterday's *Nation* respecting the prospect of a union between Orange and Green. It makes me for a moment believe that the dream of my life is about to be realised. I know that I could not recommend [in the Association] that a few hundred copies of this number of the *Nation* should be sent into the Orange districts without awakening jealousies which it is very unadvisable to raise; but I think it worth the consideration of you and Duffy, whether it would not be well to print this article on separate slips of paper, and send them by post into the heart of Fermanagh. Glorious indeed would be the spectacle of an union of the two great contending Irish parties, who have been taught to hate each other."

Davis's share of the work he projected was commonly to do half of it, and revise the other half. Here is an example. He wrote to O'Brien—

"Either you or I, or some one, should compile a short account of the geography, history, and statistics of Ireland, to be printed in fifty or sixty pages of a report, accompanied by a map, and circulated extensively. We must do more to educate the people. This is the only moral force in which I have any faith. Mere agitation is either bullying or preparation for war. I condemn the former; others of the party condemn the latter. But we all agree in the policy of education. . . . The members of the Franchise Committee should apply themselves, under your guidance, to the Grand Juries. I suppose we shall be able to work up some account of the Customs, Excise, and Post Office from Stritch's and Reynolds's reports. We should get Mr Mullin to make a report on the Poor Law Commission and its working. I shall make up the Education and Police as soon as the Estimates Report is out. Dillon and I have agreed to prepare facts, etc., on (land) tenures (Irish and foreign). Thus, I think, we are on the way of having proper materials for a statistical account of Ireland both internally and in relation to the British Empire."[1]

Dillon, who at the moment was on circuit, reported that his share of the joint task was not neglected, and described his first experiment as an advocate in terms which will help the reader to understand his modest, manly character.

"The best course I can pursue in the execution of this task is to draw up a report setting forth succinctly the Law of Landlord and Tenant, to be submitted immediately after my arrival in Dublin, and then with your assistance undertake a second, which will comprehend all the other branches of the subject, foreign tenures, changes to be suggested, etc. Perhaps it would be better not to bring any report before the Committee until our labours are completed, and then give the entire result together. . . . If I acquired any

---

[1] Cahermoyle Correspondence.

fame at Castlebar, I owe it all to the unblushing mendacity of my good friends the reporters. My speech was very weak, and I would be very much dissatisfied with myself if I had not the justification of its being a first speech to a jury, and made without even one minute to think of what I was to say. I am very much pleased at the way Barry is going on; his speeches were both exceedingly good, but particularly the first. Was not that a capital story he told about Sir Charles Napier? 'At them, you rascals, and fulfil the prophecies.'"

In another of Dillon's notes one may learn how the "ferocious hatred of the Saxon," with which the party have sometimes been credited, found expression in the private correspondence of its leaders. Their public censure of England was moderate compared to the reproaches which the philosopher David Hume discharged on that nation *apropos* of its injustice to Scotland; and was gracious courtesy compared to the habitual language of English writers respecting Ireland; and their private correspondence was more temperate and considerate than their public censure.

"You are going on gloriously in the *Nation*. There is one hint which, as an impartial spectator, I would be disposed to give, and that is, not to be guilty of incivility to Saxon sympathisers. Speaking fairly, I think they have treated us very well, and it would not be handsome to repay kindness even from them with ferocity and abuse. This hint was suggested not by anything I saw in the *Nation*, which I think has not gone one inch too far in that direction, but by some observations in the *Freeman*, prefacing a review of Venedey's book, extracted from the *Chronicle*. To assail all parties in England with indiscriminate abuse would be to follow up the blunders of O'Connell with respect to the Chartists. This, then, is the sum total of my preachment—to denounce vigorously all approaches towards compromise, but at the same time to speak with all respect and civility of those who stretch out the hand of friendship to us; and not to scrutinise too narrowly the motives of their friendship so long as they tender it unencumbered by conditions."[1]

If the fate of nations depends on the education of the young, Davis and his friends were engaged in no ignoble task. A generous Englishman, Arnold of Rugby, once conceived the project of removing to Ireland and taking pupils in a country where there was "more to be done than in any corner of the world." The basis of his system, as of Davis's, was that "Ireland was a distinct nation, entitled to govern

---

[1] Davis Papers.—Dillon to Davis, Ballaghaderrin, March 21st. MacNevin wrote in the same spirit:—"We are not animated by any malignant hatred of England or the English. No such thing. We saw revived in the glory of that great country more than the power of Imperial Rome. We recognised in her institutions the most formidable social system the world ever saw—great in arms, illustrious in arts, in science, and in literature; unlimited in empire, unbounded in the range of its power; but we saw in her too the malignant influences under which *our* national honour, *our* national glory, *our* national prosperity, withered, drooped, and died."

herself."[1] Englishmen may meditate with advantage on the problem whether a task which would be recognised as heroic in a stranger was unbecoming men of the Irish race.

To another of his friends, Denny Lane, Davis constantly opened his inmost mind on the transactions of the hour. Before the close of the imprisonment, he said :—

"Your stubborn resolve to better Cork, whether it likes it or not, is a great comfort to me. Stability, morals, and hard work—they'd better hell and make purgatory a paradise. . . . If there be a war now (with America), we must carry Repeal in six months, otherwise in three or four years, if we do our duty."

And somewhat later :—

"I learn that the best men in Cork wish to make you their representative. Our idea here was to work for your return for Mallow, but Cork is far better. I assume that both Murphy and Callaghan go out. . . . Whom do you propose to start? You and Hayes would do famously. Amongst your other duties you are to have charge of our most brilliant and kindly, but as yet headlong, friend MacNevin. All our party are most anxious to see you in the House. They are pressing me to go in, but I am positive against it. Some men of great powers are already girding their loins, and there is some prospect now of a good band of National M.P.'s. . . . We miss you much at our evening meetings, which have grown more serious."

And after Peel's concession was announced :—

"I am weary wishing you here. The events as to Maynooth will greatly weaken our enemies ; and Oregon promises well, though I trust nothing to it. For our hopes' sake do not let Cork be guilty of any meanness should the Queen come. This should be easy in Cork ; here it will be harder. But we are resolute and timely, and cannot fail ; so her coming shall be turned to good. Why don't you write more songs? Your last, to the air of 'The Foggy Dew,' was beautiful, and comes constantly on my recollection like a southern twilight. I have nearly recovered the cold winter and Repeal essays [he was one of the judges whose duty it was to read a long series of prize essays on Repeal], but have too many things to do, and so my life is a string of epigrams, which displeases me. I am left too much without affections ; but I am coldly happy and dutiful. . . . Duffy is well as a man can be who sees his young wife dying by inches. Barry and the rest of the set well and more serious than they used to be."

At the same time he engaged Maddyn's aid to make Clarence Mangan better known to the lovers of poetry in England; but unsuccessfully :—

"I think you were a reader of the *University Magazine.* If so, you must have noticed the 'Anthologia Germanica,' 'Leaflets from the German

---

[1] Stanley's " Life of Arnold."

Oak,' 'Oriental Nights,' and other translations, and apparent translations of Clarence Mangan. He has some small salary in the College Library, and has to support himself and his brother. His health is wretched. Charles Duffy is most anxious to have the papers I have described printed in London, for which they are better suited than for Dublin. Now, you will greatly oblige me by asking Newby if he will publish them, giving Mangan £50 for the edition. If he refuse, you can say that Charles Duffy will repay him half the £50 should the work be a failure. Should he still declare against it, pray let me know soon what would be the best way of getting some payment and publication for Mangan's papers. Many of the ballads are Mangan's own, and are first-rate. Were they on Irish subjects, he would be paid for them here. They ought to succeed in London nigh as well as the 'Prout Papers.''

In his notes to me at this time I find a just and graphic estimate of the books and men of the Commonwealth era in Ireland, likely to be still useful to students :—

"Carte was an Ormondite and Whig-Tory. Leland only copies Carte. Castlehaven and most of the other men acted feebly and sometimes falsely. They were half Englishmen. Owen Roe supported the ultra men, who wanted to 'cut the painter,' and thought foreign help could be best got in the name of Catholicity. He was no bigot. When a chance of getting independence by an alliance with the Puritans offered he seized it. The furious rascality of the English Parliament alone baulked him. He was the only general (as distinct from a guerilla officer) on the Irish side, during the war. I do not reckon Ormond or Murrough O'Brien as on the Irish side, though they sometimes appeared so. Ormond was a time-serving, avaricious, hard-disciplined man. Owen was just, brave, energetic, a keeper of promises, a merciful enemy, a stern leader, who was loved, feared, and trusted by his own, and dreaded and respected by his foes. Carte himself says all this. He was the Wolfe Tone of his time. The just and thorough man to whom victory would have been complete success."

And an estimate of a notable book, which will interest another class :—

"I read some forty pages of this 'Festus,' and return it to avoid reading more. It is a marvellous anatomy of soul with a sunbeam for a lancet, but I don't want theories ; I have had too much of them, and of grief—the latter chiefly at my own shortcomings. But there are dishonoured truths (such as that scorn of repentance) in the book, and when I have a longer leisure I'll ask you for it again."

In 1843 the Repeal Association had superseded Parliament; the new literature began visibly to supersede the platform in 1845.

CHAPTER VII.

THE PROVINCIAL COLLEGES.

WHEN the Maynooth Bill had passed through the dangerous stages, the Government submitted their scheme of middle-class education. The measure was explained by Sir James Graham in a speech of notable frankness. In Ireland, he said, the creed of the great majority of the people had long been treated by the State as a hostile religion; in latter times this evil was gradually abated, civil liberty had been conferred on the Catholics, the penal laws were removed, or in process of removal; but such traces of this spirit as remained were nowhere more noxious than when they tainted public education. The Government desired to establish colleges for the middle classes on the principle of perfect religious equality. It was proposed to erect one college for the south, probably at Cork, one for the west at Galway or Limerick, and one for the north at Derry or Belfast. There would be no provision made for the residence of the students within the colleges, but they would be subject to academical control. There would be no interference, positive or negative, with their religious convictions; but religion would not be neglected; it was intended to give facilities for the endowment by private benefaction of professors of theology, to train the students in the religion of their forefathers, for which purpose the use of the lecture rooms would be afforded. A new university would probably be created to grant degrees to the students of these institutions. The professors would in the first instance be appointed by the Crown, afterwards this method would be abandoned.

The measure was well received in the House of Commons. Mr Roche and Mr Morgan John O'Connell, members of the Repeal Association, and Mr Wyse and Mr Ross, Nationalists of the Federal section, welcomed it as a substantial and liberal concession. But it did not escape criticism. Mr Sheil regretted that it was not made imperative on students to attend some religious instruction; and that the

Government had not placed themselves in communication with the Catholic bishops, as they had recently done with respect to the Maynooth Bill. Sir Robert Inglis, on behalf of good old stolid, respectable Toryism, insisted that there ought to be religious teaching in all State schools, but that it ought to be the teaching of the Church of England, and pronounced the plan to be a huge scheme of godless education.

The reception of the proposal in Ireland was for a time doubtful. A moiety of the Catholic Bishops, led by the Primate, O'Brien, Davis, the National Protestants universally, and the bulk of the writers and thinkers connected with the Repeal movement, greatly desired middle-class education for Catholics, and were ready to welcome it on any fair terms; for of all the monopolies which the minority enjoyed, the most fatal to the hopes of national progress was the monopoly of education.

The proposal was immediately taken into consideration by the General Committee. A majority regarded it as a measure as generous in design as the Maynooth Bill, and which a little care would render as unexceptionable. But the minority included O'Connell and Mr John O'Connell, who amazed the Committee by denouncing the scheme as altogether and designedly evil. After a prolonged conversation, which disclosed a rooted difference of opinion, Davis advised that under the circumstances the controversy should be kept out of the Association, and conducted as the opposition to the Bequests Bill had been conducted a year earlier—in the Press and by public meetings convened for the special purpose. But O'Connell announced, in peremptory terms, his intention of opening up the question at once in Conciliation Hall. He carried out his purpose at the next meeting; and his speech was devoted to a trenchant criticism of the scheme. He adopted the phraseology of Sir Robert Inglis and pronounced it "godless." But the Government might render it acceptable by making the colleges at Cork and Galway strictly Catholic, while the college at Derry might be Presbyterian as Trinity college was Protestant. He professed himself ready, however, to abandon his opposition if the Catholic Bishops approved of the scheme.[1]

Education is a subject of supreme importance, and O'Connell's opinion upon the Government proposal was naturally entitled to grave consideration; but nothing can be plainer than that he was not justified in carrying this vexed question into the Repeal Association. The object of that body was to repeal the Union, and its constitution had been

---

[1] Repeal Association, May 12th, 1845.

modified for the express purpose of combining men who desired a native Parliament without sacrificing their individual opinions on any other question. It was idle to talk of converting the North and uniting with the Federalists if it was necessary to accept in silence the opinion of O'Connell upon subjects of this nature, or to contest them with him in the Association of which he was the leader. By crossing the street he might have held meetings on the subject without breaking the fundamental pact, and without materially diminishing the force of his opposition. A year before he had agreed to exclude from the Association the consideration of the Bequests Bill, for reasons which applied with increased force to the present Bill.[1]

If he still hoped and desired to Repeal the Union, it was plainly necessary to exhibit in Conciliation Hall that consideration for the rights of the minority which would alone induce them to trust him with power in an Irish Parliament. His disregard of these motives brought to a sharp test the fidelity and affection of his associates; but so loyal was their recognition of his authority that his speech was allowed to pass without comment.

Later in the meeting, however, Mr John O'Connell spoke on the same subject, and spoke in a tone unusually fierce, offensive, and dictatorial.

"He felt," he said, "a degree of indignation to which it was impossible not to give utterance at the melancholy spectacle which some of the Irish members had made of themselves, by presuming to commit their countrymen to the abominable scheme of education proposed by Sir James Graham. Who or what were they, that they should presume to compromise the Irish people? It was the duty of the laity to leave the question in the hands of the bishops, and for this reason he would not expatiate at any length on the subject; but would endeavour to suppress for the present his feelings of abomination and execration at this infamous attempt of the English ministers to seduce and divide where they could not hope to conquer."

This was somewhat too much. The most respectable of the Irish members were assailed for expressing their opinion in Parliament upon a measure submitted in the ordinary manner for acceptance or rejection, and the young man of mediocre talents and discretion who denounced them thought himself entitled to pronounce a far more decisive judgment upon the measure in a place where men were not assembled to pass Acts of Parliament, but to procure the Repeal of the Union; and to pro-

---

[1] "He consented, out of deference to the minority, to keep the Bequests Question out of the Association; why not this question also?" Cahermoyle Correspondence—Davis to O'Brien, December 10th, 1844.—Davis Papers.

nounce it with the full knowledge that he was speaking the sentiments of the minority only of the governing body. Dillon and Davis, who were present, felt they had no choice but to interpose. The world might make allowance for O'Connell's dictum being received in silence, but how would it interpret a similar indulgence being extended to the violence and arrogance of a personage of the calibre of Mr John O'Connell? All hope of winning the support of independent men was at an end if a stand were not made against this attempt to bully individual opinion. Davis spoke immediately.

"It was with feelings, of regret and a good deal of anxiety, he felt it necessary to express his respectful but positive dissent from some of the opinions of his friend Mr John O'Connell. He was not yet in a position, nor he feared were any of them, to judge of the details of a measure which was loosely stated by its proposer, and was not printed. He believed the people of this country were anxious to get academic education, no matter from whom it came ; for it was a gift which could not be polluted by the hands through which it passed. A liberal endowment was proposed, for which he was grateful, but it was accompanied by principles of Government interference against which he protested; for he was not disposed to surrender the selection of the instructors of the youth of Ireland into the hands of an anti-Irish Government. In any country the principle of combined education of its youth he thought a good principle ; but in Ireland, whose peculiar curse was religious dissension, that principle was invaluable. He was just as ready and willing as Mr John O'Connell to demand guarantees that the religion of the student should be protected from the propagandism or treachery of any of the professors. Were the religious discipline and instruction of the Catholic students entrusted to a Catholic dean, appointed by the Catholic Church authorities, and the religious conduct and training of Protestants and Presbyterians left to deans named by the Protestant and Presbyterian authorities, no Church could complain with any show of justice ; and he believed it was quite consistent with the general system of endowment proposed that such an arrangement might be adopted. On these grounds he dissented from the opinions expressed by Mr John O'Connell, without, however, desiring to give unqualified approval to the measure."

O'Connell rose a second time to declare that the discussion was premature and ought to terminate.

"He could not blame his friend Mr Davis for having entered into it, for it had been commenced by the member for Kilkenny and himself; but it would be more judicious to reserve further discussion till the bill was printed. Mr Davis condemned the absence of religious instruction, but the very principle of the bill was to have no religious instruction in the projected colleges or under their influence.

"Mr DILLON interposed to remind O'Connell that this was a mistake. The Government measure by no means discouraged religious instruction ; on the contrary, it contained an express provision empowering the establishment of a hall to each of the provincial colleges for the purpose of affording facilities to have the students instructed in the doctrines of their Church.

"Mr O'CONNELL: What a great advantage a hall is to teach religion in ! Really my friend is laughing at me. The Government Education Bill gives us a hall, forsooth. Why, we could give them Conciliation Hall.

"Mr DILLON: I merely wished to set Mr O'Connell right when he stated that the bill discountenanced religious instruction. That is not the fact. Religious instruction was encouraged by the bill.

"Mr O'CONNELL: Religious instruction is not encouraged by the bill which Sir James Graham brought forward; it is discouraged by it. Religious instruction is to be carefully excluded from the new colleges. Such are the terms of the bill."

It is not difficult to understand the motives that lay at the root of this controversy. The young men were Catholics and Protestants, united like brothers in a generous design; many of them had been educated together, and had learned to love each other when hearts are fresh and open, and they hoped to see the same fraternity extended throughout the nation by the same means. They knew that Catholic students in the only university in the island were lured to apostacy and hypocrisy by the exclusive system on which it was founded, and they were impatient to see colleges established on the principle of religious equality, where these temptations would disappear. They had no confidence in the judgment of Mr John O'Connell, and a very lively suspicion that he was more anxious to place the Young Irelanders in antagonism to some of the Catholic bishops than to promote or thwart any system of education. It was not necessary to doubt that, *cæteris paribus*, he preferred separate education; but they were persuaded that he carried the question into the Association, and provoked the debate which he knew must ensue, in pursuance of a design to represent them as indifferent to religion. O'Connell, as the Catholic leader, had his vigilance naturally awakened by the nature of the question, and it is probable his pride was hurt by the intrusion of any other opinion into a domain where his own used to be supreme. It is easy to misconceive critics, and he was surrounded by persons certain to put the worst construction upon any opposition to his will. He was the prey of an insidious disease, and, added to all these influences, he was perplexed by the difficulty, which has embarrassed so many kings and tribunes, of securing the succession to his authority for a feeble pretender; and he was ready to make inordinate sacrifices for this end.

To obtain education for the Catholic middle-class, and save the Association from disruption, was a task that tested the energies of the men who had both objects at heart. The *Nation* took a decided stand with this latter party. In the number following the debate Davis and the editor wrote upon the question, and it is curious to note how the

Protestant and the Catholic Nationalist, treating the same subject, relies each upon arguments and feelings drawn from the experience of his own class. Davis unburthened the heart of a man sick of the feuds and prejudices which had divided the nation into two hostile camps. The Irish had been made and kept serfs because they were ignorant and divided. The Protestant hated the Catholic and oppressed him, the Catholic hated the Protestant and refused to trust him. Any plan which would strengthen the soul of Ireland with knowledge, and knit the creeds in liberal and trusting friendship, would be better for her than if corn and wine were scattered from every cloud. If such a project could not be discussed in a reasonable and discreet way, the progress of the people to self-government was a progress to shameful ruin. The objections to separate education were immense, the reasons for it were reasons for separate life, for mutual animosities, for penal laws, for religious wars. United education was the principle accepted by Ireland in the National Schools, the principle favourable to that Union of Irishmen, for want of which Ireland was in rags and chains. An adequate provision for religious discipline was not to be dispensed with, and the appointment of the professors by the Government would be a fatal agent of seduction. Within five years after Lord Clare's Act gave the Government the appointment of assistant barristers the county bench was filled with bigots, blockheads, and partisans, and the bar, once the bodyguard of independence, became the pretorians of the Castle. The literary class must not be corrupted by the same method. But these blemishes on the scheme might be removed.

On my part I appealed directly to the Catholic middle class from which I sprang. I bade them remember that early and systematic training was among the most precious of the advantages which we had lost with the loss of a national existence. It was the basis of all practical success in life; and in this training—whether scholastic, social, or professional—we were behind nearly every civilised nation. After centuries in which the education of Catholics had been prohibited as a crime, or contemptuously tolerated but never fostered, the English minister offered us a system of large scope fettered by injurious restrictions and conditions. What was it fit we should do with it? What we were clearly not to do with it was to reject it with hatred and clamour. Of all races the Celts most needed and most profited by discipline; and the penalty we were paying for the want of it was of a very practical kind. While trained and educated Scotchmen were scattered over the world, administering its offices of trust and emolument "from Indus to the Pole," our poor exiles were sweating under its heaviest burthens and stooping to its meanest offices. Our plain duty was to strive that the objectionable provisions of the bill should be amended. As respects the objection of non-residence, non-residence was the practice in most of the Catholic colleges on the continent, and the dangers it threatened could be guarded against by a system of licensed lodging-houses under the superintendence of deans appointed by the ordinary. Another objection was well-founded—there must be two professors of history. The Middle Ages, "the Reformation," the Revolution, were fields of inquiry where concurrence was impossible. But our duty was to amend, not to reject, the scheme.

The members of the Association who held these views were not confined to the Young Ireland section. Several conspicuous men who adhered to O'Connell in the subsequent disruption of the body, and several who retired from public life rather than take sides in that unhappy contest, were eager that the bill might be rendered acceptable. A statement of their views was prepared, embodying a positive pledge to oppose any settlement which did not provide amply for religious education, and was privately presented to O'Connell in the hope of stopping further debate in public. For a moment it seemed probable that this end would be attained. At a meeting of the Association following the one just described, O'Connell stated that it was not his intention to express any opinion on the Education Bill upon that occasion; a meeting of the Catholic bishops would be held during the week, and he would accept and adhere to whatever decision they might arrive at respecting the religious portion of the measure.

O'Brien was absent from these debates, perhaps intentionally, for he shrank with wise forbearance from any contest with O'Connell. But a man cannot long escape the responsibilities of his position. Davis kept him acquainted with the proceedings in committee and urged him to resume his place. "I implore of you," he said, "to come to town before Saturday. If this difficulty be got over, we have little to fear in future."[1]

---

[1] Cahermoyle Correspondence.—Although O'Brien was in intimate relations with several of the Young Irelanders, he belonged at this time as little to their section as to the other. He aimed to maintain a complete neutrality, doubtless with a view to intervene from time to time more effectually in the common interest. But friendly critics were of opinion that he was sometimes more careful of his personal dignity than became a leader, who must be content to run risks. At this time he sent a letter to the committee respecting the colleges. Davis moved that it should be read at the next public meeting, but O'Connell took violent exception to this course—though why O'Brien should not be heard on a topic which Mr John O'Connell felt free to debate is difficult to conceive. To avert a catastrophe Davis and O'Loghlen assumed the

The return of O'Brien, and in a much larger degree the decision of the bishops, were awaited as decisive factors in the contest. The conference of the Catholic bishops had a result creditable to their sense and moderation. They resolved to accept the bill, provided certain amendments were made to protect the faith and morals of Catholic students; but failing these amendments to reject it. The amendments were neither exacting nor inordinate. They claimed that a fair proportion of the professors should be Catholics, whose moral conduct was vouched for by their respective prelates. That a Board of Trustees, of whom the bishops of the province where the college was established should be members, would be entitled to remove any officer convicted of an attempt to tamper with faith or morals; and that a Catholic chaplain should be appointed to each college to superintend the religious instruction of the Catholic students. If these concessions were not made the measure would be dangerous and inadmissible.

The supporters of the measure saw with delight that the bishops accepted the principle of mixed education, provided there were adequate provisions against proselytism; and for such provisions they were all ready to contend. Public meetings of Catholic and Protestant gentlemen and clergymen in Cork, Limerick, and Galway also approved of the bill, subject to certain amendments. The Catholics had not the least desire to see education divorced from religious sentiment and religious obligations; they would have been well content in a Catholic country to have made the Catholic Church the chief teacher, but they were alarmed at the risk of their children running the race of life weighted with the burthens which they had themselves endured. The question seemed in a fair way of being settled. But O'Connell and Mr John O'Connell, though they had promised to accept the decision of the bishops, had gone too far to follow moderate counsels; they seemed to regard their personal authority and influence as depending on the defeat of the measure.

At the subsequent meeting of the Association, Smith O'Brien made a speech designed to promote peace. Ireland, he said, was a religious

---

responsibility of postponing the letter to another day, and this exercise of discretion offended O'Brien more, I think, than was just or reasonable. Davis excused himself with good temper, "I should not have consented to the holding over of your letter, but that had it been read yesterday it would have led to a violent debate which would almost necessarily have broken up the Association. There was no second opinion as to the danger. Under such a peril I and others who concurred in your views acted as we did, though certainly I felt that our doing so might cause you much annoyance, and would be a very great liberty—one that I at least shall never take again."

nation, and he honoured the solicitude which had been exhibited by Catholics to secure religious education. He saw no difficulty, however, in engrafting on the Government plan some adequate provision for this purpose. He concurred generally in the fairness of the claims made by the Bishops, and differed from his friend Mr John O'Connell in his opinion that Catholics and Protestants should have separate colleges. It was extremely desirable that there should be united education in order that young men should cherish those friendly associations in youth which subdue the animosities of manhood.[1]

O'Connell, who followed, spoke for two hours. He came there, he said, to denounce the bill from one end to the other. If he were silent heretofore or spoke only his individual opinion, now, as a Catholic, and for the Catholics of Ireland, he unhesitatingly and entirely condemned this execrable measure.

"A more nefarious attempt at profligacy and corruption never disgraced any minister. The *Evening Post* had recently published an anonymous letter in defence of it, which he knew to be the production of a Catholic clergyman; and in this publication the writer said he had before him the private letter of a Cabinet Minister on the subject, written in August 1844. In August 1844 the State prisoners were suffering unjust captivity, and at that time a Cabinet Minister was writing to a Catholic clergyman in Dublin to win the Catholic clergy to support an Administration which had employed a packed jury and prejudiced judges to obtain their conviction! But the resolution of the bishops defeated their chance of success. The bishops had declared the system as proposed would be dangerous to the faith and morals of Catholic pupils. Was he to be blamed, then, or was the member for Kilkenny to be blamed, for their early resistance to it? Would one independent man be appointed to a professorship under the measure? Political and religious renegadism would be the highest qualification for office. But such a measure would not be accepted. He offered Sir Robert Peel his congratulations upon his success in this experiment! He rejoiced to believe that all symptoms of division and dissension in the Association were at an end. All were agreed in condemning the ministerial measure in its present shape; they were all ready to accept a bill based upon just and tolerant principles, and founded on fair and reasonable terms."

The debate was continued by Mr John O'Connell, who denied that the memorial of the bishops favoured mixed education; and Mr M. J. Barry, who said he was utterly indifferent by what name it was called, but he was in favour of such a system as the memorial of the bishops contemplated, in which ample provision would be made for religious education, and ample guarantees for faith and morals, but where Protestants and Catholics would grow up together in mutual friendliness and confidence.

Up to this point, a question full of difficulty had been debated with

---

[1] Repeal Association, May 26th.

mutual courtesy and forbearance. But the controversy was not destined so to end. There was hanging about the Association and the press at that time a young man named Conway, a person of good ability and loose principles, ready of speech and of singular self-possession, but whose want of conduct had robbed him of all personal weight. He had spoken occasionally in Conciliation Hall, and written occasionally in the national journals, and had obtained all the success which is awarded to cleverness without character. It is too little to say that he had won confidence from nobody; he belonged to a class to whom confidence is never given. On political questions his brain, when not disordered by excesses, made him worth listening to, but on questions of morals or ethics his pretending to have any conviction would have been regarded by those who knew him as an offensive jest. He was by birth and education a Catholic, but the loose hold his professed creed had upon him was illustrated a few years later by his accepting the bounty of a Proselytising Association to profess himself a convert to Protestantism. This person stepped forward to do work which a man of character would have shrunk from—which Mr John O'Connell was afraid to undertake, except in secret whispers and private correspondence—to suggest that Davis, Dillon, and their associates were favourable to the measure because they were indifferent to religion. Whether he was an agent or a volunteer was somewhat doubtful at the time; but it is possible he was a volunteer, for he was labouring under a recent personal grievance. Four or five weeks earlier he had presented himself as a candidate at the Eighty-two Club, and had been rejected. He assumed, rightly enough, I daresay, that the Young Irelanders had voted against him; and he privately appealed to O'Brien to do him justice, reminding him that he was "a Clare man with a cross of Tipperary";[1] but as he got no redress he was ripe for mischief. He broke into the debate by announcing that he was entrusted with a contribution to the Repeal funds from Armagh.

"More than a thousand years had passed over since the apostle of Irish Christianity had planted the standard of the cross on the heights of pagan Armagh. He believed St Patrick was a Roman Catholic; some claimed him as a Protestant; he had once heard him described as a Presbyterian; but at anyrate he was no friend of masked infidelity, of mixed education. His learned friend who preceded him was for the bill, and against the bill; there was an imbecility in his speech characteristic of his party and his principles; a party which the strong hand of O'Connell must not exterminate, but warn. On an essential point Mr Barry declared himself 'utterly indifferent.' Utterly indifferent! What a sentiment for a Catholic! Ireland was not indifferent

[1] Letter to Smith O'Brien dated 28th April 1845.—Cahermoyle Correspondence.

T. F. CONWAY.

Two sketches by
HENRY MACMANUS, R.H.A.

RICHARD BARRETT.

to the memorials which his own relative left behind him in the Church of God. Such a reputation as he had won was worth far more than the temporary applause of a coterie or the cheers of a baffled faction. The sentiment triumphant in the meeting that day was a sentiment common to all Ireland. The Calvinist or Episcopalian of the North, the Unitarian, the Sectaries, every man who had any faith in Christianity, was resolved that it should neither be robbed or thieved by a faction half acquainted with the principles they put forward, and not at all comprehending the Irish character or the Irish heart. Were his audience prepared to yield up old discord or sympathies to the theories of Young Ireland? As a Catholic and as an Irishman, while he was ready to meet his Protestant friends upon an equal platform, he would resent any attempt at ascendancy, whether it came from honest Protestants or honest professing Catholics."

This tipsy rhodomontade would have been forgotten as soon as it was uttered if O'Connell had not raised it into importance by taking Mr Conway under his patronage. Mr Doheny describes him as waving his cap repeatedly over his head during its delivery and cheering vociferously.[1] With something of the habitual ingratitude of sovereigns and dictators, he forgot the most substantial services in a moment of wrath; and the *nisi prius* advocate of forty years' experience was neither wanting in devices to embarrass his opponents nor too scrupulous in using them. Davis, who followed Mr Conway, glanced good-humouredly at the grotesque contrast between the man and the speech by calling him his "very Catholic friend." O'Connell interrupted him to ask if it was a crime to be a Catholic, and suggested that Davis was sneering at Catholics! Fence of this sort had perhaps been successful in former conflicts, and against a different class of antagonists, but directed against a man like Thomas Davis, in the presence of those to whom his life and labours were familiar, who loved him more than their own kith and kin, it proved a perilous mistake.. As the contest was a turning-point in the national movement, it is fit that it should be set out in detail.

"I have not," Davis said on rising, "more than a few words to say in reply to the useful, judicious, and spirited speech of my old college friend, my Catholic friend, my very Catholic friend, Mr Conway.

"Mr O'CONNELL: It is no crime to be a Catholic, I hope.

"Mr DAVIS: No, surely no, for——

"Mr O'CONNELL: The sneer with which you used the word would lead to the inference.

"Mr DAVIS: No, sir; no. My best friends, my nearest friends, my truest friends, are Catholics. I was brought up in a mixed seminary, where I learned to know, and, knowing, to love, my Catholic countrymen, a love that shall not be disturbed by these casual and unhappy dissensions. Disunion, alas, destroyed our country for centuries. Men of Ireland, shall it destroy it again? Will you take the boys of Ireland in their earliest youth

---

[1] Doheny's "Felon's Track." "Mr O'Connell took off his cap, waved it repeatedly over his head, and cheered vociferously" (p. 43).

and deepen the difference between them? Will you sedulously exclude them from knowing the virtues, the genius, the spirit, the affections of each other? If you do you will vainly hope that they who were carefully separated in youth will be united in manhood and stand together for their country. Sir, I rise to express my strong approval of the memorial of the Catholic bishops. That memorial contains four propositions, and to every one of them I yield my cordial concurrence. The first of these propositions demands that a 'fair proportion' of the professors and office-bearers in the new colleges shall be members of the Roman Catholic Church. That is a just and reasonable demand. Mark the words, a 'fair proportion,' not the entire, but 'a proportion'; meaning beyond doubt—meaning beyond reasonable dispute—that the remainder should be Protestants. That, sir, is mixed instruction. The same clause demands, too, that the bishops of each province shall be members of the governing board. Note the words 'of which,' not exclusively composing the board, but 'of which' the Roman Catholic Bishops shall be members. That, sir, is mixed management. The second clause is marked by the same care of Catholic rights, and the same adoption, by necessary inference, of mixed education. It demands that in some specified branches the Roman Catholic students shall be taught by Roman Catholic professors—the unmistakable meaning of this demand is for separate chairs in a mixed college. Separate chairs for the teaching of those subjects which cannot be taught by the professors of one creed without probable offence or injustice to the creed of others. I say that is a just demand. I fully concur also in the purpose of the third proposition in this memorial, which suggests that 'if any president, vice-president, professor, or office-bearer shall be convicted before the Board of Trustees of attempting to undermine the faith or injure the morals of any student, he shall be immediately removed from his office by the same board'—that is, by the board of which the Roman Catholic Prelates are to form a part. And now, sir, I come to the last proposition. 'That as it is not contemplated that the students shall be provided with lodgings in the new colleges, there shall be Roman Catholic chaplains to superintend the moral and religious instruction of the Roman Catholic students.' I say that such a provision is most just and most necessary. I say now, what I said before on this day fortnight, I denounce this bill for not containing such a provision.

"Mr O'CONNELL: You praised the bill.

"Mr DAVIS: I praised the bill on certain grounds, and on these grounds I praise it now, and will praise it again. The proposal runs that the appointment of each chaplain, with a suitable salary, shall be made on the recommendation of the Roman Catholic bishop in the diocese in which the college is situate, and that the same prelate shall have full power and authority to remove such Roman Catholic chaplain from his situation. 'Signed, Daniel Murray, chairman.' There could be no fitter name to authenticate that document. Dr Murray carries into the academical colleges the same principles that regulate the National Board, of which he is one of the most learned, esteemed, and honoured governors."

Mr Davis concluded his brief, persuasive, statement in these terms:—

"I offer the tribute of my sincere respect to that memorial, to the principles on which it is founded, and to the reasonings—for I have heard precisely what they were—which induced the bishops to adopt it. I denounce the bill as containing no provision for the religious discipline of

THE PROVINCIAL COLLEGES.

the boys taken away from the paternal shelter. Beyond all, I denounce the bill for giving the Government a right to appoint and dismiss professors, a right to corrupt and intimidate. For these reasons, I and those who think with me are prepared to give this bill in its present shape an unflinching opposition, and I sit down repeating my cordial adherence to this memorial."

Nothwithstanding the opposition of O'Connell, Davis's speech was received with great favour by the Association. The character of the man, the lucidity of his statement, and the singleness of purpose with which he was moved, made a manifest impression. O'Connell, who had already spoken for two hours, thought it necessary to reply to him, and he clutched at the weapon heretofore abandoned to hands like those of Mr Conway.

"One point," he exclaimed, "Mr Davis omitted altogether. He did not read the resolution adopted at the meeting of the prelates, wherein they declared that they felt themselves, anxious as they were to extend the advantages of education, bound to withhold their approbation from the proposed system, as they deemed it dangerous to the faith and morals of the Catholic people. The system was met with the unequivocal and unanimous condemnation of the venerated and esteemed body. The principle of the bill has been lauded by Mr Davis, and was advocated in a newspaper professing to be the organ of the Roman Catholic people of this country, but which I emphatically pronounce to be no such thing. The section of politicians styling themselves the Young Ireland Party, anxious to rule the destinies of this country, start up and support this measure. There is no such party as that styled 'Young Ireland.' There may be a few individuals who take that denomination on themselves. I am for Old Ireland. 'Tis time that this delusion should be put an end to. Young Ireland may play what pranks they please. I do not envy them the name they rejoice in. I shall stand by Old Ireland; and I have some slight notion that Old Ireland will stand by me."

When O'Connell sat down consternation was universal; he had commenced a war in which either by success or failure he would bring ruin to the national cause. Smith O'Brien and Henry Grattan, who were sitting near him, probably remonstrated, for in a few minutes he rose again to withdraw the nickname of "Young Ireland" as he understood it was disclaimed by those to whom it was applied. Davis immediately rejoined that he was glad to get rid of the assumption that there were factions in the Association. He never knew any other feeling among his friends, except in the momentary heat of passion, but that they were bound to work together for Irish nationality. They were bound, among other motives, by a strong affection toward Daniel O'Connell; a feeling which he himself had habitually expressed in his private correspondence with his dearest and closest friends.

At this point the strong self-restrained man paused from emotion, and broke into irrepressible tears. He was habitually neither emotional nor demonstrative, but he had been in a state of nervous anxiety for hours ; the cause for which he had laboured so long and sacrificed so much was in peril on both hands. The Association might be broken up by a conflict with O'Connell, or it might endure a worse fate if it became despicable by suppressing convictions of public duty at his dictation. With these fears were mixed perhaps the recollection of the generous forbearance from blame and the promptitude to praise which marked his own relations to O'Connell, and the painful contrast with these sentiments presented by the scene he had just witnessed. He shed tears from the strong passion of a strong man. The leaders of the Commons of England, the venerable Coke, John Pym, and Sir John Eliot, men of iron will, wept when Charles I. extinguished the hope of an understanding between the people and the Crown. Tears of wounded sensibility choked the utterance of Fox when Burke publicly renounced his friendship. Both the public and the private motives united to assail the sensibility of Davis.

O'Connell, whose instincts were generous and cordial, and who was only suspicious from training and violent by set purpose, immediately interposed with warm expressions of goodwill. He had never felt more gratified than by this evidence of regard. If Mr Davis were overcome, it overcame him also ; he thanked him cordially, and tendered him his hand. The Association applauded their reconciliation with enthusiasm. After this episode Davis resumed :—

"He and his friends, in their anxiety to co-operate with O'Connell, had often sacrificed their own predilections, and never opposed him except when they were convinced in conscience that it was a duty to do so. He trusted their disagreement would leave no sting behind. If there had been any harshness of feeling, if any person had made use of private influence to foster dissension and to misrepresent them to each other, he would forgive it, if the offence were not repeated. He would sit down with a prayer to Almighty God that the people of this country and the leaders of the people might continue united in the pursuit of liberty, in which they were so often defeated before at the moment of its apparent fruition ; and with a supplication to God that they might not be defeated again."

These were almost the last words of counsel Thomas Davis uttered, face to face with the people whom he loved so truly and served so well.

This contest not only produced a painful impression at the moment, but left behind poisonous seeds of distrust and division. It probably had still more disastrous results too subtle to be traced. Before three months elapsed the younger and more hopeful nature was extinguished in death. Before two years the historic leader was carried to his grave, having outlived in the interval the power and popularity upon which he relied so proudly for dominating in this contest. Davis's death has been referred to this transaction as one of its proximate causes; but this is a mistake. He bore away a wound which bled inwardly, but his nature was too robust to sink under it. He had the strongest incitement to live in the desire to carry his cause to success, and in the recently plighted love of one who possessed all his affections.

The reflex action of that encounter on O'Connell's influence was seriously detrimental at the moment, and perhaps finally destructive. A burning sense of wrong was excited by the foul blow struck at Davis. It made men more suspicious of the justice of O'Connell's criticism and readier to canvass his motives. The more thoughtful knew that, of the two combatants, Ireland could least spare the one of whom she knew next to nothing. The popular organisation was mainly the work of O'Connell, but the growth of national opinion among the middle class, the passionate adherence of the new generation to its aims, the respect which it had gained among opponents for breadth and sincerity, the practical projects on which it was employed, and the Protestant recruits it had won, were attributable in a far larger degree to Davis. They were persuaded that another O'Connell, distant as might be his coming, would arise before another Davis. One was a leader credited by the world, not only with the prodigious work which he actually performed, but with much that was done by others. He was living in the midst of his private friends; his nearest relatives were his agents and associates. He received an income from the people far beyond the official salary of the President of the American Republic, or of the Prime Minister of any constitutional kingdom in Europe; and he controlled an expenditure which approximated to the civil list of European sovereigns. In his youth he had tasted the supreme joy of self-sacrifice for the cause he loved, but he had long been an uncrowned king in authority and inviolability, and had come to regard the interest of his dynasty and the interest of the nation as necessarily identical, and to treat dissent as treason. The other, in becoming a Repealer, had separated in action from his family and from many of his familiar friends, and had relinquished the chance of success in his profession. He employed his splendid abilities in the public cause without reward and almost without recognition. He had never accepted so much as a postage stamp from the Repeal funds, or from any other public source, except the legitimate payment of his work as a journalist. While O'Connell's reputation was like a great river, fed by many streams which were lost in the current they helped to swell, Davis was only known, outside the circle of his friends, by adversaries who industriously disparaged him. He was content to be nothing in the common view, to see other men credited with his work ; and he would have applauded and blessed any human being, friend or enemy, who could have carried the Irish cause to success.

One of the greatest resources at O'Connell's command, had he been able and willing to use it, was the band of young men who stood, as one of them sang "like sheathéd swords around him," and now it seemed to sober spectators that co-operation between them was at an end. But if this calamity came the young men were resolved it should not come by any fault of theirs. In the next *Nation* the final reconciliation was dwelt upon more than the original dispute, and the people were admonished not to be alarmed by temporary controversies. Exact concurrence on public questions was only to be found among the ignorant and slavish; but, on the other hand, it had been the custom of the committee to prevent discussion in public on questions where differences were serious, and the maintenance of this rule was essential to the existence of the Association.

For a time there was a settled truce. At the next meeting O'Connell maintained complete silence on the bill, and his example was followed on all sides. In the course of the week he left town to attend Repeal demonstrations in the South, and an interval seemed to be secured to heal the recent scars. But Mr John O'Connell, who remained, apparently interpreted the truce to mean that his opponents were to be silent, but that his tongue was to be unchecked. He proceeded as if his aim from the beginning had been to make the continuance of Davis and his friends in the Association impossible ; and writing a generation later, after having conversed on the subject many times with men on both sides of the controversy, I believe that such was indeed his aim. At the next meeting he announced from the general committee a petition against vesting the appointment of professors in the Government, reminded the Association that points upon which there was a difference of opinion ought to be avoided ; and then proceeded to reiterate all his original objections in a speech of two hours' duration, fortifying them by letters from clergymen who denounced the measure as infidel. For the support which Protestant Nationalists gave the bill he accounted with charming simplicity. It was no doubt with an ultimate view to proselytism. He was sure they would use no unworthy means to injure the Catholic faith, but, being conscientious Protestants, it was natural to suppose that anything which would draw adherents away from it would meet their sanction and approval.

O'Brien warmly denied any such wish or purpose, and Henry Grattan deprecated the introduction of topics which gave the discussion in Conciliation Hall a polemical character. A more formidable and dangerous critic was looking on at these transactions. A country clergyman, unknown to his audience, for he was attending the Association for the first time, but of a scholarly and cultivated mien which arrested the eye, got up and declared that it had been his intention to dissent from some of the opinions expressed by Mr John O'Connell, but that gentleman had privately requested him to desist, and as it was a first request he could not think of refusing it. The priest who was silenced on this occasion often afterwards spoke with trenchant emphasis on the policy and practice of Conciliation Hall, for this stranger was Father John Kenyon, of Templederry.

When the committee re-assembled they insisted on the truce being binding on all, and at the succeeding meeting of the Association O'Neil Daunt, who was in the chair, announced that an understanding had been arrived at not to discuss the details of the "College Bill" in the absence of O'Connell. But the decision came too late; a feeling of foul play and want of faith had been created which it was impossible to eradicate.[1]

---

[1] A totally unexpected occurrence is seldom fairly judged at the moment, and Davis's generous sensibility pained and wounded some of his friends. They thought he had lowered himself, and their affection for him made them angry. MacNevin wrote to O'Brien that rather than submit to the tyranny over individual opinion exercised in this controversy he would retire from public life. "As for Davis, I know not what to say—'exit Tilburina in tears.' What was there in the vulgar assault made on himself and his friends to authorise these pearly drops or this quivering emotion?" (Cahermoyle Correspondence.)

Denny Lane, writing to Davis himself, implied the same sort of objection "Your conduct at the Hall," he said, "except 'the tears' was unimpeachable. The attack on you was altogether unexpected—and undeserved. You did nothing to provoke a collision, the only thing I can find fault with was your manner in the Committee to O'Connell, which I was informed of by a person who could scarcely be mistaken in a matter of the kind. This was the real cause of the split, it made O'Connell anxious to abuse you if he could. He has many faults, but we must take him as he is—he is the *withe* that binds together the bundle of twigs . . ." (Davis Papers.)

And for myself, I cannot remember without a sting of shame, that when I next met my friend I saluted him by reciting in a bantering tone the burden of a song in the "Spirit of the Nation"—
"We must not weep for you, dear land,
We must not weep for you!"
We were thinking too much of the humiliation of our comrade. Davis was overwhelmed by the risk to the public cause.

The weekly censor, who has always taken so liberal and humane a view of Irish affairs, interposed with a letter from Mr Punch (of *Punch*) to Mr Davis (of the *Nation*), in which the latter was graciously assured that since Marat there had not been so objectionable a person; and turned into contemptuous ridicule for presuming to maintain his conviction against Mr O'Connell. The writer of the homily was understood to be Mr Thackeray.

CHAPTER VIII

THE OPPOSITION TO THE BILL.

An agreement was come to in the Association that O'Connell and Smith O'Brien should attend the House of Commons to demand amendments in the "Colleges Bill." It seems probable that amendments, substantially yielding the chief points insisted upon in the bishops' memorial, might have been obtained. With our subsequent knowledge of Sir Robert Peel's career, it is safe to assume that he was willing to make as large concessions as the prejudices of his supporters would permit. In the previous session he had given significant evidence of his good dispositions by making, through the Executive, a concession which the House of Commons could scarcely have been induced to sanction. His "Charitable Bequests Act" provided that when it was necessary to determine who was the actual holder of any Catholic benefice to which a bequest was made, the determination should be entrusted exclusively to the Catholic bishops and Catholic laymen among the Commissioners. It was passionately objected by certain Catholic theologians that this provision interfered with the rights of the diocesan, to whom the decision canonically belongs. To meet this objection the Irish Attorney-General was instructed to frame a regulation under which the Commission were required to accept the report of the diocesan as final evidence of the fact; and this concessionary regulation was adopted. The "Maynooth Act" had afterwards given complete satisfaction by its scrupulous respect for Catholic feeling, and there was no reason to doubt that he would bring the same temper to the present measure, which was framed with the same object, of conciliating the Irish people. But his difficulties with his supporters were greatly increased by the unmeasured censure to which the bill had been subjected. If it were predetermined to reject it, unmeasured censure was permissible; but if amendments were contemplated, it was an obvious rule of prudence to insist only on such concessions as it might be possible to carry through Parliament, and not to ask them in terms which should increase the difficulty of obtaining them.

During this critical interval Davis laboured without stint to preserve peace and to save the national cause.

"O'Connell goes over [to London] to-night [Sunday, 15th June]"—he wrote to O'Brien, already in London—"and so much the better. The effort of the Repeal members (to amend the bill) should be made with all their force. It is also desirable that he should be removed for a while from the persons who suggest suspicions, alarm his Catholic feelings, and stimulate his large but vehement soul. 'Tis marvellous what evil influence such little creatures can exercise over so great a mind. We had a most serious affair in Committee yesterday, in which all Protestants who interfered in the education question were denounced in the strongest courteous language by O'Connell and his son, and by other parties in a rougher fashion."

Some impatient spirits, persuaded that a conspiracy to drive them out was formed, wished to anticipate it by a secession, but against this course Davis stood firm. Two days later he again wrote to O'Brien.[1]

"O'Loghlen [Sir Colman] and all whom I have consulted are firm against secession. O'Loghlen proposes, and I agree with him fully, that if O'Connell on his return should force the question on Conciliation Hall, an amendment should be moved that the introduction of such a question, against the wish of a numerous and respectable portion of the Committee, is contrary to the principles of the Association and likely to injure the cause of Repeal. A steady elaborate discussion for a number of days would end in the withdrawal of the motion and amendment, or in rendering the motion, if carried, powerless. An explanation would follow, and—the cause would still be safe. Secession would give Ireland up without a contest to the bigots ; it would besides be criminal and hardly honourable to secede, as if, forsooth, we had joined a retinue, not a free league, and could take up our hats and abandon the cause on receiving offence or injustice. . . . Once this peril is over all will be safe."

Much as he desired a good measure he knew it might be bought too dearly. A few days later he says, "I have been, and am, doing all in my power to prevent the injurious results of the differences on the "Colleges Bill," and have been fortunate enough to put an end to a discussion in Committee which was tending fast to mischief. In my mind any advantages to be derived from the bill are not worth even a moment's division amongst us."[2]

John O'Connell's design, though necessarily suspected from the incidents all pointing in one direction, was only suspected. But Davis could no longer shut out of his calculations the possibility of resolutions being proposed to which he and his friends must refuse their assent.

---
[1] Cahermoyle Correspondence, June 17th.
[2] Cahermoyle Correspondence, June 21st.

"I will not interfere again till an attempt be made to pledge the Association to evil resolutions. If the O'Connells wish, they can ruin the agitation (not the country) in spite of anyone. Between unaccounted funds, bigotry, billingsgate, Tom Steel missions, crude and contradictory dogmas, and unrelieved stupidity, any cause and any system could be ruined. America too, from whence arose 'the cloud in the west' which alarmed Peel, has been deeply offended, and but for the *Nation* there would not now be one Repeal club in America. Still we have a sincere and numerous people, a rising literature, an increasing staff of young, honest, trained men, Peel's splitting policy [a policy which split up the Tories], the chance of war, the chance of the Orangemen, and a great, though now misused, organisation; and, perhaps, next autumn a rally may be made. It will require forethought, close union, indifference to personal attack, and firm measures. At this moment the attempt would utterly fail; but parties may be brought down to reason by the next four months. Again, I tell you, you have no notion of the loss sustained by John O'Connell's course. A dogged temper and a point of honour induce me to remain in the Association at every sort of sacrifice, and will keep me there while there is a chance, even a remote one, of doing good in it." [1]

O'Brien replied in terms very characteristic of the man. He suspected that he, and those who shared his opinions, had been placed in a false position when they promised such unmeasured resistance, unless certain provisions of the bill were altered; but at all hazards they must be faithful to their promise.

"It is quite true that the tone taken by John O'Connell has done infinite mischief, and upon this point I have not concealed my opinion from him. But I am not disposed on that account to despond. The care which ought to be taken by the friends of mixed education with regard to the matter should not be less firm because we do not agree with the sentiments which he has put forward. We have declared that we would repudiate the College Scheme unless it gave security to religious men of all parties that religion should not be excluded wholly from these institutions—and unless public liberty should be protected from the corrupt influences of such extensive Government patronage. Whilst therefore no practical difference now arises between us and the separate educationists, we are, in my opinion, bound to sustain them in their opposition on those grounds on which we have ourselves (whether wisely or not is not now the question) proclaimed our opposition to the measure."

Davis wrote to Lane with a completer unreserve than to O'Brien. At the outset he said :—

"Should the Catholic bishops go strongly against mixed education, or should Government persist in claiming the nomination and dismissal of the professors, the plan must fail. The latter danger is the greater, as, by what

---

[1] Cahermoyle Correspondence, June 26th.

I hear, the best of the bishops are with us. Should the plan be freed from Government despotism, and be carried out, we shall have first a home provision for a literary and scientific class; second, security for educated middle and upper classes in four or five years; third, we shall have got over the last subject, short of fighting, which could break up the party. Our after course will have only front foes, and I don't care for them."

Referring to Lane's complaint that he had been too brusque in his manner of resisting opposition in Committee, he—in the language of pleading—" confessed and avoided " :—

" In Committee (which I find more powerful than you suppose) J. O'C. has been severely lectured by O'Brien and reproved by all the Catholic bar. In truth, Clements, O'Dowd, Costello, Drs Nagle and Murphy, are the only supporters of separate education among us now, for Browne is 'on mission,' and Conway is below par. What you say of my general manner is, I fear, quite true. I lose patience with the lying, ignorant, and lazy clan who surround O'C. Indeed I have to maintain a perpetual struggle to prevent myself from quitting politics in absolute scorn ; but my heart melts when I think it possible for a union of brave, patient men to lift up the country, in more ways than politics. But till the 'scene' in Conciliation Hall, O'C. and I were most courteous in manner to each other, though frequently opposed in opinion. By the way, O'C. is not sincere for separate education. In the absence of the O'C.s last autumn, O'Neil Daunt and I prepared, by order of the Committee, resolutions positively for mixed education. They were passed unanimously by both Committees—O'Brien in the chair. On Johnny's first appearance in the Committee they were read to him, and he gave them a flat negative, saying he wished Roman Catholic education to be under the Jesuits. In half an hour afterwards, O'Connell came in, heard them, and said, ' I have been for years and still am an advocate for mixed education.' He then went on to say that it would be right to consult the bishops. In a few days after he recanted this opinion, under (we have no doubt) Johnny's influence. I never intended to notice the attack in the *Pilot*, though it and the *Newry Examiner* (edited by Conway) keep constantly at me and the *Nation*. The regard for O'B. is all assumed, as I could prove to you. He was within an ace of leaving the Hall on Monday during Johnny's speech."

Meantime the two parties to the controversy were busy, through the Press and public meetings, promoting their respective views in a legitimate manner. The Archbishop of Tuam, in a letter to Sir Robert Peel, utterly condemned the bill. On the other side a petition was prepared in Dublin, and signed by the most conspicuous citizens outside the Tory party, giving it a conditional support. The petitioners admitted that the proposal to educate students of different creeds together, and to leave open the honours and emoluments to persons of all religious denominations, would tend to promote charity and extinguish religious feuds in Ireland. But the measure was defective in not providing religious instruction for youth removed from the care of their parents, and in giving the selection and control of the professors to the Crown.[1] Among the petitioners were the Young Irelanders who were already committed to the principles it advocated, and a few professional men who afterwards became officers of the colleges, and may possibly have had an interested motive even at this stage. But they included others whose names furnished significant evidence that the feeling in favour of the measure among the educated class was deep and general. In the final disruption of the Association, a year later, the barristers who took part with O'Connell were James O'Hea, Francis Brady, Robert Mullin, Robert Ferguson, Joseph Henry Dunne, and William Gernon, and all these were among the petitioners. So likewise were two other barristers, afterwards selected by the Catholic bishops to be professors of the Catholic University, John O'Hagan and D. F. M'Carthy; and a considerable number of Catholic gentlemen who were subsequently chosen to represent Catholic constituencies in Parliament, among whom were Thomas O'Hagan, Horace Fitzgerald, Robert Potter, W. H. Cogan, Denis Caulfield Heron, Sir Colman O'Loghlen, Sir Dominic Corrigan, and Sir Timothy O'Brien.

The question for which O'Connell was contending was not separate education; that point he was still willing to yield. In a private note to the Archbishop of Tuam early in the contest he said: "It is possible, though not very probable, that the appointment of professors to instruct the Catholic youth may be given to the Catholic prelates, and in that case, though the principle of exclusive Catholic education may not apply, yet I should think there would be no objection to Protestants attending the classes if all the professors were nominated by the canonical authorities of the Catholic Church."[2] Before leaving for the House of Commons he advised the same prelate, who was the leader of the party of resistance among the bishops, to yield nothing of their demands.[3] "If the prelates take and continue a high, firm, and unani-

---

[1] For petition and signatures see *Nation*, June 14th. Regarding this petition, Davis wrote to Lane: "I am glad you like my petition. If anything could change my mixed feeling of admiration and censure of O'Connell into genuine hostility, it would be the vicious adulation and lying incentives proffered to him by the little, stupid, mercenary devils about him, and his patronage of the vilest and weakest of them. They are trying to drive O'Brien, myself, and others to Secession, hoping to have the uncensured handling of public money with their gluey claws; but they shall be disappointed and beaten. . . . You would like Dublin much better than when last here."—Davis to Lane.

[2] Private letter to Dr MacHale, dated 19th Feb. '45, published in Miss Cusack's "Life of the Liberator."

[3] Published in Miss Cusack's "Life of the Liberator." The letter was dated 21st June '45.

mous tone," he said, "the ministry will yield. Believe me, they are ready to yield; you have everything in your own power." That a politician who had long taught his countrymen that Parliament would yield nothing to Irish claims, should have given such counsel would be marvellous, if we did not know that his great intellect was paralysed, and that to hinder the Tories and help the Whigs had been his policy for a decade. The result of his counsel was that no arrangement was arrived at. The bishops had a second meeting, when a new petition was prepared but rejected, and they separated without coming to any decision. The Government made several concessions, and refused several. With respect to the nomination of professors, the State must appoint in the first instance that the proportion among the Churches might be fairly regulated, but they were willing to provide that after an experiment of three years Parliament should review the system and adopt any preferable one. To protect the morals of students, the lodging-houses would receive licenses annually from the visitors, which might be revoked by the same authority. The Board of Works would be empowered to lend money for the purpose of erecting halls where the students might receive religious instruction according to the tenets of their Church, and the principals of those halls would be appointed by the visitors. A salary would not be granted to those officers, as religious endowment was contrary to the principles of the bill, but the Government were persuaded that wealthy Catholics and Protestants would contribute the necessary salary. In selecting the visitors, the heads of the religious bodies in the districts where the college was placed would be included.

After a week's attendance in Parliament O'Connell and Mr John O'Connell returned to Ireland and announced that they had failed to effect any amendment, and that the bill was hopelessly bad. It passed into law, however, and the Catholic Primate announced his intention of giving it a fair trial,[1] and the Bishops in Cork, Galway, and Belfast, where the new colleges were placed, took the same course. A little later, when a change of Government took place, the new administration consulted Dr Crolly and Dr Murray, and attended scrupulously, it is affirmed, to every suggestion they made for securing the religious instruction and moral conduct of the Catholic students.[2] They were prepared to revise the statutes of the colleges on the same instigation. But the majority of the bishops held aloof, and in time they all with-

[1] Public Meeting at Armagh.
[2] Lord Dalling's "Life of Lord Palmerston."

drew their support under instructions from the Propaganda. The result has been that during two generations a section of the Catholic youth have been educated in a system disapproved of by their religious superiors; another section have been educated in Trinity College, a purely Protestant foundation; and a large section have been entirely deprived of collegiate training, a calamity perhaps as disastrous as the famine. It is hard to estimate the suffering and humiliation which have attended the generations since launched into life without requisite discipline. Our ancestors fought with their naked breasts against Norman knights locked in iron, and it is at such odds Ireland still sends her young men to fight the battle of life. Among the friends of the measure it may be that some fixed their eyes too exclusively on the gain of rearing students in friendly intercourse, and too little on the danger to faith. But others fixed their eyes too exclusively on victory, and too little on the sacrifice at which it was to be purchased. I have since lived nearly a quarter of a century in a new country, where young mèn flock in quest of fortune, and I have seen troops of bright, intelligent young Irishmen forfeit great opportunities, and fall into inferior positions, because their education had been unpractical and defective. And it was impossible to believe that this calamity might not have been averted, when I saw in that country two universities having none of the provisions on which O'Connell insisted, where the students attend classes together and live where they think fit, without ecclesiastical or academic supervision, where there are no separate professors and no separate class of studies, and where on the council of each university there was a Catholic Archbishop. A fairer and better system than the one accepted in Australia might assuredly have been obtained in Ireland in 1845.

Peel's third measure was still more unfortunate than the second. It was spoiled by the advice of his Irish supporters; so hopeless is it to effect good through agents to whom the right is odious. Lord Stanley proposed a Land Bill which remedied none of the serious evils the Commission had disclosed. It did not recognise in any manner the costly improvements which the tenantry had already created, and it proposed to grant compensation in the future merely for drains and farm buildings; and this compensation was to be claimable only in case of ejectment. By inference it abolished the Tenant Right of the North. Davis prepared a report on the scheme, and strongly advised O'Connell and O'Brien to take up the interest of the northern farmers, and thereby

THE OPPOSITION TO THE BILL. 189

gain their goodwill and finally their co-operation. But before anything was undertaken, the measure, which was received with a shout of disapprobation North and South, was withdrawn. Lord Stanley had not succeeded in legislating on the question; but it is probable that he obtained an insight into the unjust and untenable character of the land system in Ireland, for in after years, when he succeeded to the management of the family property, he solved the difficulty for himself by selling his Irish estates.

At this period Davis proposed, for the first time, to go circuit, and the news was not received by his friends with unanimous assent. Dillon wrote to me :—

"If Davis will not attend two public dinners, I would much rather he would select Sligo than Galway. Tell him I will write to him from Sligo, and as I would say the same things to both of you, that letter will do for you, and you can show him this. I was greatly annoyed at hearing a report that he was going circuit. That, I think, would be altogether ruinous. Everyone would say that he was driven out of politics. I have been thinking that he and you ought to start a penny magazine,[1] and conduct it yourselves, making use of James Duffy to circulate it. If you would join in the speculation I am certain it should necessarily succeed, and it would be a powerful engine. 'It stands upon you' to work against the powerful confederacy that has been formed to crush you, and in your persons everything that is upright and independent in the country. May God defend the right."

On the other hand, Denny Lane approved of the design :—

"I am very glad," he wrote to Davis, "to hear that you are coming down to the Assizes. The going circuit I think more than anything else can make a man acquainted with the provincial mind of Ireland, which is really of much greater proportionate power than the ex-metropolitan mind of any other country. In fact we have no metropolis—neither the court of claret-coloured coats nor that of wigs and gowns is enough to make Dublin anything but a country town. We have no theatre, no periodical literature, no gathering of artists, no great merchants, above all no legislative assembly collecting into a focus every ray of intellect and enterprise in the country. In fact we have nothing of what makes Paris or other capitals the 'governor' of the great engine of a nation."

During the Colleges controversy a project of earlier date was carried out. The State prisoners held a levee in the Rotunda on the anniversary of their imprisonment. In the historic Round-Room, festive with flags and decorations, O'Connell and his late fellow-prisoners, standing on an elevated daïs and surrounded by the *élite* of the national party, received the felicitations of an organised nation. Deputations from the

---

[1] This project of Dillon's, to supplement a costly weekly paper by a penny sheet for the multitude, has since been successfully adopted in Ireland.

great municipalities, from the commissioners and guardians of the lesser towns, from the associated trades, and from the clergy and laity of numerous districts, were presented, thanking them for their past fidelity, and promising to co-operate with them to the end in the struggle for nationality. A pledge proposed by Smith O'Brien and seconded by Henry Grattan was adopted, declaring that the men there assembled (who were in effect a National Convention) would never cease seeking the Repeal of the Union by all peaceful, moral, and constitutional agencies till a native Parliament was restored.[1]

But Ireland by this time had had demonstrations and *pronunciamentos* enough and to spare. Perhaps indeed she "protested too much," and became liable to the suspicion which the same exuberance of sentiment suggested in the case of the tragedy queen.

One good result, however, the Levee produced; the best men of the National party scattered throughout the four provinces were brought together for a moment in the capital. They had witnessed O'Connell's assault upon Davis with feelings akin to the despair of the Dutch Protestants when Maurice of Orange, the sword of the Reformation, struck at John of Barnvelt, its brain. They desired to negotiate a permanent peace, and were profuse in good advice to both parties. But they probably took too little account of one agent, without whom peace was now impossible—Mr John O'Connell.[2]

---

[1] "The meeting on Friday was all *our* press describes it—by far the greatest popular display I ever witnessed under and outside the Rotunda. O'C. interrupted me on Monday week to confuse me, but he only roused and served me. I was famously heard, and we are great political friends now."—Davis to Maddyn.

[2] The literary projects were pressed on without regard to the controversies in the Association. MacNevin wrote to Lane:—"The country is bristling with books on all sides, Protestant, Orange, mitigated purple, bright green, dark green, and invisible green. We are all writing books, such as they are, and all about the 'dear little isle.' Now, if wealth and national learning go on together, the devil cannot arrest the progress of our cause; for I observed in reading our history that at every period when fair play was given for a moment to the national mind, it rushed to freedom with a noble instinct."

CHAPTER IX.

THE VICE-TRIBUNATE OF JOHN O'CONNELL.

WHEN the Bill passed autumn had arrived, and in autumn it was as hopeless to keep the national leaders in Dublin as to keep the House of Commons in session. O'Connell retired to Darrynane, O'Brien to Cahermoyle, and their principal associates set out for the Rhine or Mont Blanc, or on political expeditions beyond the Bann or the Shannon. Davis had volunteered to allow me a holiday, by taking my place in the *Nation* office, and my holiday was employed in an excursion through Ulster, from Rostrevor to Donegal. An Orange meeting on a scale of unusual magnitude was projected at Enniskillen to impeach Peel for his desertion of Protestant ascendancy; and in company with two or three friends I resolved to see this muster of faithful Protestants. My companions were John O'Hagan and two provincial adherents of the Young Ireland Party who now first come distinctly into view. During a residence in Belfast from 1839 to 1842, I had made the acquaintance of John Mitchel, a solicitor residing at Banbridge, who impressed me by the vigour and liberality of his opinions, as well as by his culture and suavity. He was the son of a Unitarian Minister, had been educated at Trinity College, and at this time was under thirty years of age. He was rather above the middle size, well made, and with a face which was thoughtful and comely, though pensive blue eyes and masses of soft brown hair, a stray ringlet of which he had the habit of twining round his finger while he spoke, gave it, perhaps, too feminine a cast. He lived much alone, and this training had left the ordinary results; he was silent and retiring, slow to speak and apt to deliver his opinion in a form which would be abrupt and dogmatic if it were not relieved by a pleasant smile. He was already happily married, and lived contentedly among his books, in a little village on the pastoral Bann, without one associate of his own sex for his mind or heart. During his rare visits to Dublin I introduced him to Davis, with whom he was much taken, and though he had not yet given us any effectual assistance as a writer or speaker, he was reckoned by the young men as one of their reserve. We had shown our estimate of him by placing him on the Council of the Eighty-two Club, and by inviting him to contribute a volume to the Library of Ireland, which after some hesitation he undertook.[1]

It was with Mitchel I had originally planned this expedition, and as the time approached he announced himself ready. In the middle of July he wrote from Banbridge :—

"Did I not predict truly of the July weather? [It was raining cats and dogs.] Surely we shall have a glorious August for this. The assizes and all other attorney work will be at an end (or suspended) before the 1st August. So that if you and O'Hagan fix any day about then, and let me know a day or two before, I will meet you in Newry, then we will see Rostrevor, and on our way to Banbridge batter and reduce Loughorn but spare the garrison [Loughorn was the residence of Mr John Martin, one of the proposed tourists] and so on to Belfast : or else in a north-west direction, as may be decided in solemn council of war, to be held in Banbridge, over a map of Ireland.

"Will none of the rest—Dillon, Barry, MacNevin—be persuaded to join us, even for a part of the time? About the books [the Library of Ireland, of which the first volume had just appeared] Mr Davis writes to me that he will not have his 'Tone' ready as the advertisement promises, and I have been making some exertion to have 'Aodh O'Neill' finished soon, to put in its place—I fear a sorry substitute. Still if yours [the 'Ballad Poetry of Ireland'] and Mr Carleton's 'Rody' are really to be published as announced, I should have time enough, and moreover I should have (which I much desire) your advice upon some passages that Davis rather takes exception to—I should hardly say that, but desires me to reconsider—and those very passages I am unwilling to alter seeing they are as I conceive justified, both historically and otherwise. It is a delicate period that I have fallen upon ; and one upon which *conciliatory* writing is difficult. Besides, I confess that I am

---

[1] Mitchel had written one review for the *Nation* (a notice of a pamphlet on the estates of the London Societies in Ulster, by his uncle Mr Haslet, Mayor of Derry), one letter of no significance, one leading article (Convicted Conspirators, March 2nd, '44), and half another. The latter appeared in No. 33 (May 27th '44), and is entitled "The Anti-Irish Catholics" (Lord Beaumont, etc). The first portion was Davis's ; it is Mitchel's from the following sentence to the end ; a sentence interesting as marking his opinions at that period. Davis republished in the "Voice of the Nation" his own portion of the article, omitting the remainder :—" In the year 1843 the native country of that servile lord is still a province, but making a noble struggle for its independence ; violating no human, no divine law ; forming no dark, secret associations, but working by the peaceful might of concentrated opinion alone ; collecting in the open day the suffrages of her unarmed and sober millions, under the sanction of religion, and the guidance of religion's anointed ministers, until every Irishman shall have pronounced his opinion whether his country shall be once more a nation or not." The articles in the "Voice of the Nation" signed M——, which have sometimes been attributed by critics to Mitchel, were written by John Fisher Murray.

inclined to ultra vehemence in speaking of that time, and really thought I had restrained myself admirably. But you shall see.

"I hope you are in good health and that you will be able for the hills when we start. For Mrs Duffy I am almost afraid to ask.

"Be sure to give me warning before you come that I may have a day or two to put my office in order. I hear you have the 'Battle of Maghrath' [one of the publications of the Archæological Society], and that there is a learned appendix upon Irish Military Standards. Will you lend it to me? Remember to bring it with you."

The excursion began early in August, and its aims and enjoyment were a type of the practical and imaginative characters of the party inspired by Davis. I borrow a brief account of it from a note-book of the period :—

O'H. and I rested at Drogheda, where we fought the battle (of the Boyne) over again, map in hand, then proceeded to Lurgan Green, where a Scotch engineer has conquered a tract from the sea at a cost which makes it feasible to have the same result repeated in many places ; thence to inspect the Catholic church of Dundalk [the most successful of the Gothic revivals which had recently begun], and on to Faughart, where tradition declares Edward Bruce lies buried after his disastrous Irish campaign. Next day to the old keep of Narrowwater, over Ferry hill, where the divine bay of Rostrevor—lying between guardian mountains, with Carlingford and Cooley on the right, and on the left Mourne and Warrenpoint—might realise a painter's dream of ideal beauty. Here our northern friends met us and we spent a day at Kilbroney, a valley in the heart of the Mourne mountains, where the bleach-green and beetling mills of Mr Martin's elder brother renewed our acquaintance (we were all Ulstermen bred among flax and linen) with the most successful of Northern industries. Thence to "castle-filled Carlingford" where a mediæval fortress fit to shelter an army sits on a huge rock rising perpendicularly out of the sea, unapproachable, except by the flattest and lightest boats, and still seems to guard, as of old, the "Pass of the North." At Loughorn we made another pause. Mr Martin—the eldest of the party—was a gentleman farmer of unusual culture, but whose gentle manners and feeble health gave little promise of political action. He had been Mitchel's schoolfellow, and his life then and thereafter was undoubtedly ruled by this fact. From Loughorn our course to Bryansford lay through a district which, after seven generations, still bore the character impressed upon it by the Plantation under James I. There were Catholic districts and Protestant districts, Protestant towns and Catholic towns like Rathfriland and Hilltown, and the original population, who had been driven from the rich valleys to the soil which the " plantators " disdained, were still known as the "mountainy men." At Fofaney we found the name of the National School painted in the Irish character, and vowed to have this example followed in the Repeal Reading Rooms. At Bryansford (the residence of Lord Roden), the leader of the Orangemen has made himself a home of matchless beauty, in an ancient seat of the O'Neils, and what is better, established an hotel which was [in those days] a model of comfort and convenience. I can scarcely record without inward laughter and some self-reproach the incidents at Bryansford. You are required to write your name in a book at the lodge before entering Lord Roden's domain, and two of the travellers, against the plaintive remonstrance of their comrades, insisted upon entering themselves as Aodh O'Neil of Tyreoghen, and Roger O'More of Leix, two historic names malign to the house of Jocelyn. When we returned to an excellent dinner we found on every toilet table a Protestant Bible conspicuously displayed. [Lord Roden was one of the modern saints.] One of us called attention to the fact, and vowed he would not let Lord Roden thrust his Bible upon him till he asked for it. "Certainly not," said Mitchel; "I'll ring the bell and order the waiter to carry them off forthwith." Martin, who acted as general peacemaker, insisted that the Bibles were doing us no hurt, that we were not forced to read them, that Lord Roden meant well, and so forth, which produced small results, till at length he urged a final motion in arrest of judgment. "Well, for my part," he said, "I want to read a chapter before I go to sleep." The idea of a Bible on every toilet table of four being necessary to enable our friend to read his chapter was so irresistible, that we broke into a chorus of laughter, and compromised the case by piling all the Bibles on Martin's table for his personal comfort.

From Bryansford we went to Newcastle, and ascended Slievedonard. As we mounted a mist came plump down, through which we could not see three yards, but we toiled on towards the summit. After a little the mist drifted away almost as rapidly as the lifting of a curtain, and disclosed a scene which none of us will ever forget. The whole Mourne chain lay beneath us, and out of the valleys the mist was steaming up as from huge cauldrons. The sea was a dazzling spectacle ; a shower of rain turned a stretch of the bay from deep blue to jet black, while nearer the shore it became emerald green, and the harbour of Dundrum seemed to rise silver white out of the brown plains, to meet the changing sky. Through the breaks of the mountain we could discern in the distance the lough of Carlingford and the bay of Dundalk. The mists as they rose flew about the mountain, now chasing each other round its base, now hooding its head in darkness. During the entire period of our slow descent it was raining in some part of the vast plain exposed to our view, and the contest between the sun and the storm looked like a pitched battle of pagan gods. A vast army of clouds would take possession of a town, and pour a fierce storm of rain upon it ; suddenly the sun would be seen advancing in its rear and driving it to sea. Presently the rain would rally round some hill-top, and the clouds flocked to this new *rendezvous*, leaving the former battlefield in possession of the enemy. Again, when the sun would seem to be in complete command of a town, a reinforcement of heavy clouds would rush round a mountain spur and beat back the sunshine. We watched the conflict with constant interest, though occasionally flying parties of the storm took us in flank and galled us considerably.

We pursued our journey by way of Dundrum, where John de Courcy erected one of the castles through which that great Norman soldier held his grasp on the North, and made our way to Downpatrick, where Thomas Russell, the friend of Wolfe Tone and the ally of Robert Emmet, lies buried in the parish church ; and where an unprotected sod, which the piety of pilgrims constantly diminishes, is shown as the grave of St Patrick. The day ordinarily finished with refreshment for mind and body which we fell into the habit of distinguishing as 'Tea and Thomas'—Thomas being the philosopher of Chelsea [whom we all loved for having taught so well to scorn pretence and hold by truth and duty, without sharing one in twenty of his opinions on men or events]. While we were sipping the social beverage, and listening to 'Sartor Resartus' read aloud by one of us, in an inn in

Downpatrick one evening, a dapper little Cockney commercial traveller in stress of accommodation was shown into our sitting-room, and served with brandy and water at a table apart. After listening in mute amazement for a quarter of an hour he could stand it no longer. "Forgive me, gentlemen," he said, "for interrupting you, but you don't mean to say that all that blessed nonsense is printed in that book." When he was assured that it was so set down in the record, he requested to be told the name of the author. "Carlyle!" he said, "Ah! I am not surprised at that fellow. I often saw his shop in Fleet Street with the devil in one window and a bishop in the other." Some of us intimated that his Carlile and the author of "Sartor Resartus" were not identical, any more than the Solomon who had recently been convicted as a "fence" was identical with the personage of the same name who built the Temple of Jerusalem; but it was in vain. "Ah," he repeated, "I saw his shop in Fleet Street with my own eyes, and there was a bishop in one window and the devil in the other."

From Downpatrick we went to Ballynahinch, where in '98 the United Irishmen, Presbyterian and Catholic, fought against the English troops for six hours; a man named Innes, who had carried a pike that day, was still living and showed us the battlefield. Thence along the river, whose low hills were covered with white and brown linen, to Banbridge, where Mitchel resided. Next morning two of us went to mass in the village chapel, and saw a scene singularly solemn and impressive. A venerable old man, whose head I thought I would recognise as the head of a Christian bishop if I met it in an African desert,[1] was receiving a public offender back into the Church. He questioned him as to the sincerity of his repentance, then prayed over him, and exhorted the congregation, in language wonderfully impressive, to be charitable to their erring brother, as they too might fall. From Banbridge we passed through the pleasant orchards and farmyards of Armagh, to the ecclesiastical capital where the Protestant Primate had spent thirty thousand pounds to re-edify the ancient cathedral, and the Catholic Primate was engaged in planning a new cathedral which it was said would throw it into the shade; and on to Enniskillen, where the Orangmen were to bring Peel to judgment for his backsliding.

But the pleasure of the day was turned into gloom whenever we fell in with the Dublin newspapers. In the absence of the legitimate leaders, Mr John O'Connell was in undisputed control of the Association, and was deliberately destroying the labour of years, and the hopes of a generation. He played the part of dictator at that time with a dogmatism which his great father after a life of public services rarely assumed. At every meeting the chair, which used to be an object of honest ambition, was occupied by some of his private retinue; and at every meeting there was some personal conflict or some gross violation of the neutrality on which the Association rested. One day a respectable solicitor who had been engaged in the great Clare Election of 1829, and constantly afterwards in public affairs, was asked "how dare he come there" to controvert an opinion of Mr John O'Connell's on the question of negro

---

[1] Right Rev. Dr Blake of Dromore.

slavery.[1] Another day was occupied with an angry contest over the private affairs of the Dublin Corporation. The comments of the English press on the Holy See, the proceedings of a body of dissenters who called themselves the German Catholic Church, were in turn debated at great length. But the climax was reached when he occupied the Association for half an hour with a denunciation of a Whig newspaper for having referred disrespectfully "to an adorable relic, an unseamed garment exhibited at Treves, supposed to have been worn by the blessed Redeemer during His Passion"—the authenticity of which, however, was not a fundamental principle of the Repeal Association. His first escapade came to hand as we sat down at Mitchel's table for the first time, and for some of us dinner was at an end. Each week brought new troubles, and though youth is not easily depressed, for a day after the receipt of fresh bulletins of ruin the sunshine and beauty seemed to vanish from the noble scenery in which we were travelling, and from life itself. The correspondence which these disastrous proceedings produced among our comrades went to the *Nation* office; but a note from MacNevin followed me to the north. "John O'Connell," he said, "is the most mischievous public man in Ireland. The Association is now merely a Catholic Association. Repeal or any high or honourable principle of nationality is never heard there. . . . Look at the corporation. Is that the spirit of municipal freedom? Oh, Brussels, Bruges, Ghent, and Anvers!" It was needless to add, what his correspondent would know, was implied in the fact that to turn the Repeal Association into a Catholic Association was to break faith with the Protestant members, and to forbid the hope of recruiting to its ranks independent men of any section. The sentiment of nationality was beyond Mr John O'Connell's power, but the instrument by which nationality might triumph was being blunted and broken.

The Enniskillen meeting proved an impressive and significant phenomenon. There was a muster of twenty thousand men, making no account of women, children, and stragglers. Elsewhere in Ulster the Orangemen were commonly servants, shop boys, and the class generally without discipline or influence; here they consisted in a great part of the solid middle-aged farmers of Fermanagh and Tyrone, led by the smaller gentry. Large in person, stern in feature, erect in carriage, they

[1] Mr Richard Scott of Ennis. Mr Scott observed that he condemned slavery as much as any one, but there was an Anti-Slavery Society which met at the Royal Exchange, and he considered that platform, not Conciliation Hall, the proper place for denouncing it. The present time, when there was a cloud in the west, was not a fit one for gratuitous interference in American affairs.

Quebec, 1861.

*Yours affectionately
Thos D'Arcy McGee.*

were the manifest heirs of the planters and Puritans, and as they filed over the northern bridge the tourists agreed that they had never seen a body of undisciplined men so military in their bearing and movements. The gay genial air and elastic step of the men who mustered at Tara and Mullaghmast were replaced by a serious and even gloomy demeanour, but we recognised the serviceable qualities it covered, and eagerly desired to see this solid force added to the national strength, and serving Ireland in its own fashion. The faces of the men did not promise too ready a reception for new opinions, and the tone of their spokesmen furnished even less ground of hope. The speeches were painfully driftless; mere idle rant or brute bellowing. The mass writhed with pain and fear of change, but there was no intelligible voice to express either their hopes or their fears. "It ended in a roar; it might have ended in a revolution."

From Enniskillen we turned to Donegal to revel in the grand ocean-beaten scenery of the north-western coast. As we arrived after a long day's travel at Donegal, the little town where the pious labours of the Four Masters preserved the early annals of Ireland, I found a letter announcing alarming news from my home. It was necessary to separate from my companions on the instant, and travel back the same route through the night. When I reached home, happily all immediate danger was declared to be over.

Davis urged me to rejoin the northern tourists and complete my holiday, under penalty of being unfit for the work of the coming winter. This was not to be thought of, but as a compromise I agreed to spend some days in Wicklow, within a few hours' drive of Dublin. A week before I started on the northern tour Wilson Gray had introduced a young Irish-American to me, whom the proprietors of the *Freeman's Journal* had brought home from Boston, to become one of their contributors. The young man was not prepossessing. He had a face of almost African type, his dress was slovenly even for the careless class to which he belonged, he looked unformed, and had a manner which struck me at first sight as too deferential for self-respect. But he had not spoken three sentences in a singularly sweet and flexible voice till it was plain that he was a man of fertile brains and great originality; a man in whom one might dimly discover rudiments of the orator, poet and statesman, hidden under this ungainly disguise. This was Thomas D'Arcy M'Gee. I invited him to breakfast on some early day at his convenience, and as he arrived one morning when I was engaged to breakfast with Davis I took him with me, and he met, for the first and last time, a man destined to largely influence his life. When the Wicklow trip was projected I told Davis I liked this new-comer, and meant to invite him to accompany me. "Well," he said, "your new friend has an Irish nature certainly, but spoiled, I fear, by the Yankees. He has read and thought a good deal, and I might have liked him better if he had not so obviously determined to *transact* an acquaintance with me."

During the run in Wicklow a letter from the northern tourists reached me which will complete the record of that pleasant time.

"We have had a most delightful tour through Donegal" (Mitchel wrote), "and only arrived here yesterday, but we missed you sadly. On Sleive League, at Dunlewy, at Horn Head, and wherever the earth and the heavens were grandest, we thought with regret that you should have been turned back from the very threshold of such glorious scenery, and by so melancholy a cause ; but we shall meet again in Donegal, and end the tour another day. O'H.'s journal ought to be good, for he spends a good deal of time writing it. He has turned out a capital mountaineer, and will tell you of strange passages that he and I have gone through amongst the hills ; how we walked five-and-twenty miles through woods and morasses one day, and were at last benighted about fifteen miles from any shelter, in the midst of a pathless wood, that stands now as wild and shaggy and savage as it was a thousand years ago : how we struggled on all night, having fortunately moonlight, and not liking to lie down to sleep in the wood, inasmuch as we were wet to the bones : how towards morning we reached the hotel, weary, wet and famished with hunger, etc. In short, I have good hopes of making a tourist of him yet—if he survive my instructions. Poor Martin has had a good deal of illness, but he has pushed on gallantly. However, he was not out with us in the night adventure.

"I am hurrying home and intend to be in Banbridge on Tuesday, when I will work hard till I finish 'Aodh' [his volume for the Library of Ireland], and will carefully refer to my Index Expurgatorius of Carlylish phrases [to which his correspondent and another of the tourists had taken exception]. We got the *Nation* yesterday, and simultaneously asked each other which of *us* was the enthusiastic gentleman referred to in 'Answers to Correspondents' who requires his letters to be addressed to the Merman of the Rosses and roaring Meg. We approve highly all of us of our correspondent's account of the Enniskillen meeting, and *disapprove* of giving so much good language to the treacherous *Evening Mail!*"[1]

The MS. of "Aodh O'Neil" followed speedily, and in reply to some further objections to Carlyleisms which had escaped his promised revision, Mitchel wrote a fortnight later[2] :—

"Now as to the Carlylean phrases you mention ; the printer might omit the last clause of that paragraph beginning ' Though in a mercantile point of view, etc.'—it is unnecessary, though I think *not* Carlylean. 'The Good Heavens for what service?' *has* a tinge of Thomas. It might stand thus 'for some unknown service.' It is hard of you to cut down my fine writing !"

---

[1] Londonderry, Aug. 22nd, '45, Mitchel to Duffy.
[2] Mitchel to Duffy, Banbridge, Sept. 7th.

CHAPTER X.

THE DEATH OF DAVIS.

AFTER a week's absence I returned home at the beginning of September, relieved Davis from duty, and urged him to start immediately on his autumn tour. But he was correcting a new edition of his "Curran" at the moment, and would not consent to go till it was finished, or before the time originally fixed for the close of my holiday, and the beginning of his—a date still two or three weeks distant.

The condition of the national cause, when I resumed my place, was one to justify discouragement and even dismay. Wherever the eye turned one discerned disasters or reverses, grave mistakes committed, or great opportunities thrown away. Among our most notable successes in 1843 might be counted the sympathy awakened in France and America; but at this time France and America were sullen or exasperated. Frenchmen had been wounded by O'Connell's gratuitous declaration that he would rather abandon Repeal than owe it to France; and America had received a more wanton and intolerable provocation. Peel's concessions were referable to his apprehension of a war between England and the United States, and by bringing the English minister into such a temper the United States had proved a most serviceable ally to Ireland. To knit closer a friendship which had proved so useful was the plain duty of the Irish leaders; but instead of taking this course O'Connell declared that the Irish people, on certain conditions, were ready to turn on their ally and smite him into the dust. They would help England to "pluck down the American eagle in its highest pride of flight."[1] This maladroit declaration was received with dismay in Ireland, and with mingled rage and derision in America.

---

[1] "We tell them from this spot that they can have us—that the throne of Victoria can be made perfectly secure—the honour of the British empire maintained—and the American eagle in its highest pride of flight be brought down. Let them conciliate and do us justice, and they will have us enlisted under the banner of Victoria—let them but give us the Parliament in College Green, and Oregon shall be theirs and Texas shall be harmless."—Speech of O'Connell at the Repeal Association, April 4th, 1845.

"Everybody," Dillon wrote to Davis, "is indignant at O'Connell meddling in the business. His talk about bringing down the pride of the American eagle, if England would pay us sufficiently, is not merely foolish, but false and base. Such talk must be supremely disgusting to the Americans, and to every man of honour and spirit. He lectures the *Spectator* for saying that the loyalty of the Irish may be secured for a 'consideration,' and he says the same himself the next moment. The plain policy of the party now is to assume a menacing attitude : for either there will be a war, or England will be obliged to shrink."

In America the natural rage of the native press and the native party was largely shared by Irish Americans. The Repeal Associations in Baltimore, New Orleans, and other populous and important districts, were dissolved, and all further connection with Conciliation Hall repudiated. The few Associations which remained in existence did not attempt to justify O'Connell's language, but pleaded the paramount claims of the mother country. Whatever blunders leaders might commit, the Irish exile must be true to the Irish cause. At home mismanagement produced even more disastrous results than abroad. The Federal movement, the proposals of the Whig peers, the project of a Rotatory Parliament, but beyond all these, the temper and language of the Tory gentry, and their representatives in the press, had disclosed a condition of mind singularly favourable to a formidable national union. O'Brien, who was slow to predict pleasant things, assured Davis that such a union was no longer impossible, if only the Repeal party did not throw away their chance.

"From many circumstances which came to my knowledge whilst I was in London," he wrote, "but which I do not feel myself at liberty to particularise, I am induced to think that the period of such an union is much nearer than our fondest hopes could lead us to believe—that is, if we do not spoil our own game. This I am afraid that we do at each moment, when there is the best ground for hope."

It was effectually spoiled by Conciliation Hall being made, week after week, more and more odious to the men who were gravitating towards the national cause. With a great league authentically representing the bulk of the Irish people, having Catholics and Protestants standing shoulder to shoulder in its foremost ranks, a league treated with confidence and deference in Paris and Washington, the gentry might perhaps negotiate; but with a sectarian society, where Mr John O'Connell harangued on negro slavery, German Catholics and the Holy Coat of Treves, and which nations the most friendly to Ireland repudiated with scorn, negotiation was impossible. The sweet temper and forbearing nature of John Dillon were so embittered by John O'Connell's presumption that he counselled immediate resistance, in language from which his habitual moderation almost entirely disappeared.

"I have just read," he wrote to Davis, "with inexpressible disgust the speech of John O'Connell, and the scene which followed between himself and [Richard] Scott. It behoves you to consider very seriously whether the *Nation* is not bound to notice this matter. I feel very desirous that you personally should avoid any further encounter with the O'Connells for some time. . . . In truth, from the turn matters are now taking, a decent man cannot frequent the public meetings ; for he must either create dissension or have his reputation damaged by silently listening to the absurd and mischievous stuff that is talked there. But I doubt much whether a newspaper can, without compromising its character, allow these proceedings to pass unnoticed. My notion is that Scott has a right to protection, and that the public will, or ought to, feel indignant if this protection be withheld. The *Nation* could not possibly get a better opportunity of reading a long-required lecture to Johnny. The immediate topic is one on which public opinion is universally against him." . . . [Scott was an old man long associated with O'Connell, who, having no relations with the Young Irelanders, made a slight effort to pacify America by excluding from Conciliation Hall negro slavery, Texas, Oregon, and the whole range of transatlantic questions upon which O'Connell and Mr John O'Connell had been haranguing.] "Can anything be more evident than the puerile folly of it ? When the Americans were engaged in their own struggle, only fancy one of their orators coming down to the Congress with a violent invective against the abuses of the French Government of the day ! Any man who is thoroughly in earnest about one thing cannot allow his mind to wander in pursuit of things not merely unconnected but inconsistent with that thing. It is impossible latterly to bear with the insolence of this little frog. There is no man or country safe from his venom. If there be not some protest against him, he will set the whole world against us."[1]

MacNevin was also deeply discontented and disquieted; but his vehement nature was moved rather to the scorn that rejects further responsibility than to the zeal that sets to work to amend what is wrong.

"Dillon wrote me a letter, and he is sick of the abomination of desolation on Burgh Quay. It never opens its sooty mouth on the subject of Repeal now. By the way, where *is* the Repeal agitation ; is it hunting at Darrynane ? . . . My parliamentary mania is cured ; I would not accept the representation of any constituency at the beck of such a body. I will work with you and Davis, but no more with that base *mélange* of tyranny and mendicancy. I am glad that Davis does not go to the Association ; I shall not go when I return."[2]

This danger to the public cause was supplemented, as I speedily

---

[1] Davis Papers. Dillon to Davis. Ballina, August 6, 1845.
[2] MacNevin to Duffy. Rose Park, September 15, 1845.

discovered, by danger to the party and the journal for which I had a more immediate responsibility. Mr John O'Connell—so friends whom we could altogether trust assured us—had been as busy in undermining the *Nation* as in disorganising Conciliation Hall. Doheny reported to Davis from Tipperary that a journal which a few weeks before was a synonym for public spirit and public confidence had now many enemies.

"It [the *Nation*] is in great disrepute among the priests. I met a doctor at Nenagh who lost two subscribers to a dispensary for refusing to give it up. . . . I was thinking of writing an article on the subject. If you and Duffy don't approve of it when you see it, it can be left out. O'Connell's *hints* are taken to be corroborative of the ruffianism of others."

The *modus operandi*, it seems, was to attribute to the Young Irelanders opinions and designs which, says Doheny, are as authentic "as if the *Nation* were described as a monster with an adder's sting and the scales of a crocodile." Dillon wrote to me from the West in the same tone :—

"I trust the *Nation* has not suffered materially in circulation by the rascally conspiracy that has been formed against it. It would be a most cheering thing if it pass through this trying ordeal. The scoundrels are betaking themselves to the provincial papers to circulate their calumnies. I perceive the *Sligo Champion* has an article now regularly upon Young Ireland. It is to be attributed to the influence, if not to the pen, of Dillon Browne. I will be in Sligo on Friday. I have met only one priest here who is not an enemy to Young Ireland, always excepting those who know nothing about them. The name of that priest is Coghlan, . . . and his good opinion is worth that of all the rest."

There was plainly much need of a conference of my friends, but there were none of them at hand to consult except Davis; and he was engrossed in long-deferred work of his own.

Early in the second week after my return to the *Nation* office, instead of his usual visit, I got a note. It was a hasty scrawl, written in bed, the lines blurred, and as few as could convey his meaning intelligibly.

"*Tuesday Morning.*

"MY DEAR D.—I have had an attack of some sort of cholera, and *perhaps* have slight scarlatina. I cannot see anyone, and am in bed. Don't be alarmed about me, but don't rely on my being able to write.—Ever yours,
"T. D."

Disease, or deficiency in any sort of strength, seemed so incredible in the case of Davis, that the few friends to whom his illness was necessarily known, because to see and talk with him was part of their daily life, regarded it as of no importance. The complete absence of

Tuesday morning

My dear V/ I have had an attack of some sort of cholera & perhaps have slight scarlatina. I cannot see anyone & am in bed. Dont be alarmed about me but dont rely on my being able to write.
ever yours
VD

[204]

any suspicion of danger will be best understood by the terms in which the news was announced and received by his comrades. Among MacNevin's correspondence I find this note, which I addressed to him on the same day as Davis's note to me :—

"I sympathise with your desire for a new and an Irish subject. What say you to the 'Plantation of Ulster'? A good title, a good topic, and a useful one. It would begin the day Mitchel's book ends, and end where mine begins [a projected History of the Rising in 1641]. The subject would suit you. It is civil, not military, near enough our own time to need no antiquarian research, and full of strong pictures. If you determine upon this subject I can give you books, pamphlets, and other assistance. . . . Davis is confined to his bed with English cholera ; but it is passing away, so do your best for the *Nation* next week."[1]

MacNevin replied by return of post :—

"I am quite delighted at your suggestion about 'the Plantation of Ulster.' It is an excellent subject, the more peculiarly as I shall be an isthmus connecting Mitchel and Duffy. I suppose the materials are abundant, and I am sure you will give me the best assistance ; and I shall dedicate the 'Plantation' to the Fishmongers' Company. Is there any way of tracing the names and families of the plunderers who displaced the native Irish, and the names of the latter—I mean as connected with each locality? I consulted O'Brien, strange to say, upon the propriety of writing provincial histories of robbery, beginning with Charles ; but he thought it smacked too much of the literature of confiscation. But no objection lies to my new subject. . . . Is it not Davis's book on 'Tone' that comes out next? I am glad he is getting better of his 'English cholera.' Why the d——l did he not get an Irish cholera?—his stomach is too Saxon."[2]

To Davis himself he wrote in the same bantering tone :—

"I regretted very much to hear that you had been unwell, the more especially as your ailment took so unpatriotic a turn as 'English cholera.' The unfortunate disease won't remain long in your Celtic constitution. I suppose you are quite well by this time. . . . Will you write me (and pray do it at once if you are well) a list of places and books to find all about the 'Ulster Plantation' in ; as I have, greatly to my pleasure, been awarded that subject by Charles Duffy. It is not too antiquarian ; and I am quite sick of modern patriotism. . . . Pray do now write me one line from your couch, where ' *Tityre tu recubans sub tegmine—quilti.'*"[3]

After a couple of days Davis wrote again ; the handwriting was tremulous and scratchy, but the tone was so tranquil and confident that it was impossible to feel any alarm. Tossing on a bed of fever, his first thought was to provide against the chance of the ill news alarming

---

[1] *Nation* Papers. Duffy to MacNevin.
[2] *Nation* Papers. MacNevin to Duffy.
[3] Davis Papers. MacNevin to Davis.

one who was very dear to him, his second that a trivial duty for which he was responsible might not be neglected.

"DEAR D——I have had a bad attack of scarlatina, with a horrid sore throat; don't mention this to *any* one, for a very delicate reason I have; but pray get the Curran speeches read, except the Newry election. Have Conway's *Post* of 1812 sent back to him, and read and correct yourself so much of the memoir as I sent. In four days I hope to be able to look at light business for a short time.[1]—Ever yours, T. D."

Before the end of the week he improved so much that he insisted on driving out for an hour; for what purpose we may safely conjecture. On Sunday and Monday he was again in bed, and denied to his friends; but he was in the midst of his family, watched by the loving care of his mother and sister, who had still no serious misgivings; and the idea that his life was in danger probably did not enter the mind of any human being. On Tuesday morning[2] I was suddenly summoned to his mother's house in Baggot Street, to see the most tragic sight my eyes had ever looked upon—the dead body of Thomas Davis. He had grown rapidly worse during the night, and at dawn he died in the arms of a faithful servant named Neville, who had lived in his family for many years. He was confident of recovery, Neville assured me, almost to the end; and spoke impatiently of interrupted work; work which was now to remain unfinished for ever. To me the spectacle I was summoned to witness was like the light suddenly gone out of the sky. The friendship that sweetened life, the sympathy that made labour easy, the confidence of ultimate success for our cause, which rayed out of his virile and luminous nature, seemed laid low with him. And when I retired from that fatal bed it was to send to the friends who loved him best, without a moment's warning or preparation, news that would leave them as desolate as I was.

Though it was the season when Dublin was emptiest of the cultivated class, a public funeral was immediately determined upon by

---

[1] After five-and-thirty years my answer to this note has come back to me (in the Davis Papers), and nothing can more clearly exhibit the absence of all thought of danger, for his condition is made the subject of a pleasantry.

"MY DEAR DAVIS—I will do all you desire forthwith. When may I hope to see you? Leave word with your servant when you are well enough to be seen. I cannot now keep your illness a secret, because I told John O'Hagan and McCarthy yesterday; but I will prevent them going to see you. John says you have an opportunity of rivalling Mirabeau, by dying at this minute; but he begs you won't be tempted by the inviting opportunity.—Always yours, C. G. D."—Davis Papers Duffy to Davis.

[2] September 16th, 1845.

Dear W/ I have had a bad attack of scarlatina with a horrid sore throat. Don't mention this to any one for a very delicate reason I have; but pray get the Curran Speeches read except ~~message to~~ the henry election; Have Conway's Part of 1812 sent back to him & read & correct yourself so much of the memorandum as I sent;

In 4 days I hope to be able to look at light business for a short time

ever yours
JD

a few leading men, and the assent of his family obtained. But it was no cold funereal pageantry that accompanied him to the grave. In all the years of my life, before and since, I have not seen so many grown men weep bitter tears as on that September day. The members of the Eighty-Two Club, the Corporation of Dublin, and the Committee of the Repeal Association, took their place in the procession as a matter of course; but it would have soothed the spirit of Davis to see mixed with the green uniforms and scarlet gowns men of culture and intellect, without distinction of party and outside of all political parties. The antiquarians and scholars of the Royal Irish Academy, the Councils of the Archæological and Celtic Societies, the artists of the Royal Hibernian Academy, the committee of the Dublin Library, sent deputations, and the names best known in Irish literature and art might be read next day in the long list of mourners. He was buried in Mount Jerome Cemetery, in latter years the burying-place of the Protestant community, but once the pleasure-grounds of the suburban villa where John Keogh, the Catholic leader, took counsel with Wolfe Tone, the young Protestant patriot, how to unite the jarring creeds in a common struggle for Ireland. The Whig and Conservative Press did him generous justice. They recognised in him a man unbiassed by personal ambition and untainted by the rancour of faction, who loved but never flattered his countrymen; and who, still in the very prime of manhood, was regarded not only with affection and confidence, but with veneration, by his associates. The first proposal for a monument came from a Tory; and Whigs and Tories rivalled his political friends in carrying the project to completion. To the next meeting of the Association O'Connell wrote : " I solemnly declare that I never knew any man who could be so useful to Ireland in the present stage of the struggle." O'Brien on the same occasion described him as one who " united a woman's tenderness with the soul of a hero."[1] Even Mr John O'Connell discovered, somewhat late in the day, that "if there did exist differences of opinion " (between him and other Nationalists), " they were differences of honest and sincere conviction." But the bulk of the people throughout the island little knew the calamity which had befallen them. A writer of the period compared them to children who had lost their father, and were unconscious of all the danger and trouble such a fact implied. In Dublin it was necessarily different; many of the

---

[1] I fear that I could not have said so much *vivâ voce*, for that letter was blurred by many a tear which would have stifled my utterance in a public meeting.— Cahermoyle, Sept. 20, '45.

industrious classes knew and loved him ; and it was noted as a strange instance of unsought popularity that the ballad singers of the Liberties, who had no longer, as of old, a Swift or a Goldsmith for their poet, sang a lament for Davis to street audiences in the traditional tropes and jingles which he had so long laboured to supersede by poetry and sense. "Each brave Milesian, of Erin's blessed nation" (was invoked by the poets of Meath Street) "to join in the mournful theme for the brave son of Granu, young Davis the hero, who never knew terror or shame."

Judging him now a generation after his death, when years and communion with the world have tempered the exaggerations of youthful friendship, I can confidently say that I have not known a man so nobly gifted as Thomas Davis. If his articles had been spoken speeches his reputation as an orator would have rivalled Grattan's; and the beauty and vigour of his style were never employed for mere show, as they sometimes were by Grattan. He fired not rockets, but salvos of artillery. If his programmes and reports, which were the plans and specifications of much of the best work done in his day, had been habitually associated with his name, his practical skill would have ranked as high as O'Connell's. Among his comrades who were poets, he would have been chosen laureate, though poetry was only his pastime. And these gifts leave his rarest qualities untold. What he was as a friend, so tender, so helpful, so steadfast, no description will paint. His comrades had the same careless confidence in him men have in the operations of nature, where irregularity and aberration do not exist. Like Burke and Berkeley, he inspired and controlled all who came within the range of his influence, without aiming to lead or dominate. He was singularly modest and unselfish; but the phrases employed to express modesty and unselfishness are weak and absurd when applied to him. In a long lifetime I have never known any man remotely resemble him in these qualities. The chief motive-power of a party and a cause, labouring for them as a man of exemplary industry labours in his calling, he not only never claimed any recognition or reward, but discouraged allusion to his services by those who knew them best. Passionate enthusiasm is apt to become prejudice, but in Davis it was controlled not only by a disciplined judgment but by a fixed determination to be just. He brought to political controversy a fairness previously unexampled in Ireland. In all his writings there will not be found a single sentence reflecting ungenerously on any human being. He had set himself the task of building up a nation, a task not beyond his strength had fortune been kind. Now that the transactions of that day have fallen into their natural perspective, now that we know what has perished and what survives of its conflicting opinions, we may plainly see that, imperfectly as they knew him, the Irish race—the grown men of 1844—in the highest diapason of their passions, in the widest range of their capacity for action or endurance, were represented and embodied in Thomas Davis better than in any man then living. He had predicted a revolution; and if fundamental change in the ideas which move and control a people be a revolution, then his prediction was already accomplished. In conflicts of opinion near at hand a prodigious change made itself manifest, traceable to teaching of which he was the chief exponent. During his brief career, scarcely exceeding three years, he had administered no office of authority, mounted no tribune, published no books, or next to none, and marshalled no following; but with the simplest agencies, in the columns of a newspaper, in casual communication with his friends and contemporaries, he made a name which, after half a century, is still recalled with enthusiasm or tears, and will be dear to students and patriots while there is an Irish people. It is well that it should :—

> Keep but the model safe, new men will rise
> To study it, and other days to prove
> How great a good was Luria having lived.

In the language of the Celtic annalist, "a new soul came into Ireland" with Davis, and his death was followed by such discouragement and dismay that for a time the soul seemed to have fled again. A few days after his funeral I followed my young wife to the grave, and when I left my desolate home to muster my comrades for the work to which we stood pledged, I found that misfortune had not come single, but in troops. Of the little band of his fellow-students in the university who were the life and light of the Young Ireland party, there was not one ready to take up his task; by a calamitous mischance there was scarcely one who was not at that moment disabled from doing his ordinary share of public work. At the beginning of autumn John Dillon had been ordered to his native air for a chest disease, and was an invalid when the fatal news reached him. He had burst a small blood-vessel at the scene between O'Connell and Davis in the debate on the Colleges Bill, and had never wholly recovered.

"Your letter [he wrote me] was like a thrust from a dagger. I had not even heard that he was unwell. This calamity makes the world look black. God knows I am tempted to wish myself well out of it. I am doing you a grievous wrong to leave you alone at this melancholy time. I was preparing to be off by the post-car, but my friends have one and all protested against it, and I verily believe that they would keep me by force if nothing else would. God help us, my dear fellow; I don't know how we can look at one another when we meet."[1]

He was peremptorily ordered to refrain from all business, but it was impossible to keep a man like Dillon from coming to the aid of his friends in such a conjuncture; and it is a touching evidence of the difficulties under which he made the attempt that his contribution proved unfit for use, even when aid was so much wanted. For the first time he found himself a rejected contributor in the *Nation;* and the manner in which he received the news will illustrate his sweet and generous character.

"I am very much pleased," he wrote, "that you did not insert that letter. Even when I sent it I knew it was below mediocrity; but it was the best I could do in the state I was in. In fact, nothing could have induced me to write at all but the impossibility of refusing your request under such circumstances. The *Nation* has surpassed itself in the last two numbers. The one before the last was amongst the very best, and the article headed 'Another Year' in yesterday's, in my judgment, has never been surpassed in the *Nation* or elsewhere. It was a trumpet blast. While I read it my heart bounded with hope for the first time during many weeks. Who wrote it? It is not like your style, and yet I do not know where else to look for its strength and extreme clearness of thought. It is replete with manliness, sound sense, and strong genuine feeling, without the slightest tinge of obscurity or fustian.[2] It vexes me much that I can do nothing at this time to lighten the load of your labour and sorrow. I would have gone to town if the state of my health did not absolutely forbid it. I have got a return of that ugly cough which brought on some startling symptoms before I left. I am combatting it with the sharpest remedies I can. While I write I have two troublesome blisters on my neck and breast. I trust, my dear Duffy, you will make a brave stand against this affliction. It requires no little fortitude to pursue an occupation every act of which calls to your mind the remembrance of one you loved so well."

In the end Dillon was sent to Madeira for the winter by his medical advisers, and for many months his wise counsel and effectual aid were lost to the party which he had helped to create.

MacNevin was also in the country, not consciously an invalid, but disturbed by the first symptoms of an unknown disease, which proved in the end the most painful affliction that can befall a man of intellect. On receiving the calamitous news he wrote :—

"I have been in a state of the greatest agony since I got your letter last evening. I could have lost nearer than he with less anguish ;—he was such

---

[1] *Nation* Papers, Dillon to Duffy. September 19th.
[2] The article referred to was written by the editor.

a noble, gentle creature. And to me always exaggerating my good qualities, never finding fault, and never, never with an angry look or word. He was more than a brother; and I loved him better than all the brothers I have. Our bond of union is broken; what mournful meetings ours will be in future! I cannot go up; it is *impossible*. There is no use in troubling you with the reason. But I will go up early in October, and meanwhile will do all I can for you. Can we ever repair this damage? What shall we do to replace him? My God, how horror-struck will be Dillon and Smith O'Brien! I never closed my eyes since I got the fatal news. It is the most dreadful visitation that could have fallen upon us, and to come upon you just at this period of your calamity. I sent up some pages of notice of him. I could not write anything else."

A few days later he wrote again :—

"It is some sort of consolation to find that all the country is paying its duty to his memory. As for myself, everything I see, every book, every subject that I think of, brings him before me with all his worth and kindness. I feel so lonely and bereaved, the soul has gone out of all my hopes for the future, and even the conviction of the dear friends I have still goes but a short way to reconcile me to a loss that I know is irreparable. I had a mournful satisfaction in reading the beautiful tribute in the *Nation* to his extraordinary virtues. . . . I have a great favour to ask of you—that you will lend me your portrait of Davis to get a copy done of it.[1] I know I am not wrong in thinking you will collect all that he has written of any value; and what did he write that was not vital with genius?"

The insidious disease which was preying on MacNevin was no doubt aggravated by pondering on all we had lost; a little later he announced that he was done with speech-making, and that I must not even count upon his writing regularly for the *Nation*.

"I endeavoured, my dear Charles, to write what you wished, and I found it to be utterly impossible. However well I knew the subject, I could not write a sentence. In fact, the feeling has grown on me daily that it is not honest of me to continue our present arrangements. The difficulty of composition is every hour growing greater, and the result more worthless. . . . I will write for the *Nation* as often as I can, and I never will fail to make the effort. But the good that was in me has, I fear, passed away; my spirits are gone, and I cannot look at my pen and paper without a shudder. This is a humiliating confession; but it is truer than any of Jean Jacques'."

In his ordinary temper MacNevin was gay and sparkling, exploding in epigrams and joining cordially in the laughter he provoked. When he returned to town I found him silent and morose; at times he broke

---

[1] The only portrait of Davis in existence was a cabinet picture painted for me by Henry M'Manus, R.H.A., sketchy and rude, but a vivid likeness. Mr Burton, after Davis's death, drew from memory, with the aid of this rude portrait, a grand and impressive head, which, however, represented the soul and spirit rather than the physical features of his friend. It was lithographed, and has been freqvently reproduced on wood and steel,

into sudden merriment, but in the state of feeling among his associates at the time, his laughter was more painful and ghastly than his reveries. Though he struggled for months before finally succumbing, the brilliant gifts and generous nature of MacNevin were lost for ever to the cause and the men whom he loved so well.

To complete our difficulties, two other of Davis's college friends, united to him by the ties of confidence and affection, John O'Hagan and John Pigot, were about to enter a pleader's chambers in London, and would necessarily be absent for a year—a year that promised to be critical and decisive in Irish affairs. Neither of them had written much, nor spoken in public; but one of them brought a rare insight and sagacity, and the other a constant fire of enthusiasm, to the counsels of their friends. When I add that M'Carthy and Barry wrote only verses or occasional critical papers, and Mangan and Williams verses exclusively, and that Doheny's strength did not lie in journalism, it will be understood at what disadvantage the paper and the party were about to be placed. The entire staff, indeed, on which both depended, were either fatally disabled for present work, or absent from the centre of action for an indefinite period.

Outside his political circle Davis had friends who helped the journal from personal good-will. Mr Maddyn had contributed valuable critical and historical papers from the beginning, and edited one of the "Library of Irish Orators"; but he did not sympathise with our main purpose, and he was connected with the Conservative Press in London, and unwilling to run the risk of being misunderstood. He would not positively promise any further contributions; but he was eager to unite with us at least in making the genius and character of his friend known in both countries.

"I need not say," he wrote to me, "how your letter stunned me. I can hardly credit the intelligence still. With no one in this world did I more sympathise. I never loved any man so much, and I respected him just as much., But we all felt the same way towards him: let us see what we can do to honour his memory and to preserve his fame. The man Thomas Davis ought to be exhibited in as strong colours as consist with truth, not only to his countrymen, but to the citizens of this Empire. The world must be told what his nature was, how large and patriotic were his designs, and how truly pure were his purposes. For he was one of those spirits who quicken others by communication with them. For the purpose of recording his career in a literary shape, I venture to suggest that his personal friends should meet and determine that his life should be given to the public, and that all of them should contribute whatever materials they could to such a work. You ought to be the recorder of his life; for that office you of all his friends are the most fitted, not alone by talents and literary power, but by thoroughly close and catholic sympathy with the noble Davis in all things. There was more of the *idem velle* and *idem nolle* between him and you than between any other of that large circle who admired him living and lament him dead. Your close intimacy and identification for the last three memorable years, your agreement with him on all practical and speculative questions of Irish politics, your personal cognisance of the extent of his unseen labours to serve the country he loved—these things seem to command that you honour yourself and your friend by taking charge of his memory. Let me entreat of you to resolve upon doing so."

They have read history to little purpose who will feel any surprise that faction was busy during this period of confusion and discouragement, making bad worse. It offered a favourable opening for Mr John O'Connell and the little knot of conspirators who desired the destruction of the Young Irelanders, and they eagerly seized on it. In the Association there was decorous grief and solemn lamentations for the loss the country had endured, but in private the retainers rubbed their greasy hands with glee that the enemy of the Liberator and the Young Liberator was gone. Before he was a week in his grave we heard from the provinces whispered disparagements of his memory, traceable, as we believed, to a common source;[1] and the *Pilot* renewed its warnings against the concealed adversaries of religion who had too long got the ear of the people. Maurice O'Connell's instincts, which were generous, and his capacity, which was considerable, drew him towards the young men, and away from these cabals; and he wrote a personal tribute to the memory of Davis, perfectly sincere, I am persuaded, which was altogether incompatible with any belief in the romances manufactured at the Corn Exchange, and which was published at the period of their briskest circulation.[2]

---

[1] *Ex. gr.*, "Miss N—— asked me the other day, with the most mysterious curiosity, about Mr Davis. She had heard from Fr. D—— that he was an infidel, and that his death was a great blessing," etc.—Private letter from H. M'L—— *penes me.*

[2] For Maurice O'Connell's letter, see note in Appendix.

It is worth noting that just so much knowledge of Davis began to prevail among literary men in England as resulted in confounding him with one of his comrades. Lord Jeffrey wrote to his daughter at this time—"Granny (Lady Jeffrey) went to church, and I read a very interesting little volume of "Irish Ballad Poetry," published by that poor Duffy, of the *Nation*, who died so prematurely the other day. There are some most pathetic and many most spirited pieces, and all, with scarcely an exception, so entirely *National*. Do get the book and read it. I am most struck with 'Soggarth Aroon,' after the two first stanzas; and a long, racy, authentic, sounding dirge for the Tyrconnel Princes. But you had better begin with 'The Irish Emigrant,' and 'The Girl of Loch Dan,' which immediately follows, which will break you in more gently to the wilder and more impassioned parts. . . . . God bless all poets! and you will not grudge them a share even of your Sunday benedictions" (Lord Cockburn's "Life of Lord Jeffrey," vol. ii. p. 405).

Somewhat later Miss Mitford, in her memoirs, devoted a chapter to Davis.

And now it might well seem that Young Ireland was approaching its extinction. Its leaders were dead or disabled; and its enemies, like camp followers after a disastrous battle, were stabbing the wounded and plundering the dead. But not so does a true cause perish. The cause so baffled and repressed speedily found new outlets; and as for the party, whatever is commonly known of Young Ireland—whatever is associated with the name in the brief and misleading notices of contemporary history—nearly all that will be permanently remembered of the labours or sufferings of the men who composed it—were events accomplished after the death of Davis and the apparent rout and dispersion of his friends. Meagher had never seen Davis except in some public place, and Meagher was destined to rival Vergniaud in the suddenness and splendour of his success as an orator. M'Gee had seen Davis only once, and M'Gee, in wide sweep of imagination, in the persistency and variety of his labours, in everything but in the moral qualities, where Davis was unapproachable, closely resembled the master who was lost. Devin Reilly had pursued Davis in the streets to feast his eyes on one whom he so greatly honoured, but he had never exchanged a word with him. James Finton Lalor was living the life

---

Speaking of his last poem, "The Sack of Baltimore," she says: "The more we study this ballad, the more extraordinary does it appear that it should have been the work of an unpractised hand. Not only is it full of spirit and of melody, qualities not incompatible with inexperience in poetical composition, but the artistic merit is so great. Picture succeeds to picture, each perfect in itself, and each conducing to the effect of the whole. There is no careless line, or a word out of place; and how the epithets paint—'fibrous sod,' 'heavy balm,' 'shearing sword'! The Oriental portion is as complete in what the French call local colour as the Irish. He was learned, was Thomas Davis, and wrote of nothing that he could not have taught. It is something that he should have left a poem like this altogether untinged by party politics, for the pride and admiration of all who share a common language, whether Celt or Saxon."

It is proper to notice that there was one exception to the general chorus of regret. Mr Edward Kenealy, in latter times called Dr Kenealy, and known for his connection with a popular delusion in England, contributed a paper on "Maclise" to the *University Magazine*, in which he took occasion to express his contempt for the hopeless monomania under which Ireland laboured when men "raised altars and busts to a dog-faced demagogue of nine-and-twenty." In the next number of the magazine the editor apologised for this libel and utterly repudiated it. While Davis was living Mr Kenealy held widely different language. "I am glad," he wrote to Davis nine months before his death, "I am glad you have disabused my mind of its error, as from what I know of you and the noble spirit which animates your writings, I cannot suppose the bearing of the *Nation* towards me was intentional, and because it has relieved the party before alluded to from what was an unfounded suspicion. For the very courteous and gentlemanly spirit in which you replied to my intemperate outburst, you have my warm thanks. Believe me, you are the last person in the world of whom I would have said or written a word of bitterness." Davis Papers: E. Kenealy (Cork, January 2nd, 1845) to Thomas Davis.

of a hermit, and knew literally no one outside his own family; but Lalor came in the end to modify the action of the party more than anyone then living. None of these men had written a line in the *Nation* at this time, or, except M'Gee, knew that they could write. Mitchel's "Life of Aodh O'Neil" was still unpublished, and few suspected the remarkable powers as a writer and speaker he was destined to develop. Smith O'Brien loved and honoured Davis, but up to the era of his death he had stood apart from Young Ireland; his identification with it dates, as we shall see, from later transactions. And there were still to come names of both sexes, as significant as any of these, with whom the reader will make acquaintance later.

But those succours were distant, and the future depended in no small degree upon what might be done on the instant. The one thing—which none of Davis's friends thought permissible—was to abandon our task: the question was simply by what method it might be best promoted under the new conditions. Appeals and remonstrances were made to me, from all the friends who remained, to take up the relinquished work. Before this time I had lived a journalist's life, hating, as students commonly do, the platform and personal exhibition of any sort. I knew that the singular influence which Davis exercised over the judgment and conscience of his contemporaries was a personal gift which had passed away as completely as his personal life; I knew how unapproachable were his endowments and attainments; but something might be done to carry out his programme, to fill up the fatal gap in our ranks, and to keep the green flag flying. I answered the appeal by giving up literary leisure and the luxury of books and reverie; and from that time forth my life was passed in the fever and tumult of political action. I can scarce recall without stirring the fountain of tears the generous help that came from many quarters. The two young barristers who were soon to leave for London set to work with a zeal which in the barren remnant of life I have rarely seen men employ except for their personal interests. They took up the tangled thread of Davis's labours in the learned societies, they conferred with his Conservative friends to make sure of a statue by a competent artist, they helped to collect his scattered writings, and their alacrity and success in this work furnished the measure of the loss their absence would entail. Among the Cahermoyle Correspondence of that time I find a hasty note of mine to O'Brien, which exhibits the purpose kept in view in all that was being done.

"*We* know what he was to the Committee of the Association, to the Press, to his fellow-labourers; but what do the people know of this? Our duty is to make his name familiar and household to Ireland—to make him to his country more than Burns is to Scotland, more than Franklin is to America. It is my conviction that neither of these men matched him in vigour and variety of powers, much less in his great loving heart. What you can do for him is to put yourself at the head of a movement which a multitude of men are anxious to make, to give him a monument, a statue, and a portrait. If the Association will vote £300 towards his monument, I have no doubt his friends will subscribe twice as much. We have caused a cast to be taken from his face, and with this, an admirable portrait which I have of him, and his own knowledge of him, Christopher Moore will be able to make a perfect likeness in bust or statue.[1] The portrait I will send to London to be engraved in the best style, to be published as we may hereafter consider best. His greatest monument will be his writings and his Life, which I will have published in the 'Library of Ireland,' when there is leisure to consult on the most suitable method. Out of his grave he will kindle new hearts to complete his labours. Death has dissipated calumny and jealousy, and he will be listened to now as the man of his generation."[2]

That death had not quite dissipated calumny we have seen; but I regarded the *Pilot* as outside the pale of controversy. To answer imputations by such a man as Mr Barrett on such a man as Thomas Davis seemed to me little short of ignominy. I was persuaded he could damage no one in the end but his patrons. Some of my friends thought differently, or thought, at any rate, that the end which would see this sort of poetic justice accomplished might be unpleasantly remote. They urged me to interpose. Dillon, on the eve of his departure for Madeira, wrote on the subject for the second or third time, as much in a passion as was possible to his sweet and considerate nature. "The notion of listening in silence," he said, "to these attacks is altogether absurd. There is no calumny so outrageous that ignorant people will not believe it, if it be not contradicted." As far as credulity is concerned, Dillon doubtless was right. Ireland afterwards passed through the agony of a famine, through a despairing attempt to snatch her rights, and through a campaign of parliamentary agitation, and at every stage honest men (echoed by many more who were not honest) reiterated these calumnies with a rooted belief in their truth. How far contradiction would have availed is another question. The policy of the *Nation* from the beginning had been to engage in a contest with stipendiaries and camp followers under no circumstances, and from this policy I would not depart. But the *Pilot* maintained a precarious

---

[1] Moore made a small model of a bust, which I gave in later years to the National Gallery in Dublin.
[2] Cahermoyle Correspondence. Duffy to O'Brien.

THE DEATH OF DAVIS.

existence solely by favour of the O'Connell family, and I resolved to pass by the agents and hold the patrons responsible. A conflict with the Association at the moment would have found the young men ill prepared; but to a party which means to live by honest arts, there are many things more disastrous than defeat. In the next *Nation* I opened the subject, and warned all whom it concerned that if the slanders did not cease it would no longer be a safe recreation. "The humblest of Davis's friends," I said, in language which was much canvassed at the time, "would (if the necessity arose) take by the throat the highest head that breathed a slander upon him."[1]

The attacks on Davis stung MacNevin into a rage, and he flew to his pen for relief. A lecture on the state and prospects of the National question was the result, which he printed and sent to me from the country, in proof. I had no suspicion at the time of his mental condition, and I read it with consternation. In defending our friend fiercely we were within our rights, but in assailing the leader of the cause we served, while peace was possible, we would have imitated the offence which moved MacNevin's scorn; and this was a fault into which he fell. I strongly recommended the suppression of the pamphlet, or, if he would publish, large and fundamental alterations in the text. This was his answer:—

"You may be sure, my dear Charles, that I accept with thanks, and adopt with pleasure, your advice. You never gave me bad advice, and I know your warm interest in me, and which, be assured, I deeply reciprocate. But pray look at the last part of the lecture . . . I am profoundly indifferent to the opinion of that class of politicians. I have done with them entirely. I mean to resume writing for the *Nation*, but only for love and good-will. I wish you would send me to-morrow the proofs, altered as you please, because adopting your suggestions is just as pleasant as adopting my own original thoughts."

It is possible—it is, perhaps, even probable—that a conflict with the Association at that time could not have been long postponed, but for an exposure which befell the *Pilot* and covered its friends with confusion and shame. The decision of the Catholic Primate to give the new Colleges a fair trial had greatly exasperated the gentlemen who were watching over the interests of religion in that journal, and it was determined, it may be surmised, to punish him with the only weapon at their disposal; the same poisoned weapon which had been brandished against Davis. It was whispered among the people that the Archbishop

---

[1] *Nation*. October 4th.

was about to become a Protestant, and no wonder—so the whisper ran—for his mother had been a Presbyterian. After a little, when the time was supposed to have arrived for another stroke, the *Pilot* announced in large type, in its leading page, that the Archbishop was insane—a circumstance which doubtless would account for everything in his conduct which had perplexed the people. " He was incapable of attending the meeting of bishops at Maynooth owing to the unsound state of his mind, and he must relinquish the discharge of his duties and live in retirement for some time to come." The announcement was copied into nearly every journal of the Empire, and this publicity was its ruin. The *Pilot* had so miserable a circulation and so miserable a character that its slanders were permitted to enjoy the immunity of contempt. But when the statement was read in respectable journals there was a clamour of indignation. The Primate at the very time was conducting a conference of bishops at Maynooth, over which he had presided during six days, and his mental and physical health was perfect. The statement was immediately contradicted, but several numbers of the *Pilot* were issued without any withdrawal or modification of the original falsehood. An archbishop, however, is a personage who cannot long be misrepresented with impunity; the clergy of the Archdiocese of Armagh, in district after district, met to express their disgust and indignation at what they described, in language not too strong for the provocation, as an atrocious calumny.[1] Before the long array of ecclesiastics who signed these angry protests, the journal had of course to recant and apologise. And for a time it was no longer of any service as an organ of ingenious inventions. For a time indeed it was dangerous to employ Mr Barrett in the only work in which he was serviceable, for men of character fled from a cause with which his name was associated.[2]

---

[1] Declaration of the Clergy in various districts of the Archdiocese of Armagh, advertised in the *Nation*, Oct. 12th and 19th, 1845.

[2] Frederick Lucas was, beyond comparison, the most gifted and trusted of Catholic journalists in that day. In authority and knowledge he stood nearly alone among his class. He has left on record his estimate of Mr Barrett's conduct in this transaction, and generally as a party hack; and as Mr Lucas differed *toto cælo* from the ecclesiastical policy of the Primate, it may be accepted as testimony wrung from an honest man by frank scorn of an unworthy ally.

"The only thing that could diminish its weight" [the libel on the Archbishop] "or make it of little importance, was the character of the mouthpiece through which it got vent. If the character of the *Pilot* be such that an enormous lie told of the highest individual becomes suddenly of little importance, solely because it is elaborately stated in the *Pilot's* largest type, the case is very easy of comprehension. It must be that no one thinks of believing the *Pilot*; that the character of its editor for honour

A truce ensued. The Collection of Davis's Essays and Poems, the publication of a memoir in the *Nation*, of a portrait by the most accomplished painter, and a statue by the most renowned sculptor in Ireland, fixed the public attention on his memory till the people gradually came to know in some degree what sort of a friend they had lost.[1]

The temporary dispersion of the Young Irelanders left a more visible gap in Conciliation Hall than in the *Nation* office. Among O'Connell's personal staff there was not one man capable of doing more than echoing the policy of his leader, and, from the time the *rammolissement* set in, the policy of the once resourceful leader had been little else than schemes only mooted to be abandoned, or a languid acceptance of proposals originating with O'Brien or the Young Irelanders. During the three months of Mr John O'Connell's management the Association had constantly lost ground, and it was now destined to recede more and more, for want of the higher faith and clearer purpose which were withdrawn. For a time the people probably saw little of this. It is only an expert who knows with

---

and veracity are at the lowest ebb ; and that no human being dreams of regulating his belief or disbelief by the voucher of such a being. . . . If any respectable Catholics, lay or ecclesiastical, are really the founders of *Old Ireland*" [*Old Ireland* was a weekly paper then recently established], "we venture to give them one friendly warning. It is, to sell that part of the stock-in-trade which goes by the name of 'Mr Barrett,' if they can find a purchaser ; if not, to get rid of him upon any terms—to sweep him and everything that belongs to him out of the street door—and to put forward some sounder and less tainted name in the front of their battle."— *Tablet*, Oct. 18th, 1845.

Mr Lucas differed widely from Davis on the Colleges question, and probably in his aims and agencies generally ; but how he estimated the character and nature of the man will be gathered from a note he wrote me immediately after Davis's death :—

" The loss of so dear a friend, and that loss so sudden, is almost more afflicting for the moment than the other, which had been longer prepared and expected. I think I can enter in some degree into your feeling in regard to him you have lost, and I am the more glad that I once passed an evening with him, because the impression I received of his amiable and noble qualities enables me the better to appreciate the hold he must have had on the warmest feelings of your heart. I have, after my fashion, paid a short tribute to his memory in the *Tablet*, and I hope you will find in what I have said no word or phrase that offends reverence for the memory of the departed. May God have mercy on both ! I shall have Mass said *for both*" [Davis and my wife] "at the earliest opportunity, that I may by this act at least, if by no other, enroll myself amongst the list of mourners."

[1] The statue by Hogan stands over his grave in Mount Jerome. The likeness is not striking, but the figure and attitude are characteristic. The ideal is that of a German student, spare, slender, and thoughtful ; the action is that of an orator gathering up his robe with one hand while the other rests on a manuscript. For this action and for the truth to nature, there ought to be greater breadth of chest. Davis did not give the idea of a speculative, but of a vigorous and practical man.

certainty when the tide is going out, as it covers its retreat by a constant succession of apparent advances; and with this party on the ebb, the noise and movement of the popular flood were still heard, and there was a great historic three-decker on the waters with all sails set, bound as it seemed for a distant port, a spectacle of constant interest to sightseers; but in truth the tide was slowly retiring, and the three-decker lay hopelessly becalmed.

There was one harvest, however, which Conciliation Hall had not gathered and could not waste. Nationality had made prodigious progress among the cultivated classes. It was said that all who did not profit by the Union were now weary of it; and many who did profit by it shared the feeling; for nationality, like the air of heaven, penetrates into places most jealously barred against it. To some it came like an absorbing passion which loves great sacrifices; with some it was a mere sentiment; but an unequivocal change was felt throughout the entire community—a change which it might be hoped would bear fruit later; for opinion is the root from which action springs. It was a fact of great significance that the Irish names best known to the Empire and to Europe in the peaceful professions—Stokes and Anster, Kane and Burton—were found on the committee to commemorate Davis's career by a public statue. They did not, any of them, share his political aims, but assuredly no one who had held and preached the same opinions since the Union would have been selected by them for such a distinction. And Ferguson, who lay on a bed of sickness when Davis died, impatient that for the moment he could take no part in public, asked me to come to him, that he might ease his heart by expressing his sense of what we had lost. He read me fragments of a poem written under these circumstances, the most Celtic in structure and spirit of all the elegies laid on the tomb of Davis. The last verse sounded like a prophecy: it was at any rate a powerful incentive to take up our task anew.

> "Oh, brave Young Men, my love, my pride, my promise,
>   'Tis on you my hopes are set,
> In manliness, in kindliness, in justice,
>   To make Ireland a nation yet.
> Self-respecting, self-relying, self-advancing,
>   In union, or in severance, free and strong;
> And if God grant this, then, under God, to Thomas Davis
>   Let the greater praise belong!"

The measures by which the Young Ireland party was reorganised, by which it repelled the devices planned to ruin it, by which the national cause was re-animated, and by which the direct and public attempt of O'Connell to destroy the party, with the purpose of renewing his relations with the Whigs, were encountered, and the disastrous results of the French Revolution in Ireland, remain to be told in the sequel of this narrative, published under the title of "Four Years of Irish History."

APPENDIX

[226]

# APPENDIX.[1]

READERS OF THE *NATION*.

THE readers of the *Nation* were estimated to exceed a quarter of a million. At that time every copy of a newspaper bore a penny stamp, which carried it free through the post, and the quarterly return of stamps issued from the Custom House showed the quantity of each paper printed. The stamps consumed by the *Nation* exceeded ten thousand for each issue, a number far in excess of any other Irish journal. As the price of the paper was sixpence a copy, the people paid £250 a week for it. And it is to be noted that the special distribution of the *Nation* increased enormously the actual number of its readers. Three hundred copies went to newsrooms and Teetotal Societies, and were read by at least fifty persons each. Eleven hundred copies went to Repeal Wardens to be read aloud at weekly meetings, and each copy served from fifty to a hundred persons. Nine thousand copies were sold by agents or went directly to subscribers ; and as the *Nation* was handed about like a magazine, and preserved for binding, it is certain that each of these copies reached more than a dozen readers, probably more than a score. Its local distribution was still more remarkable. In almost every town in Ireland the circulation of the *Nation* exceeded the circulation of the local papers representing the same opinion in the district. Old men still describe the fever with which they waited for its weekly issue, and the delight with which they lingered over it. This attraction extended to the official class, through whose hands the paper passed, and there were constant complaints of copies missing, and agents' parcels deficient of their proper numbers. To remedy this inconvenience it was suggested, by some person wanting in reverence for constituted authority, that an additional paper should be attached to each parcel with the inscription, " Please to steal this copy."

A stamp return of the period will enable the reader to understand the relative position of the Dublin journals as regards circulation :—

	Average Number of each Publication.	
	Quarter ending 30th Sept., 1843.	Quarter ending 31st Dec., 1843.
The Nation	9,500	10,730
Weekly Freeman	6,650	7,150
Weekly Warder	6,000	7,230
Weekly Register	2,461	3,154
The World	2,077	2,038
Evening Mail	940	886
Evening Post	2,769	2,932
Evening Packet	1,371	1,948
Pilot	1,615	1,923
Evening Freeman	859 / 333	1,146 / 448
Daily Saunders	2,314	2,461
Daily Freeman	1,293	1,410

[1] Most of the NOTES which, in former editions of " YOUNG IRELAND," were placed at the ends of chapters, and one of which is so referred to at page 131 (*note* 1), Vol. II., have been transferred to this Appendix.

And to these details must be added the fact that its leading articles and verses were copied extensively in the Colonies and wholesale in the United States.

THE FEDERAL CONTROVERSY.

THE tone of the leading Irish journals may be gathered from the subjoined *précis*, and a knowledge of it will greatly help the reader to understand the composition and character of the national party at that time.

The *Freeman's Journal*, then the only daily paper on the popular side, thought that the merit of Federalism was a question of degree. If the people of Ireland listened, as a final settlement of their relations with England, to the Federalism which some men talked, they would be justifying all the contempt and contumelious wrong which that connection had inflicted on them. But Federalism like Mr Grey Porter's was worth considering. And O'Connell, it might be assumed, would not have distracted the people by a new controversy without some practical end in view

The *Cork Examiner*, the leading national journal in Munster, gave forth an uncertain sound. It desired to be more clearly informed what was Federalism? An Irish Parliament composed of the Lords, Commons, and legitimate monarch of Ireland was intelligible to all minds ; but the people did not understand the complicated idea of Federalism. What constituted the local affairs over which a Federal Legislature would have control ? What did they include and what did they exclude ? Mr Duffy's letter had some forcible reasoning, but O'Connell must not be embarrassed in the effort to benefit Ireland.

The *Belfast Vindicator*, the organ of the Repealers of Ulster, spoke more unreservedly. It could not deny that Mr O'Connell's letter had caused some alarm among the ranks of men originally enlisted under the banner of definite principle, whose leading orator and journalists had been imprisoned for the assertion of a definite principle, namely, the establishment of an independent Parliament in the kingdom of Ireland, free from the control or limitation of England. But people were more frightened than hurt. For the declaration of a preference for Federalism was Mr O'Connell's individual preference, which he was too wise and just to attempt to force on the Association. The General Committee or the Association itself had, as Mr Duffy insisted, as little right to pledge the people to Federalism as the Irish Parliament had to betray the trust reposed in them.

Among the Repeal papers in Leinster, outside the capital, the *Kilkenny Journal* held a leading place. Some of the most capable and experienced men of the national party were resident within the range of its circulation, and, in turn, it was understood that it lay within the range of their influence. This journal was of opinion that it would be treason to the country and injustice to the country's leader not to declare that the people viewed Federalism with suspicion. They desired to maintain the Crown as the only bond of connection between Great Britain and Ireland. O'Connell had himself taught them this principle, and it was a work which could not be done and undone like Penelope's web. Mr Duffy was right in declaring that a sudden change of policy, however justifiable in an individual, would argue fickleness, vacillation and want of purpose in a nation.

The *Limerick Reporter* thought Federalism was good, bad, or indifferent according to the form in which it was proposed. Mr Duffy thought Federalism did not go so far as Repeal, but it might go farther. If, for example, Ireland did not send an equal number of members with England to the Imperial Congress, it would be a one-sided and inadmissible system.

The *Tipperary Vindicator* contended that the time when Federalists were admitted into the Association was the proper period to condemn Federalism, if it were a bad thing. At present it would be better to leave time to develop the views of the transcendently able leader than pronounce opinions one way or the other.

The *Newry Examiner* defended O'Connell from the imputation made by Tory journals, that he struck the national ensign from the flagstaff, and was about to substitute some motley *tricolor* for the historic Green. On the contrary, he had merely intimated the courteous purpose of hearing what an important party had to propose. Mr Duffy had asserted the right of free opinion in language sturdy enough, but never wanting in the respect due to O'Connell. There was one of his propositions from which it would be criminal to withhold immediate and cordial assent. It would be a flagrant breach of faith with the nation to attempt to force Federal opinions upon the Association, or to pledge that body to anything but the general principle of Repeal.

The *Southern Reporter*, which was the organ of Federalism in Munster, applauded the frankness and manliness of Mr Duffy's remonstrance, but considered that unlimited and implicit obedience to a single leader was the necessary condition of success in a national movement.

The *Kerry Examiner's* share in the controversy was noted because it was the local newspaper of the county where O'Connell resided, and where he was supposed to be supreme. But this journal declared that Federalism was not to be preferred to Repeal. Fortunately, however, O'Connell had not declared an absolute, but only a conditional preference for the Federal plan. The greatest Irish lawyers and statesmen had pronounced the Union to be a fraud by which Ireland had been robbed of her Parliament; she demanded a restoration of it, but Federalism was not a restoration—on the contrary, it was an abandonment of that claim.

Of the English journals which had advocated Repeal, the *Tablet* was the ablest and best informed, because Mr Lucas did not give the question merely a casual attention, but brought the whole force of his subtle intellect to solve a great political problem. On this occasion he declared that he did not agree with all the objections taken by Mr Duffy; but considered the general scope of his letter exceedingly sound and full of wisdom. Mr Porter's scheme of Federalism would not find favour in England because no scheme for a reconstruction of the Empire would be supported there; but if the Northern Protestants, who were then considering the question, proposed a reasonable and plausible arrangement, it would have a better chance of success than simple Repeal.

The *Leeds Times* did not regret the present controversy. Mr Duffy's remonstrance marked an important era in the movement. It formed the commencement of a discussion of the *means* by which the liberty of the Irish people was to be gained. Hitherto the movement had been popular and impulsive; it had now arrived at a stage when it must become reflective and legislative. The plan must be proposed, discussed, and decided upon by which Repeal was to be achieved and the Government of Ireland afterwards carried on. How were taxes to be levied, armies to be raised and paid, treaties with foreign countries to be formed? All these questions must be discussed and settled before a sufficient amount of moral force could be brought to bear on the British Parliament to compel them to repeal the Act of Union.

O'CONNELL'S LETTER TO O'BRIEN ON THE FEDERAL PLAN.

DARRYNANE ABBEY, 21*st October* 1844.

MY DEAR O'BRIEN,—It was only yesterday I received the paper of which you have enclosed a copy. It is the "first project" of the Federalists; its history or its contents are not to reach the press *from us*, nor is there to be any commentary in the papers until it has appeared authentically as the act of subscribing Federalists. Subject to this caution, I submit it with the least possible delay to you for consideration. The principal actor in Dublin in the arrangement is William Murphy, called of "Smithfield." He is a man who has acquired enormous wealth and has long been a principal "brains carrier" of the Irish Whigs. A most shrewd, sensible man, Thomas Hutton, the very wealthy coachmaker, has assisted and is assisting. I could mention other influential—highly influential—men. There is to be a Federalist meeting in Belfast on the 26th. Caulfield, brother of Lord Charlemont, leads or presides. Sharman Crawford, Ross, the member for Belfast, and other notabilities attend. Hutton, who is a Presbyterian, goes there and passes through Armagh to muster as many important Presbyterians as he can, or at least to procure their signatures. O'Hagan the barrister attends the registry, and will be at the meeting on the 26th. I do not know whether it will be a public meeting, but a publication will emanate from it. In short, the movement is on foot. The effect must in any case, as it strikes me, be useful. It annihilates mere Whiggery.

I had nothing whatever to do directly or indirectly with the composition or the material of this document. I was merely sent a copy of it by a third person so soon as it was put into publication; and to you alone do I send a copy of it. I do not further adjudge its contents than considering them as a mere sketch. But this I say to you, that your accession to the Repeal cause has been the efficient cause of this advance, and I do not hesitate to say further and to *pledge* myself not to assent to any plan for the restoration of the Irish Parliament, or to any of the details of any such plan, that meets with your disapprobation. *We* go together; that is, you go with me, because I certainly will not go a single step without you. No man living has been more fortunate than you in the opportunity of showing personal independence. Whatever you do will be the result of your own judgment, and differ with me who may I will not differ with you. If you were in my opinion so wrong as to violate principle I would *retire;* I would cease to act, and would do so rather than join in any course I deemed unjust or injurious. But while I *do* act I will act with you. I am thoroughly convinced that without your accession to the Repeal cause years upon years would elapse before we made any impression upon the general Protestant mind. Ireland owes you an unlimited debt of gratitude, and the popular confidence in you can never be shaken. Consider then the document I send you attentively. Be prepared for its authentic publication. You probably will not commit yourself respecting its contents without *conference* as well as mature consideration. It is but a skeleton, and wants nerves and sinews and flesh. There is enough for conference—and there are some promising limbs—but there must be more before we can consent to give it vitality.

I will not take one single step about it without giving you *previous* intimation and consulting with you fully and deliberately.

Believe me to be respectfully and faithfully yours,
DANIEL O'CONNELL.
W. S. O'BRIEN, M.P.

It need only be noted that these professions of a determination to act together were made ten days after O'Connell had written his public letter, declaring his preference for Federalism, on which he had not consulted O'Brien. They were made also several days after the *Nation* had opposed the scheme, when O'Brien's neutrality had become highly important.

EXTRACT FROM THE FEDERAL PROJECT, ENCLOSED IN THE FOREGOING LETTER.

"While all matters of foreign, commercial, and ecclesiastical policy, as well as the general taxation and expenditure of the United Kingdom, would by such an arrangement remain as now, within the exclusive control of the Imperial Legislature, such matters as the regulation and disposition of local taxation, the relief of the poor, and the development of the natural resources of the country would be provided for by the local assembly, which must necessarily be better qualified to discharge such functions.

"We utterly disclaim any intention of rendering the proposed measures in any degree subservient to the severance of the *legislative* connection between Great Britain and Ireland, which, thus reformed, we shall deem it our duty, as we believe it will be our interest, by every means in our power to maintain."

O'CONNELL'S LETTER TO DAVIS. [*Referred to in page* 130, Vol. II.]

DARRYNANE, 30*th October*, 1844.

MY DEAR DAVIS—My son John has given me to read your Protestant philippic from Belfast. I have undertaken to answer it, because your writing to my son seems to bespeak a foregone conclusion in your mind that we are in some way connected with the attacks upon the *Nation*. Now I most solemnly declare that you are most entirely mistaken—none of us has the slightest inclination to do anything that could in anywise injure that paper, or its estimable proprietor; and certainly we are not directly or indirectly implicated in the attacks upon it.

With respect to the "Italian Censorship," the *Nation* ought to be at the fullest liberty to abuse it: and as regards "the State Trial Miracle," the *Nation* should be at liberty to abuse not only that, but every other miracle from the days of the Apostles to the present.

But we Catholics, on the other hand, may be permitted to believe as many of these miracles as we may adopt either from credulity or convincing proofs; at the same time I see no objection to a Catholic priest arguing any of these points or censuring, in suitable and civil terms, opinions contrary to his own.

As to the Cork attack upon a Protestant proselyte, you know that I publicly and most emphatically condemned it ; as did the Catholic Press of Cork.

With respect to the *Dublin Review*, the word "insolence" appears to me to be totally inapplicable—all the *Review* did (and I have examined it again deliberately) was to insist that a man who from being a Catholic became a Protestant, was not a faithworthy witness in his attacks upon the Catholic clergy. Now, independent of that man's religion, of which I care nothing, there never lived a more odious or disgusting public writer, with one single exception, and that is the passage in which he praises you.[1]

The "insolence" of the *Dublin Review* consisted, as I have said, of merely stating that a pervert from Catholicity, who abused the Catholic clergy, was a suspicious witness in declaring their guilt. Would you not have a right, if a person who, from being a Protestant became a Catholic and abused the Protestant clergy, to state that his evidence against them ought to be considered as suspicious, or even unworthy of belief? Yet for no greater offence than that, the *Review* is attacked, and a high and a haughty tone of threatening assumed in speaking of it.

I really think you might have spared the insinuation that you and other Protestants were "pioneering the way to power," for men who would establish any sort of Catholic ascendency. I know this, and I declare it most solemnly, that in the forty years I have been labouring for the public I never heard one bigoted expression, not only in our public meetings but in our committees and private discussions, from a Catholic ; but I have often felt amongst SOME of the Liberal Protestants I have met with that there was not the same soundness of generous liberality amongst them as amongst the Catholics.

I hate bigotry of every kind, Catholic, Protestant, or Dissent, but I do not think there is any room for my interfering by any public declaration at present. I cannot join in the exaltation of Presbyterian purity or brightness of faith, at the same time that I assert for everybody a perfect right to praise both the one and the other, liable to be assailed in argument by those who choose to enter into the controversy at the other side. But with respect to the *Dublin Review*, I am perfectly convinced the *Nation* was in the wrong. However, I take no part either one way or the other in the subject. As to my using my influence to prevent this newspaper war, I have no such influence that I could bring to bear : you really can much better influence the continuance or termination of this bye battle than I can. All I am anxious about is the property in the *Nation*. I am most anxious that it should be a lucrative and profitable concern. My desire is to promote its prosperity in every way I could ; I am besides proud as an Irishman of the talent displayed in it ; and by no one more than by yourself. It is really an honour to the country ; and if you would lessen a little of your Protestant zeal, and not be angry when you "play at bowls in meeting rubbers," I should hope that, this skirmish being at an end, the writers for the *Nation*

---

[1] Smith O'Brien had a very different opinion of Maddyn. Davis wrote a little earlier : " O'Brien is in delight with your book. He says not three men in the empire could write so well, and hopes and expects you to be with us and for us. God grant it."—Davis to Maddyn, 28th September, '44.

APPENDIX. 233

will continue their soul-stirring, spirit-enlivening strains, and will continue "to pioneer the way" to genuine Liberty, to perfect liberality, and entire political equality for all religious persuasions.

If I did not believe that the Catholic religion *could* compete upon equal and free terms with any other religion, I would not continue a Catholic for one hour.

You have vexed me a little by the insinuations which your letter necessarily contains, but I heartily forgive you; you are an exceedingly clever fellow, and I should most bitterly regret that we lost you by reason of any Protestant monomania.

We Papists *require* co-operation, support, combination, but we do not *want* protection or patronage.

I beg of you, my dear Davis, to believe, as you may do in the fullest confidence, that I am most sincerely,

Your attached friend,

DANIEL O'CONNELL.

PEEL'S CONCESSIONS AND THE YOUNG IRELANDERS.

Among the serious misconceptions and savage misrepresentations to which the writers of the *Nation* have been subjected in England from time to time, it is worth while, in the interests of truth, to take notice of how their conduct in this business impressed a party journalist, opposed to the Government whose measures they welcomed. The *Morning Chronicle*, a Whig organ at that time, said :—

"Notwithstanding irreconcilable differences of opinion with our Dublin contemporary the *Nation*, and the Young Ireland of which it is the representative, we have long thought well of the spirit of political independence and earnestness observable in the conduct of both. That the *Nation* is not always civil, nor even decently just to the Whigs and ourselves, does not lessen the pleasure we have in acknowledging that it at least does something to create in Ireland one of the things which Ireland most wants—an independent public opinion. We have noted also with satisfaction, that on general questions of policy connected with the material and moral improvement of Ireland this influential journal is fully as earnest as on Repeal itself. It shows no sneaking kindness for special grievances for the sake of their reaction on political discontent, and would, we do believe, cheerfully relinquish the finest grievance in the world without a thought of the political capital into which it might be improved. The tone of this important organ of Irish opinion has always been sound on the subject more particularly of education. It has not been backward on fit occasions to do ample and handsome justice to the system of primary schools established in 1831-2, although that system was the work of an Imperial Legislature, and not only of an Imperial Legislature but of a Whig Cabinet, and not only a Whig Cabinet in general but of Lord Stanley in particular. In the same spirit we are glad to see it go heart and hand with Mr Wyse in his endeavours to press on Parliament and the Ministry the subject of improved and extended academical education. Young Ireland asks no question about Mr Wyse's soundness in the Repeal faith, cheers him on, all tainted as he is with the heresy of Imperialism, and is prepared to hope all things and thankfully accept any really good thing even from the Cabinet that wrongfully imprisoned Mr O'Connell and Mr Duffy."

It may be noted that the policy pursued did not meet universal assent among the party. MacNevin, who was the most sensitive to opinion and the least able to stand alone, took alarm from the talk of his country neighbours that Repeal was to be sacrificed for these concessions, and was so disheartened by the ignorance of the Western peasantry that for a moment he was in despair. I find among his letters one from a friend who answered his objections and quieted his fears :—

"Touching Peel and O'Connell, let me say, with the Duke, there was no compromise, there is no compromise, and there shall be no compromise. Peel may bid as high as he pleases, but he can bid nothing equivalent to what must be abandoned. Rest you easy in your rural groves, and fear nothing on the score of a new *Pacata Hibernia*. I deny and repudiate your theory about the people. If they were all bred the serfs of Connaught squireens, their independence—I mean their *personal* independence, their recognition of the fact that they are men with certain human powers and human rights—would be distant. But you must not judge the people of Ireland by your present neighbours. Did you ever make a *kaylie* with an Ulster farmer? He would puzzle you, I promise you, on any subject within his range; on the Bible for example, or crops, or profit and loss (he is rather too wide-awake on the last point). Look at the Munster peasantry; they have not the shrewdness of the Northerns, but they have a higher and manlier nature, more imagination, more sympathy, more self-denial. Remember that some of the best songs in the "Spirit" were written by Munster peasants in intervals of their daily labour. You find selfish and barbarous notions about Repeal among the people. To be sure. Do you think the Barons at Runnymede knew any higher meaning for liberty than privileges and immunities to be enjoyed by themselves? They wanted freeholds like the poor Connaught men, and had as little sense of abstract right or wrong. Trust me, 'tis a sense which has to be sedulously cultivated, and by no means grows wild. But why don't you plant Reading Rooms among them? It would be pleasanter employment, to my thinking, than interchanging hospitalities with the Squire Ulicks and Squire Anthonys of the West."[1]

The Library of Ireland.

In the Library of Ireland the issue continued unbroken till public events interrupted it. The "History of the Volunteers," by MacNevin, was followed by the "Ballad Poetry of Ireland," by Gavan Duffy, the third volume on the list was a "Life of Wolfe Tone," by Thomas Davis, for which had to be substituted, under tragic circumstances, the "Life of Aodh O'Neill," by John Mitchel, a new recruit at that time. These were succeeded by memoirs of Irish writers by M'Carthy, and D'Arcy Magee, another recent recruit, a "National Story," by Carleton, a "History of the American Revolution," by Michael Doheny, "Collections of Songs and Ballads," by Barry and M'Carthy, and a "History of the Confederation of Kilkenny," by the Reverend Charles Meehan. Among volumes

---

[1] Duffy to MacNevin.

announced but never published were—"The Rebellion of 1798," by M. J. Barry, the "French Revolution," by David Cangley, the "History of Irish Manufactures," by John Gray, "History of the Great Popish Rebellion" (1641), by Charles Gavan Duffy. The *Nation* not only interpreted to the people and popularised these works, but supplemented them by others in the same spirit. At the opening of the New Year a series of papers was announced and immediately commenced which sufficiently indicates the nature and character of the education which its writers aimed to give to the people. This was the list of *Nation* essays :—

I. Sketches of Distinguished Irish Soldiers, Statesmen, Ecclesiastics, Artists, and Authors.
II. Papers on the Study of the Irish Language.
III. A Series of Critical Articles on Continental Literature.
IV. Historical Essays on Memorable or Obscure Periods of our National History.
V. Popular Summaries of the Principles and Facts of Political Science.
VI. A Series of Critical Papers on the Great English Poets.
VII. Biographical and Critical Essays upon Obscure Writers of Merit.
VIII. On Popular and National Sports.
IX. On the Social, Moral, and Intellectual Condition of the Labouring Classes, with suggestions for their Improvement.
X. Retrospective Reviews of the leading Irish Books in History, Fiction, and the Drama, intended as a guide to students and popular reading-rooms.
XI. Translations from the Irish.
XII. Accounts of Colonial and Continental Legislatures.
XIII. The Contemporary History of Europe.
XIV. Sketches of Modern Revolutions—France, Belgium, Canada, Greece, etc.

MAURICE O'CONNELL ON DAVIS.

DARRYNANE ABBEY, 14*th October* 1845.

MY DEAR DUFFY—I have not addressed you since the death of our beloved friend, because the crowd of condolers would give the air of conventional compliment even to an expression of sincere sorrow ; and next, though not least, that I grieved to know that you had other and more sacred matters of sorrow. May the Giver of All Things console you in that bitterest of afflictions. I enclose a few verses framed, I think, in a tone which poor Davis himself would approve of—as my offering to his memory.[1]

Amidst this wilderness of song and testimonial, surely the most effectual tribute to his memory will not be neglected. His writings should be collected and published as soon as possible. They were his offerings to

---

[1] The verses will be found in the *Nation* of November 8th, 1845, and in the "Spirit of the Nation."

his country, and should be perpetuated. It will be an interesting study to trace the workings of his mind, and to point out to the future men of Ireland how much he did to advance her literature and her liberty, and in how short a space, by strenuous, unremitting devotion to her cause.

Yours, my dear Duffy, most truly,

MAURICE O'CONNELL

CHAS. GAVAN DUFFY, Esq.

INDEX TO VOL. II.

ART in Ireland, letter to Davis, 154.

BANIM, John, union of parties to secure an annuity for the widow of, 65, 101, 103.
Barrett, Richard, 6, 7, 9; *note*, 68, 112, 218.
Barry, Michael Joseph, 52, 54; letters to Davis, 115, 173, 214.
Belfast Meeting to address State Prisoners, 55.
Bright, Right Hon. John, 146.
Brewster, Mr, 5.
Brougham, Lord, 72.
Browne, Dillon, a marplot in Conciliation Hall, 67.
Burton, Judge, passes sentence on O'Connell and others, 47.
Butt, Isaac, political leader of Young Conservatives, 64; *note*, 131.

CANTWELL, John M'Namara, 4, 16.
Campbell, Lord, 72, 73.
Carleton, William, occasional contributor to the *Nation*, 66, 159, and *note*; his wit, 97, 98.
Codd, Francis, 17.
Cloncurry, Lord, on jury packing, 6, 144, 151.
Coltman, Mr Justice, 71.
Conway, Michael George, 174.
Conway, Frederick William, *note*, 113.
Corbally, Matthew, 17.
Corrigan, Sir Dominic, 17, 92, 93.
Crolly, Archbishop, 134, 187.
Colleges, Provincial, 165.
Cottenham, Lord, on the trial of the State Prisoners, 72.
Crampton, Mr Justice, approves of the manner in which the Chief-Justice put the evidence against the Traversers, 45.
Crawford, Sharman, 41, 87, 109, 113, 114, 118, 123, 146.

Curry, Eugene, 98.

DARRYNANE, visit to, 101, 102, 105.
Daunt, W. J. O'Neill, 52, 133, 181, 185.
Davern, Rev. Father, death of, 90.
Davis, Thomas, 51, 52; disgust at being "hamstrung from behind," 68; attempt to introduce Irish nomenclature, 99; letters to Duffy, 102, 103, 109; letters to O'Brien, 115, 117, 124, 128, 145, 155, 160, 161; letters to O'Brien and Duffy on Sectarianism in the Repeal Association, 127; projected Life of Wolfe Tone, 156; indefatigable worker, 160; letters to Denny Lane, 163; speech on Provincial Colleges, 168, 170, 171, 176, 177, 178; letters to O'Brien and Denny Lane, 184, 185; proposes for the first time to go circuit, 189; *note*, 190, 197; letter from sick-bed to Duffy, 202; his last letter, 206; his death, his funeral, estimate of his character, 210: letters of intimate friends on his death, 211, 212, 213; condition of Young Ireland party at his death, 211; *note*, 216; proposal for a monument, picture, and life, 218; collection of his essays and poems, memoir in the *Nation*, portrait, and statue, 221.
Denham, Lord, on trial of State Prisoners, 72.
Devon Commission, report of, 142.
Dillon, John Blake, 52; letters to Duffy, *note*, 75, 144, 161, 162, 189, 202, 211, 212, 218; letters to Davis, 200, and 201.
Disraeli, Mr, 37, 40, 77.
Dixon, S., *note*, 57.
Doheny, Michael, *note*, 33, 53; *note*, 54, 96, 119, 202.
Doyle, John ("H. B."), 66; caricature,

O'Connell dropping poker inscribed "Federalism," 121.
Doyle, Martin, one of the survivors of '98, 101.
Duffy, Charles Gavan, trial of, 4, 33; *note*, 63; tour from Dublin to Darrynane, 101; letters to Davis, 104, 105, 106, 118, *note*, 131, *note*, 206, *note*; hoists the danger-signal, 109; remonstrance to O'Connell in the *Nation* on the declaration that Federalism was better than Repeal, 110, 111, 116; projects the "Library of Ireland," 156; letters to MacNevin, 99, 157, 158; *note*, 160, 170; *note*, 181, 200, 205; tour in Ulster, 193 *et seq.*, 199; estimate of Davis, 210, 217, 219.
Duffy, James, 97, 98, 99; *note*, 159.

ENNISKILLEN, Orange meeting, 196.
Eighty-Two Club, 151.

FEDERAL Movement, O'Connell favours, 107; letter of Duffy, in the *Nation*, to O'Connell, 110; opinions of Irish Press upon, 112, 113; O'Connell breaks with the movement, 120.
Ferguson, Samuel, 64, *note*, 65, 222.
Fonblanque, Mr, 123.
Foreign Policy for Ireland, 62.
Ford, William, 74, 75.
Ffrench, Lord, 34.

GARTLAN, Peter M'Evoy, 4.
Graham, Sir James, 147.
Grattan, Mr Henry, M.P., 6, 83, 152, 177.
Gray, Dr, 4, 32.
Gray, Wilson, 197.
Greene, Solicitor-General, 5.
Gregg, Rev. Tresham, 138, 139.
Guizot, 41; interview with O'Connell, *note*, 42.

HAUGHTON, James, 138.
Hawarden, Lord, 73, 90.
Haggarty, Edmond, 74.
Hogan, John, sculptor, 101, *note*, 221.
Holmes, Robert, Counsel against O'Connell, 5; challenges Barrett, of the *Pilot*, 6.
Hume, Joseph, M.P., 149, *note*, 150, 162.
Hutchinson, Hely, 51.

INTRIGUES, religious, at home and abroad, 125.
"Irish Society" in London, 66.

JOINVILLE, Prince de, pamphlet on condition of French Navy, 62.
Jury Packing, 12.

KANE, Professor, *note*, 92, 222.
Keogh, John, 52, 209.
Kemmis, Crown Solicitor, 7, 16.
Kenyon, Father John, first appearance in Conciliation Hall, 181.

LANE, Denny, 97, 103; letter to Davis, 153; letters from Davis, 163; *note*, 181.
Lalor, Fintan James, 217.
Le Fanu, Joseph Sheridan, 64 and *note*.
Lever, Charles, 64 and *note*.
Leyne, Maurice, joins the Young Irelanders, 59.
"Library of Ireland," 156.
Lords, House of, Writ of Error in case of O'Connell and others, 74.
Lucas, Frederick, on the Repeal Movement during O'Connell's imprisonment, 67; on character of Mr Barrett and *Pilot*, *note*, 220; letters to Duffy on Davis's death, 221.
Lyndhurst, Lord, 72.

MACAULAY, Lord, 37, 40, 146, 148, 149 and *note*.
Maddyn, Daniel Owen, 163, 214; letter on Davis's death, 214.
MacHale, Archbishop of Tuam, condemns Provincial Colleges Bill, 185.
Maclise, 101.
MacCarthy, Denis Florence, 95, 96, 101, *note*, 155, 214.
M'Carthy, J. J., 96.
M'Gee, Thomas D'Arcy, description of, 197, 216, 217.
M'Knight, Dr, *note*, 66, 67.
Mangan, Clarence, 163.
Mahony, Pierce, 4, 12, 129.
MacManus, Terence Bellew, 152.
MacNevin, Thomas, Smith O'Brien's estimate of, 51, 53, 96; letter to Duffy, 100, 131; distrust of Protestant gentry, 145, 152; *note*, 131, 181, 201; letters to Davis and Duffy, 205.
Mathew, Father, in his home, 101; his Teetotal Reading Rooms, 104, 105.
Martin, John, 54, 152, 198.
Maunsell, Dr, 87, 138.
Maynooth Grant, 137; bill to further endow, 143, 145.
Meagher, Thomas Francis, 102, 152, 216.
Meehan, Rev. Charles P., 127, 156.
Mitchel, John, 152, 191; letters to Duffy, 192, 193, 217.

INDEX. 239

Mockler, Captain John, 83.
Monahan, Attorney-General, 17.
Moore, Mr, 4.
Murray, Archbishop, 134.
Murray, John Fisher, 66.
Mitford, Miss, her appreciation of Davis's poetry, 216.

Nation newspaper, 56; action for Libel against, *note*, 91 *et seq.*; answers to correspondents, 94; on Peel's Concessions, 133, 137.
Napier, Sir Charles, 36.
Napier, Mr, 5.

O'BRIEN, William Smith, *see* Smith O'Brien.
O'Connell, Daniel, how he was tried, 3 *et seq.*; defence of himself, 26; proposes to abolish the Association, 31, 32, 34; visits England before his sentence, 40; called up for judgment, 46, 47; imprisoned, 49, 51; life in Richmond Penitentiary, 58 *et seq.*, 74; released from prison, 75; state of parties after his release, 81; first speech at Repeal Association after his release, 83; banquet on his release, 86; can no longer control national sentiment, 87, 89; in his own home, 102; approves of Federalism, 107, 110, 112, 113, 115, 116, 117; public entertainments in Tipperary and Limerick, 119; breaks with the Federalists, 120, 121, 122, 130, 136, 149; letter to Davis on Sectarian controversy, 131, and *Appendix;* 166, 168; president of the Eighty-Two Club, 151; attack on Davis, 177, 179, 182; letter to the Archbishop of Tuam, 186; 187, 191, 199, 209, 223.
O'Connell, Daniel, junior, 61, 74.
O'Connell, John, trial of, 4, 33, 59; released from prison, 75; intrigues against the Young Ireland Party, 125, 130; letter to Davis, 149; opposition to Provincial Colleges, 167, 169, 173, 180, 181, 183, 187, 190, 195, 209, 215, 221.
O'Connell, Maurice, 52, 60, 86, 115, 125, 215.
O'Connell, Morgan John, 6, 66, 165.
O'Donovan, John, 98.
O'Gorman, Richard, 52.
O'Hagan, Thomas, 4, *note*, 93; extract from his address at O'Connell's Centenary, *note*, 82.
O'Hagan, John, 101, 214.

O'Loghlen, Sir Colman, 4, 183.

PALMERSTON, Lord, 62, 69, and *note*.
Imperial Parliament, Irish State Trials, 31.
Parke, Baron, 71.
Peel, Sir Robert, 63, 65, 77 ; concessions to Ireland, 136.
Pennefather, Chief-Justice, charge in Trial of O'Connell and others, 46.
Perrin, Mr Justice, 6, 21.
Pigot, D. R., 4, 17, 66.
Pigot, John, 214.
Pilot newspaper, 112, 115, 218, 219, 220.
Policy, Foreign, for Ireland, 62.
Porter, Grey, 83, 88, 89; joins Repeal Association, 139, 140, 150, 160.
Potter, Sir Thomas, 41.
Presbyterian marriages and chapels endangered, 54.
Primate, the slanderers of, in the *Pilot*, 219.
Purcell, Peter, 113.
"Prout, Father," 66.
Provincial Colleges, 58, 165.

RAY, Thomas Matthew, 30, 97.
Regium Donum, *note* 55.
Reilly, Thomas Devin, 4, 216.
Repeal Association, O'Connell's proposal to dissolve, 31 ; members of the Press retire, 33; action after the State Trials, 50; first meeting after release of O'Connell, 83; reading rooms, 102; O'Connell on Federalism, 111 ; accession of Mr Grey Porter—his speech, 139; Smith O'Brien replies to Macaulay, 147 ; Grey Porter and MacNevin, 148; action of Mr Hume, M.P., and how it was met, 149; Dissensions on the Colleges question, 166 ; speeches of O'Brien, O'Connell, Michael George Conway, and Davis on the Colleges question, 172 *et seq.;* Davis's emotion, 177; the Vice-Tribunate of John O'Connell, 191; feelings of France and America, 199 ; declaration of O'Connell, 199; action of John O'Connell and his associates, 200.
Richmond Penitentiary, O'Connell and Traversers imprisoned there, 49 ; under control of Dublin Corporation, 58 ; the Traversers' manner of life, 58 *et seq.;* rejoicings there at news of O'Connell's release, 74 ; triumphal car bears O'Connell and his son away from, 75.
Richmond Gazette, *note* 59.
Russell, Lord John, 22, 35, 40.

SHAW, Right Hon. Frederick, 13, 66, 144.
Sheil, Richard Lalor, 4, 38, 39, 40, 90, 165.
Smith O'Brien—his relation to O'Connell after the State Trial, 32, 33, *note;* letter of Davis to, 34; method of joining Royal Dublin Society, 35; leadership entrusted to, 49; measures he inaugurates, 50 *et seq.;* his associates in the work, 54; support given to, by the *Nation,* 56: letter to, on Federalism from O'Connell, 122, and *Appendix;* from Davis on religious intrigues, 127, 128; to Davis on same, 130; further letters to Davis, 130, 136, 144, 161, 171, and *note,* 221; insists on Davis presiding at the Association, 131; his reply to Macaulay, 147; refusal to attend "the call of the House," 149; opinion of the new literature, 161; his attitude in relation to the Colleges Bill, 171, 184; and to "Young Ireland," 217.
Smith, T. B. C., Attorney-General, 4; his speech on trial of O'Connell and others, 38, 39.
"Spirit of the Nation," 98.
Stack, Moore, 58, 65.
State of parties after O'Connell's release from prison, 81.
State prisoners, their religions, *note* 57; before the House of Lords, 69; reversal of the judgment in the Queen's Bench, 74; procession from the jail, 75; levee in the Rotunda, 189.
Sugden, Sir Edward, 55.
Sturge, Joseph, 33, 41.

TENNANT, Mr Emerson, *note* 55, 66, and *note.*
Tierney, Rev. Thomas.
Times newspaper on Federal Union, 89.

Thackeray, W. M., attack on Davis in *Punch,* 181.
Traversers, released, 75.
Trial of O'Connell and others, 3; the indictment, 7; application for list of witnesses refused, 11; special jury list, 12; striking the jury, 16; public meeting respecting the exclusion of Catholic jurors, 17; challenge of the array, 19; jury selected, 20; the Attorney-General's statement of the case, 21; case for the defence, 24; Solicitor-General's reply, 26; charge of the Chief Justice, 27; verdict, 30; opinions in Parliament, 31; motion for new trial, 44; Judge Burton pronounces sentence on O'Connell and others, 47; popular feeling in Ireland, 55; the judgment in the Lords, 74.
Tyrrell, Father, death of, 18.

"VOICE of the Nation," reference to, 109.

Warder newspaper, 89.
Wellington, Duke of, 324.
Whigs, Irish, propose sitting of Imperial Parliament in Dublin, 87.
Whiteside, 4, 15.
Wilde, Sir Thomas, 39, 40.
Wyse, Thomas, M.P., 109, 165.

YOUNG ENGLAND, 37.
"Young Ireland" in Conciliation Hall, 49.
"Young Liberator," the, 125.
Young Irelanders, recreations of, 94; their weekly meetings, 97; *bons mots* of, 95 *et seq.;* their excursions, 101; unjust suspicions held by some of the clergy, 126; repudiated by Father Meehan, 127; workshop of, 151; literary prospects of, 156; hostility of Mr John O'Connell to, 215.

PRINTED AT THE EDINBURGH PRESS, 9 AND 11 YOUNG STREET.

www.ingramcontent.com/pod-product-compliance
Lightning Source LLC
Chambersburg PA
CBHW031937230426
43672CB00010B/1958